Bear With Me

Bear With Me

A Cultural History of

Famous Bears in America

DANIEL HOROWITZ

Duke University Press · *Durham and London* · 2025

© 2025 DUKE UNIVERSITY PRESS. All rights reserved
Project Editor: Lisa Lawley
Designed by Courtney Leigh Richardson
Typeset in Garamond Premier Pro and Sophillia
by Westchester Publishing Services

Library of Congress Cataloging-in-Publication Data
Names: Horowitz, Daniel, [date] author.
Title: Bear with me : a cultural history of famous bears in America /
Daniel Horowitz.
Other titles: Cultural history of famous bears in America
Description: Durham : Duke University Press, 2025. | Includes biblio-
graphical references and index.
Identifiers: LCCN 2024050922 (print)
LCCN 2024050923 (ebook)
ISBN 9781478032373 (paperback)
ISBN 9781478028826 (hardcover)
ISBN 9781478061045 (ebook)
Subjects: LCSH: Bears—Folklore. | Bears—United States—Folklore. |
Bears. | Bears in literature. | Bears in art. | Bears (Gay culture)
Classification: LCC GR730.B4 H676 2025 (print) | LCC GR730.B4
(ebook) | DDC 398.24/52—dc23/eng/20250210
LC record available at https://lccn.loc.gov/2024050922
LC ebook record available at https://lccn.loc.gov/2024050923

Cover art: Smokey Bear, 1944. 1989 U. S. Forest Service poster based
on Alfred Leete's and J. M. Flagg's war-era "Lord Kitchener/Uncle Sam
Wants YOU/" posters.

※

TO PEOPLE WHO LOVE

AND PROTECT BEARS,

※

REAL AND

MAKE-BELIEVE ONES

※

Contents

Preface

Polar Bears, Franz Boas, and Me

The COVID-19 pandemic; three previous books I authored; my long history with imaginary bears; playful pillow talk about one polar bear in particular; and learning how Franz Boas encountered polar bears on Baffin Island in the 1880s. All this somehow led me to research and write about how over centuries bears—mostly representational but some real ones—became celebrities in the United States. Initially, I naively hoped that immersing myself in stories of how American bears became so famous would provide me with some measure of relief from the threats of a global pandemic, the rise of authoritarian threats to democracy, increasing evidence of the threat of climate change, and wars in Ukraine and in the Middle East. Well, it turned out that though I might pleasurably revel in stories of Goldilocks and the Three Bears, Garfield's Pooky, and victories of UCLA's Bruins, evidence about some celebrity bears underscored how precarious the world was.

Each of us has in mind the date when we realized how dangerous COVID-19 might turn out to be. For me, it is March 16, 2020. I was on a Metro light rail going from downtown Los Angeles to Pasadena, where my wife, the historian Helen L. Horowitz, and I spend winters in the company of other retirees who gather around the Huntington Library. Having just had lunch in LA's Grand Central Market, where I worried not at all about contagion, I suddenly realized that a dangerous virus might be lurking all around me, including on the metal pole I held on to as the train lurched forward. Helen and I rushed to our condo, cancelled plans to go to Charlotte, North Carolina, for a Business History Association conference, packed up, and made arrangements to return to Cambridge, Massachusetts, where we spend most of the year. At the time, I was finishing up a third scholarly book—this one on residential real estate, and the two previous ones on the problematic promises of happiness and entrepreneurship—in which inequalities of wealth and income, as well as racism, were dominant themes.[1]

To wander off into what I thought would be reassuring worlds, I could have turned my attention in any number of directions. But somehow, I alighted on bears as I tried to figure out how, when, and why some of them emerged as such famous animals in America over centuries. I gradually realized that bears had long been part of my imaginative life. Like many children, I had a teddy bear and my parents read books to me about bears before I could read them myself. As a child I saw bears perform in circuses and zoos. Not long after we married in the summer of 1963, Helen and I began what turned out to be well over half a century of travels in the American Southwest. Sometimes we brought back reminders of what we had seen, including two Zuni fetishes. To Zuni people, bears, guardians of the West, represent the power to heal and protect. One tiny fetish, which we still possess, pays homage to a medicine man with abundant powers, with the arrowhead on top signifying an offering of gifts anticipated or received. The arrow on the other one, which sits on a shelf in my study, is a lifeline that begins at the mouth and then heads to the soul, the location of inner strength and faith.[2]

Only when I was far along in researching and writing this book did I realize that these fetishes stood on a shelf near where I wrote. I also recalled buying an Inuit carving in Montreal over forty years ago, one that did not reference a bear but offered a representation of women's work. Only recently did I realize that it is from Cape Dorset, now called Kinngait, a hamlet on the southwestern tip of Baffin Island that is the center of Inuit art.[3] I remembered that Helen and I read books about Paddington and Winnie-the-Pooh to our children, and that bears were among the many stuffed animals that seemed to fill their bedrooms. More immediately, I know that the smaller collection pictured here resides in the bedroom Helen and I share.[4] We began to collect them, almost thirty years ago, after our nest became empty. They provide sentimental examples of how we seek comfort from stuffed animals. Besides two small Smith College mice, the basket holds the large "Winter Bear," who hibernates in the appropriate season and has a snood over his head; "Travel Bear," who is small enough to

Basket of bears in the home of Daniel and Helen L. Horowitz. Photo by author.

accompany us on trips; and the most recent acquisition—"T Bear," with the routes of the Boston-area MBTA crisscrossing its body.

If you, dear reader, promise not to report me to mental health authorities, I will also describe the pillow talk involving imaginary animals that Helen and I engaged in as we drifted off to sleep. This practice may have begun in the spring of 2005, while I was teaching at the University of Hamburg, when Helen encountered, or so she claims, two mice—Gemein and her husband Gesell—who made her feel at home in our apartment. So, as she often does, Helen engaged in writing behavior, in the end producing a still unpublished book on how Mr. and Mrs. Schaft accompanied us back to Northampton's Smith College, where they began careers as cheese entrepreneurs. Much later, as COVID-19 drove us into lockdown mode, a polar bear named Polar entered our sleep-approaching nights. Along lines that are now difficult to recover fully, we spun elaborate stories about how Polar migrated from Baffin Island to Massachusetts, where he enrolled in medical school and then became a psychiatrist who saw patients in the freezer section of a local supermarket, giving him easy access to fish as payments for his service. The stories became elaborately fanciful, principally about his prior life on Baffin Island. Baffin is the world's fifth-largest island, part of Canada located west of Greenland, with only thirteen thousand people, half of whom are Inuit.

Early in 2020 I had learned about Baffin Island when I read Charles King's recently published *Gods of the Upper Air: How a Circle of Renegade Anthropologists Reinvented Race, Sex, and Gender in the Twentieth Century*. This wonderful book opened my eyes to how over time the experiences of Boas on Baffin Island in 1883–84 profoundly shaped how we understand culture. As King notes, through his encounters with the Inuit, Boas was coming to realize that "being smart was relative to one's circumstances and surroundings."[5] In 1888, at age thirty and more than a quarter of a century before he would emerge as America's most influential anthropologist, Boas published *The Central Eskimo: Sixth Annual Report of the Bureau of Ethnology to the Secretary of the Smithsonian Institution, 1884–1885*. Here he highlighted the lives of polar bears in two ways. On the one hand, he offered moving evidence of a reciprocal cross-species relationship when he related a story of a woman who adopted a cub a few days after its birth. On the other hand, as if to underscore the connection between affection and violence, he described how Inuit hunt polar bears, something that had become much easier and less dangerous to the hunters, Boas reported, with "the introduction of firearms in Arctic America."[6] So it turns out that if sometimes the Inuit killed polar bears, at other moments they told loving, gender-inflected tales that endowed humans with empathy and bears with ample intelligence and emotional powers.

As I carried out research for this book, at idle moments I let my curiosity run wild about the comfortably distant Baffin Island. I spent hours online trying to imagine what it was like for people to live there. I used Google Earth to travel to Iqaluit, with just under seven thousand inhabitants the island's most populous location. Although I am not sure I was serious, I unsuccessfully tried to persuade Helen to join me on a vacation on and around Baffin. We'd spend an unaffordable tens of thousands of dollars per person for a three-week trip to "a land where the sun never sets and polar bears roam." We'd be lowered to small inflatable Zodiacs that would enable us to approach and "get a glimpse of one of the Arctic's most iconic animals: the polar bear."[7]

As I read about polar bears, I learned that some observers consider Baffin Island "Polar Bear Central," possessing as it does five of the world's nineteen subpopulations of the species. With as many as 2,800 polar bears, by some estimates they comprise more than 10 percent of the world's population of the species.[8] I carefully read Andrew E. Derocher's *Polar Bears: A Complete Guide to Their Biology and Behavior* (2012). A text by an eminent biologist, the book is lavishly illustrated, mostly with pictures that present the bears as beautiful and cute, rather than threatening or threatened. Yet Derocher asserted that "most people find something mystical about a huge, potentially dangerous, pure white predator." The bears were so popular, he continued, because of the contrasts between adorable cubs and their "mysterious lifestyle" that contributed to a "frisson of fear." I found out that polar bears, one of eight extant species, live only in the Arctic, typically on sea ice. They have a powerful sense of smell, eat seals as their principal source of food, and can be as tall as ten feet and weigh as much as 1,700 pounds. Inuit on Baffin and elsewhere hunt and kill them because they rely on them for food and materials. Threatened by humans but rarely threatening them, they are overharvested, especially on Baffin Island. Endangered by climate change, their futures are uncertain.[9]

What Boas revealed about polar bears from his year on Baffin Island is part of a story, eons in the making, of relationships between bears and people. At one end we see merciless and often wholesale endangerment or slaughter, the result of humans causing environmental degradation as they hunt for sport, profit, and sustenance. One step over are bears held in captivity at zoos and in circuses. At the other end, in imaginative renderings that emphasize caring and reciprocal relationships, are all sorts of bears in folklore, children's literature, and toys, as well as most recently fresh and sympathetic understandings of the lives of actual bears.

And so I wondered why and how we tell so many stories about bears, some of them affectionate. People relish such narratives even though they act in many ways that threaten bears' existence. Having learned about Boas, Baffin, and polar bears, I turned to find out about how all varieties of North American bears in all manners of settings have compelled people to represent them in media from oral traditions to video games. People did so in ways that turned bears into celebrities that we perceive as both cuddly and dangerous, actual animals and ones we know principally through fabricated stories. Having started out to take comfort in the lives of bears at a time when dangers loomed large near and afar in my life, I discovered that precarity also prevailed.

Once I embarked on this project, I found bears here, there, and everywhere. After family members, friends, and Google's algorithm became aware of my interest in them, I received a seemingly unending stream of stories of bears invading human spaces. For my birthday in 2022, one friend sent me an e-card

Jar of Teddie Peanut Butter. Photo by author.

that pictured many teddy bears wishing me well by singing and playing musical instruments. Two other friends gave me a cap with a grizzly embossed on the front. At one point, Helen emailed me an ad for the commercial possibilities that Build-A-Bear offered, including gifts for every occasion, as well as its workshop near me. On my iPhone, Google, relying on my search history, alerted me to how a camera captured a live bear cub bathing in a swimming pool with a toy bear he had found. Common were stories of bears finding their way into residential neighborhoods, such as one that circulated about Hank the Tank, a 500-pound grizzly who invaded dozens of homes in search of food in the South Lake Tahoe, California, area.[10]

And bear with me for offering examples of bears' commercially oriented, representational presence. Think of the logo for Behr paints. Or how Teddie peanut butter deploys a not very natural, recumbent, and smiling bear on its label. At the supermarket in Cambridge where I usually shop, I encountered a large display featuring stacks of Polar Seltzer sodas, produced in nearby Worcester, with a friendly toy polar bear sitting on top. In a Robitussin ad, a bear appears at a window and offers a woman honey to relieve her cough. Ads for Charmin toilet paper feature smiling, cartoon bears who encourage users to "enjoy the go"

Polar bear on top of bottles and cans of Polar Seltzer, Star Market, Cambridge, Massachusetts. Photo by author.

as a bear wiggles its bottom and sings, "I'm grinning cheek to cheek." Finally, in the world of sports, to name only a few, there are the Chicago Bears and Chicago Cubs, UC Berkeley's Golden Bears, Brown University's Bears, Baylor's Bears, the Kutztown Golden Bears, and Touchdown—the Big Red Bear of Cornell University.

The rest is history.

Introduction

Bear With Me: A Cultural History of Famous Bears in America focuses on the ways media have made bears omnipresent in the everyday lives of Americans for over two centuries. Although the book stretches back to bears in the heavens and in the Bible and acknowledges the importance of stories imported from abroad, this is nonetheless an American story of how high and popular culture have transformed bears into celebrities that have permeated our imaginative lives.[1] Although some real bears make appearances, I concentrate mainly on representational ones, principally those presented by Euro-Americans from the colonial period to the present. *Bear With Me* explores how depictions have evolved from a focus on human domination to cross-species reciprocity and emotional engagement, even intimacies.

Indeed, portrayals have often ricocheted from deadly anthropocentrism to loving empathy. As bears came to appear more like us, they became less threatening and instead sources of emotional and spiritual strength. Yet it remains an intriguing question of whether the proliferation of bear stories, even ones in which affection plays a central role, shoulders some responsibility for the threat humans pose to bears. Much of popular culture promotes sympathetic identification with bears, yet demographic and economic forces drive us to threaten them. Some stories, such as those about the dangers of global warming, should impel us to protect them. Others, like news of bear attacks, drive us to fascinated fear and even murder of bears.[2]

I present chapters in the order in which bears appeared on the scene. In the United States, widely circulated stories began in Native American, African American, and Euro-American oral and folk traditions, transitioned into print, and then intensified in the 1850s when Grizzly Adams displayed grizzlies he had captured in California before he moved to New York in 1860 and teamed up with P. T. Barnum. This was a key moment, in part because the middle of the nineteenth century was when news of the American West spread more widely, driven by new engines of popular culture. Early in the next century the connection between Teddy Roosevelt and teddy bears provided the first major example of the extensive commercialization in many genres and across the nation. Now, an observer noticed in 1906, teddy bears had "become a fad. Automobilists carry bears as mascots. Children cry for 'em, and even 'society' is taking up the toy as a novelty."[3] However, it was in the years following World War II that bears and popular culture came together in full force into the lives of so many Americans through multiple media—including songs, films, television shows, stuffed animals, tchotchkes, video games, and newfangled options such as Facebook. With the Disney empire playing an outsize role for baby boomers, the culture industries in postwar America helped spread the word and images about bears as celebrities.

The standard historical explanation of what happened is that when, with urbanization, wild animals disappeared from most people's lives, bears appeared not as dangerous but as innocent and lovable.[4] Yet many dramatic stories of famous bears underscore the necessity to question the widely accepted story of linear progression from threatening to cuddly. There is no one-to-one relationship between proximity to wild nature, actual threats, and a sense of danger that stories convey. How imagined bears enter our lives depends on genre, the power of traditions, cultural and historical contexts, and audience.

Moreover, even though cross-species empathy can be powerful, our separation from and commodification of nature may well have intensified threats to the lives of bears. Affectionate representations are more prevalent even as some species struggle to survive in the wilderness. It is perhaps too optimistic to say that these very forces have opened up the possibility that sufficient numbers of Americans will defend and protect bears. Indeed, driven by the increasingly powerful forces of culture and capitalism, stories of bears do two conflicting things that accentuate the moral dilemmas that suffuse our reactions. By offering such wondrous varieties of bears with which we identify, they present the possibility of empathetic cross-species relationships. At the same time, by distancing us from actual bears and instead offering us cuddly ones, multiplying narratives may limit the effectiveness of environmental policies that might help bears thrive in the Anthropocene.

Recently, rewilding had led to encounters between bears and people, including in American suburbs and cities. This process upends the long-held belief that modern Americans have less direct experience with wild animals. The environmental studies scholar Peter S. Alagona adds a hopeful note about rewilding in his 2022 book, *The Accidental Ecosystem: People and Wildlife in American Cities*. The more people came to live with such animals, he insists, "the more they viewed these creatures not as threats but as natural and beneficial members of multispecies urban communities." Alagona notes that "beginning in the 1980s, surveys showed that Americans—having grown up with Teddy, Smokey, Winnie, and Yogi—thought of bears as intelligent, attractive, similar to people, and worthy of protection."[5]

For bears to become well known and omnipresent requires figures whose fame can be enhanced; an ample and engaged audience; and powerful media that provide the grist for what Susan J. Douglas and Andrea McDonnell call, in their study of famous human beings, "the celebrity production industry." Bears have potential notoriety because of the importance of the sensational and exotic, their complicated emotional resonances, and what many see as their resemblance to humans. Sufficient audiences developed beginning in the middle of the nineteenth century, when increasing numbers of people with more ample leisure time resided in and around large towns and cities. Economical postage, the telegraph, and railroads helped create a national market facilitating popular culture's spread. Other media platforms took hold—initially local urban institutions such as performance spaces and widely circulating stories in inexpensive newspapers. Over time a full range of national media developed, from magazines to radio, film, and television, and eventually contemporary social media. "Our ability to relate to and identify with celebrities," Douglas and McDonnell note in ways that apply to bears, "also allows us to use stars as a way of considering our own identities, values, and beliefs. In our media-saturated world, being a fan is often integral to our own self-formation," something children have experienced when reading books about bears and adults when encountering them in the wild and in captivity.[6]

Why bears? Putting aside household pets such as cats and dogs, perhaps more so than any other animals they capture the imagination of the widest possible range of Americans. Elephants and horses do not do that so extensively. Even monkeys and chimps, which in important ways are more humanlike than bears, are not consistently presented and do not present themselves in such a manner. The most common explanation for bears' prominent presence is that they are unusual because they stand erect on their hind legs, face us, and in myriad ways act like us.[7] "For many of us today," the nature writer Jon Mooallem insists, "who spend our days slumped over spreadsheets or quarreling with our banks over hidden fees, bears look like the composed and competent survivors we wish we still were."[8]

In many ways bears are not at all like us, although we do our best to pretend they are by projecting human traits onto them. We do so in ways that amplify often contradictory characteristics. In the wild, real bears are majestic and threatening—and at times playful and seemingly friendly. As represented, they evoke a wide range of feelings: cuddly or dangerous; family members or lone avengers; lordly or timid; smart or stupid. More than domesticated animals and most wild ones, bears evoke strikingly opposite responses from humans, including domination, cross-species reciprocity, and emotional engagement. All this provides rich fodder that the engines of popular culture mobilize to turn them into celebrities.[9] Bears rampant in popular culture are more like us than are the wild ones who live in nature. If bears inhabit our imaginative worlds because of their posture and facial expressions, powerful commercial interests play upon, amplify, and exaggerate the many characteristics that make them so prevalent in many modern media.[10]

Of course, real bears vary in the ways they look, where they live, and how they behave. Of the eight types, the four that live in North America provide this book the most abundant material for cultural representations. Pandas exist in North America exclusively in captivity. North American black bears (*Ursus americanus*) live in places ranging from Florida to Alaska; brown bears (*Ursus arctos*, a category that includes grizzlies and Kodiaks) live not only in Russia and Western Europe but also in the Canadian and the American West; and polar bears (*Ursus maritimus*) inhabit the Arctic region.

Adults range from 400 to 1,700 pounds, with brown and polar bears the largest. Bears have an unusually strong ability to hear and even more so to smell. They tend to travel alone or in small groups rather than in large packs. Stories of bears, especially fictional ones, pay remarkably little attention to their diets; they are omnivores, with many of them more likely to consume plants than animals.[11] Despite how often they are depicted as slow and dumb, they are intelligent and capable of learning. They are aware of how our lives affect theirs. Species such as grizzlies and polar bears, notes a PBS special, are "considered by many wildlife biologists" to be among "the most intelligent land animals of North America," having as they do "the largest and most convoluted brains relative to their size of any land mammal." Their intelligence compares favorably with "that of higher primates." They keep track of other members of their group, perform complex tasks, can learn and apply information, are able to deploy self-awareness, and possess powerful memories.[12]

Compared with large cats such as cheetahs, bears are not especially fast. However, capable of reaching a speed as high as thirty miles per hour, they can outrun humans. North American bears typically hibernate, even though many bear stories pay relatively little attention to that practice. Unless they feel hungry or threatened, especially if a mother faces the prospect of losing her cubs, they are much more likely to avoid rather than confront people, but they are fully capable of dismembering and killing human prey when necessary. "Sensational reports of bear attacks," notes Bernd Brunner, "may make for exciting reading, but they can easily create a false impression. For the most part, bears are far less interested in us than we are in them."[13] News of bear attacks circulate widely, but it is important to balance such stories with statistical evidence. Over a long period of time in Yellowstone National Park, there was only one injury for every 1.5 million visitors. In the United States far more deaths occur due to bites from venomous animals or to lightning than from attacks from grizzly bears. Up until 1980 at Glacier National Park, 150 people died but only 6 of them from the paws of grizzlies, with drowning, auto accidents, and falls more likely to be fatal. In almost all cases, bears attack people because they are protecting cubs, food, or territory. However, such incidents may be increasing as people travel more frequently into areas where bears live and vice versa.[14]

In Western cultures serious interest in the relations between humans and animals dates back at least to the writings of Thomas Moore and Jeremy Bentham. In the 1960s writers began to develop fresh understandings. Animal studies scholars, animal rights activists, postmodernists, posthumanists, scientists, conservationists, and environmentalists have come to insist on the importance of reciprocity between humans and animals. They have removed humans from our long-held position at the center of the world. Profoundly shaping how to think about our relationships to animals, they have blurred the boundaries between humans and animals as they oppose dualisms of mind/body, human/animal, culture/biology. They deemphasize notions of separation, exclusivity, and difference. Instead, they stress the importance of respect, mutuality, a sense of shared destiny, and cross-species similarities. They understand that animals can represent the instinctive, unconscious, and more natural aspects of human existence. They insist that, with complicated emotional lives, animals are more similar to us than we have often realized—albeit not in the ways popular culture represents. They underscore how animals such as bears have complex and intricate systems of organizing themselves and communicating with each other, use tools in problem-solving, possess some abilities than humans lack, and interact with one another in complex, emotionally laden lives.[15] These anti-hierarchical perspectives have risen to prominence among influential writers in ways that raise fundamental questions about power, citizenship, and the historical tendency to separate culture and nature. We can hope that such transformative visions will lead to policies and practices that protect rather than destroy wildlife.

Influenced by these intellectual and experiential changes, scholars, especially those in the field of animal studies, have explored the issue of how to write the history of the relationships between humans and animals.[16] I have drawn on the insights they and others offer, for example by exploring how in some cases representational bears are understood as having emotions and intelligence. I do this even if, as a cultural historian, in important ways I offer different perspectives but not necessarily better ones.

I wish I could claim that from the outset I had in mind a detailed research plan. Instead, the conditions under which I worked profoundly shaped how I proceeded. On February 3, 2021, I received my first COVID-19 vaccination. Six and a half weeks later, I began the process of submitting my previous book manuscript, on the crises in American residential real estate, for review at a university press. This meant I could begin to work on another project. Initially, with library collections inaccessible, to a considerable extent I had to rely on the internet—Google and Wikipedia especially—as research tools. Being hunkered down in front of a computer opened up worlds in ways that meant bears quickly appeared everywhere, immediately, and in every corner of newly discovered worlds. Although I eventually gained access to the holdings in libraries, the worlds I entered through my computer screen had lasting impact. Several things happened simultaneously and often in contradictory ways. Bears—actual and representational ones, in the wilderness and in captivity—proliferated in digitized historical documents, book reviews, YouTube videos, and Facebook sites. An unending number of bears floated on my screen as if they were everywhere and nowhere at the same time, torn out of historical, cultural, and physical contexts. As a reader for Duke University Press suggestively asked, "Does this story begin with the industrial cooption of fairy tales (a la the Grimms)—move through the print revolution, mass pop culture and subcultural responses (gay bears) to mass culture—and end with everything-everywhere-all-at-once internet hyper-proliferation and fragmentation?"[17] If in this book I had included references to and stories about every bear that friends and the World Wide Web brought to my attention, there would be no end to my work or to the length of *Bear With Me*. Instead, I have done my best to tame representational bears and place them in historical and cultural contexts—and to give such hyper-proliferation some sense of order.

Throughout the book, I grapple with several issues. One involves the relationship between anthropomorphism and anthropocentrism. Humans have increasingly deployed anthropomorphism to give animals agency, intelligence, and rich emotional lives, including in children's literature and folklore. Anthropocentrism is also prominent, especially given that bear narratives are more about humans than about bears, which is to say that if under so many conditions images of anthropocentrism lead to assertion of our dominance, anthropomorphism can challenge domination in ways that give animals agency and acknowledge their capacity for intelligence and emotion.[18]

Then there are the complicated, often reciprocal relationships between real and representational bears. Actual bears abound throughout this book, albeit often quickly moving to representations on pages and screens. I recognize how important it is to understand actual bears even as I know that most of us encounter only representational bears, on which I lavish so much attention. Yet when I do so and when the evidence makes it possible, I acknowledge the genuineness of the powers that bears have. In the end I find problematic any sharp distinction between real and representational bears, as is clear, for example, in the stories of Smokey Bear.[19]

Conservation and environmentalism also command our attention. Public policy and economic forces significantly affect bears, often adversely. Again and again in *Bear With Me*, we encounter moments when what humans do, or fail to do, as citizens with political or corporate power significantly impacts the lives of bears. This comes under discussion at several key points but especially with struggles over public policies and the meaning of Smokey Bear beginning in the late 1960s.[20]

White men dominate so many bear tales. Yet members of diverse groups make appearances. By and large, class remains implicit or unexplored. Female bears are frequent, including mothers protecting their cubs. Yet rarely do we find feminist perspectives or women authors. Among humans, we encounter assertive manly men, including gay bears. African Americans appear early as historical figures and more often as folkloric ones. Then in the late twentieth century, African American writers take center stage as they recast traditional, frequently racist stories. Especially with narratives that originate with encounters between humans and bears in western America in the nineteenth century, Indigenous peoples have prominent roles. In multiple stories they often appear as undifferentiated and essentialized people. Even though I pay relatively little attention to Indigenous Americans' experience of bears, we catch glimpses of distinctive and enduring traditions. As original tales transform into more modern versions, it is possible to track shifts from racist depictions of Indigenous peoples to more sympathetic ones. Yet even in many modern instances, responses are problematic, with stereotypes often prevalent and identities up for grabs.[21]

✕ ✕ ✕

The preface focuses on how I came to write this book, the presence of bears in my imaginative life, and the polar bears Franz Boas encountered on Baffin Island in the 1880s.

"Folkloric Bears and Actual Ones: Sacred and Profane from the Bible to Contemporary Celebrities" follows the introduction. It ranges from the bears in the Bibles carried by early settlers, to the tales many Native Americans passed down in rich oral traditions, and eventually to contemporary video games. It ends with stories of famous real bears, such as Wyoming's Grizzly 399, that scores of wildlife photographers and millions of tourists follow.

"The Stories of Hugh Glass: The Case of a Disappearing and Reappearing Dangerous Bear" is the first of three legendary narratives of violent bears. Told and retold since 1823, the tale originates with a record in a local newspaper and then quickly became part of regional folklore, later reinterpreted by writers from vernacular storytellers to skilled literary practitioners. Eventually it expanded into other media, most famously in the award-winning 2015 film *The Revenant.*

"Out of Hibernation and Into Children's Literature" begins with *Goldilocks and the Three Bears* and continues to contemporary tales in almost every conceivable medium. Ever changing along the way, the trajectory moves resolutely toward reassuring relationships between youngsters and bears. In contrast, the demands of the genre of video games meant that in the early twenty-first century some bears were often more ferocious than friendly.

Then comes "Grizzly Adams: Bears He Tamed, Those He Displayed, and Those Responsible for His Death," which involves how a bear attacked John "Grizzly" Adams, a mid-nineteenth-century mountain man who left Massachusetts to travel throughout the West and eventually joined P. T. Barnum in Manhattan. This is another dramatic and violent story told and retold first in print and later in other, more modern media, most notably in the simply made but wildly popular 1974 film *The Life and Times of Grizzly Adams.*

"Captive Bears and Their Captors as Workers" begins on April 10, 1871, the date of the founding of what would eventually become Ringling Bros. and Barnum & Bailey Company. From then on captive bears appeared in natural history museums, zoos, homes, films, theme parks, and video games, where their presence expands our notion of representation beyond the usual books and films. With these presentations, contrived to varying extents, the agency of humans rather than of bears powerfully persists.

Attention turns to "Teddy Bear: Another One Quickly Disappears and Frequently Reappears." The story begins in 1902 when President Theodore Roosevelt encountered a bear whose life he refused to end. The ensuing narratives mark a major turning point as bear stories exploded out of print and into an enormous range of expressions in popular culture, with a second wave beginning soon after World War II.

Then there is the story of Smokey Bear, told in "Off the Poster and Out of the Zoo: Smokey Bear Goes Everywhere." Much more so than what is true with teddy bears, Smokey's history was persistently and deeply implicated with conservation politics and public policy. With Smokey, in addition to the one that appeared on posters announcing, "Only YOU Can Prevent Forest Fires," there is at least one actual bear, discovered hovering up a tree in New Mexico, residing in the National Zoo, and then buried near where he was originally found. Beginning in the last decades of the twentieth century, critiques of the uses of both teddy and Smokey developed and then intensified.

If in all other cases mass media spread stories of bears throughout much of America, "Out of the Closet: Bears in the Gay World" provides an interesting case of how a bear-referenced world remained contained within a largely separate media world. In almost all other cases, people impute human characteristics onto bears. But in the gay male subculture that emerged in the 1980s, the reverse is true. In this context, hairy and hefty gay men were characterized as bears but showed little interest in actual ones. My status as an outsider among people who study and encounter real bears is more vexed when it comes to my writing about gay bears. Neither a member of the LGBTQ+ community nor an expert when it comes to queer history, I nonetheless focus on this subculture because of its distinctive relationship to media and its reversal of the usual projections when it imputes ursine characteristics to humans.

"Timothy Treadwell and Marian Engel: Bears, Humans, and Dangerous Eroticism" offers two stories that, like many others, mix danger and attraction. Treadwell sought salvation among Alaskan grizzlies, yet in the end the result was death not rebirth. Engel's highly regarded *Bear: A Novel* (1976), like Treadwell's story, involves emotionally charged, erotic, and violent encounters between a human and a bear. This novel is unusual because while manliness has dominated so many bear stories and men have authored most of the best-known narratives, a woman wrote this one from a feminist perspective.

I end the book with a coda that focuses on Arctic polar bears as symbols of the danger of climate change.

1

Folkloric Bears and Actual Ones

SACRED AND PROFANE FROM
THE BIBLE TO CONTEMPORARY CELEBRITIES

✕

Early settlers from Europe arrived on American shores with copies of the Bible and, less commonly, versions of *Aesop's Fables*, both of which contained stories of bears. They encountered communities of Native Americans who immersed themselves in tales of bears that had been passed down over the ages in rich oral traditions. Over time other narratives that included bears spread from the heavens, Bible, oral traditions, and folktales to a wide range of media—about Reynard the Fox; from the Brothers Grimm; in *Goldilocks and the Three Bears* and its offshoots; featuring Baloo from Rudyard Kipling's *The Jungle Book*; and tales of Uncle Remus in the original based on oral traditions of enslaved people, rendered into racist expressions by Joel Chandler Harris, and later recast by the African American Julius Lester. In our own time, actual bears emerged as celebrities. Commercialization enhanced the fame of bears, conveyed in every possible medium, including oral traditions, print, movies, cartoons, mascots, and video games. As with bears in children's literature, folkloric tales accomplish important cultural work. They reveal how adults use stories to teach children important lessons, something made possible by images of bears as friendly and like us. They underscore how bear narratives illuminate issues of gender, race, and imperialism, as well as the increasing power of the connections between commerce and culture.

Looking into eternity though the Bible or the heavens, reading or listening to folktales, and seeing imaginary bears in movies and cartoons, Americans encountered them during their daily lives. They captured people's imaginations and offered some information on actual bears but more significantly about our mostly imagined relationships to bears.[1] Drawing on age-old mythological traditions, for centuries Americans have deployed bear stories to inspire a wide range of evocative beliefs. In these narratives stretching from seventeenth-century oral traditions to multimedia today, bears vary greatly—smart and dumb; wild and threatening or tame and friendly; enemy or friend; dangerous or endangered; sacred or commercially profane; representative or actual. Whether polar, panda, grizzly, black, brown, or sometimes unspecified, myriad bears captured Americans' imaginations and opened them to experiences that could be wondrous, humorous, terrifying, and unknowable. Stories ricocheted between empathy and fear, affectionate cross-species engagement and deadly domination. Examples offered opposing but simultaneous depictions, such as how the Bible contained references that bears were warlike and peaceable. Sometimes images were constant and at other times shape-shifting; animate as wild animals or as close as possible to being a human—or as an inanimate stuffed animal that came alive for children. Generally speaking, bears emerged as increasingly anthropomorphic, often in ways that challenge the assumption of human superiority or wisdom. Yet such variations, including how harmless or less dangerous they seemed, occurred unevenly. In the end it is hard not to be struck by how fabulous bears were emotionally variable and border crossing.

Likely because the Holy Land was not a common bear habitat, they appear relatively rarely in the Bible—only fourteen times by one count. This pales in comparison with references to sheep, lambs, goats, horses, bulls, and lions—each of these species mentioned well over hundreds of times.[2] In some instances bears inspire bravery. In 2 Samuel 17:8, for example, people are "as fierce as a wild bear robbed of her cubs." More often, rather than being models of bravery, they are themselves hostile to humankind—lying in wait for livestock prey. Then there are at least two examples of extreme evil—in 2 Kings 2:24 a bear mauling forty-two boys and in Proverbs 28:15 one resembling a "wicked ruler" lording it "over a helpless people." There is apparently only one instance where a bear provides inspiration for positive good. Isaiah 11:7 narrates how the cow "will feed with the bear, their young will lie down together, and the lion will eat straw like the ox." This story from the Hebrew Bible is a more modest version of another immediately before in Isaiah 11:6, which reads "The wolf also shall dwell with the lamb, and the leopard shall lie down with the kid; and the calf and the young lion and the fatling together; and a little child shall lead them." This second one inspired the American Quaker Edward Hicks in the early 1830s to paint many versions of a "Peaceable Kingdom." To be sure, no bears there, but this nonetheless suggests that wild animals could live peacefully with domesticated ones as well as with humans.

If you look for inspiration in the heavens, you will encounter the Greater Bear and the Lesser Bear, Ursa Major and Ursa Minor, nearly always visible in the northern skies unless clouds intrude. From prehistoric days this stellar configuration, a series of otherwise random stars in one of the largest constellations, has represented two bears. Different cultures interpret these configurations in distinct ways, but at least since the second century AD, when Ptolemy listed it as one of four dozen constellations, it is a story that has both varied and endured. In the version from Roman mythology, Jupiter's wife Juno suspects that her husband had a son named Arcas, born, she believes, from his amorous relationship with the nymph Callisto. The angry Juno prevents Jupiter from lusting after Callisto any longer by transforming her into a bear. Arcas, not realizing that the bear is his mother, almost kills her when she is embodied as a bear. Jupiter, determined to avoid such a tragic consequence, transforms Arcas into a bear; he then places the bear that was once Callisto into the sky as Ursa Major and her son, the bear that was once Arcas, there as Ursa Minor.[3] In the long, multifaceted histories of representations of bear, these heavenly ones are in most ways outliers. Although like many others they involve shape-shifting, they are comforting only through their association with advantageous celestial navigation. If they provide any threat to humans, it is not because the bears might attack them physically. Rather, as the product of an extramarital love affair among gods, they might remind knowledgeable people who look skyward of the danger not of vicious bears but of lustful desires.

Then there are the bears that abound in traditional teaching, folklore, and fairy tales, conveyed both orally and in writing. Among them, several stand out for their enduring power: abundantly and varied among different groups of Native Americans; "The Bear and the Two Travelers" from *Aesop's Fables*; Bruin the Bear from the trickster Reynard the Fox; "Bearskin" and "Snow White and Rose Red" from the Brothers Grimm; Brother Bear or Brer in the Uncle Remus stories; Baloo from *The Jungle Book*; Pooky in Garfield cartoons; and all sorts of bears as mascots and in video games. Together they offer a wide range of possible representations of bears, some more influential in the United States than others, some more menacing than others, and some providing precedents for others to follow.

Bears occupy central positions in the rituals and beliefs of many Native Americans. Albeit with variations from group to group, from deep into the past and into the present bears have played central roles as teachers, medicine men, and shamans. They occupy key positions in initiation rites as well as stories of hunting and healing. Members of many Indigenous groups in North America both feared and revered them. They celebrated cross-species border crossing, with bears being transformed into people and vice versa. Indigenous peoples often blurred distinctions by believing that bears, now sacred, were once humans or, alternatively, that bears could transform themselves into humans. They anthropomorphized them—seeing so much in common, both physically and in their fierce maternalism, with people. As Paul Shepard and Barry Sanders insisted in *The Sacred Paw: The Bear in Nature, Myth, and Literature* (1985), the bear "is a kind of ideogram of man in the wilderness, as though telling of what we were and perhaps what we have lost."[4] Or as David Rockwell wrote in *Giving Voice to Bear: North American Indian Rituals, Myths, and Images of the Bear* (1991), "Native Americans imitated the bear in countless rituals. They danced to bring the spring, to heal the sick, to ensure abundant plant food, to guard themselves against their enemies. By imitating the bear, men and women celebrated and honored the animal and, even more important, the aspect of the sacred that it represented."[5]

We can also turn for inspiration to *Aesop's Fables*, which are among the most ancient of mythological stories, ones collected by Aesop, who is believed to have lived in Greece about a century before the classical period that began in the fifth century BC. Collected and reissued, codified over time, they offer didactic stories for American children—the first of many instances underscoring how useful bear are as instruments of moral education because they are emotionally variable and accessible. Among the fables by Aesop that feature a bear is the relatively little-known "The Bear and the Two Travelers." A bear, described as "huge" and a "savage beast," confronts two men walking through the woods. One of them, interested in protecting himself, climbs up a tree. The other, who remembered hearing that a bear would avoid touching a dead body, lies quietly on the ground. The bear, who approached the man on the ground, concluded that he was indeed dead and simply walked away. When the other man climbed down from his perch in the tree, he asked his companion what the bear had whispered to him. The answer was "that it was not at all wise to keep company with a fellow who would desert his friend in a moment of danger." The lesson was clear: "Misfortune is the test of true friendship."[6] In this story the bear is anthropomorphized only by the ruse that it spoke wise words. Though potentially dangerous, the bear decides not to maul the man pretending to be dead.

A series of legends that centered on Reynard the Fox is more recent in origin among the fabled bear stories. They originated as tales told in northern Europe during the late medieval period and appeared in modified versions up to the present, conveyed in bedtime stories. At their center was a trickster, an anthropomorphized red fox who outwitted his adversaries, one of which was Bruin the Bear. Together Reynard the Fox and Bruin the Bear, the narrative relates, had purchased a cask of butter. Asleep near one another, Reynard sneaks off time and time again to eat some of the butter. When Bruin asks why the fox's girth is growing larger, Reynard answers cleverly that he has been at a feast for a child named Just-Begun or an event for Licked-to-the-Bottom. Bruin, half wondering at such strange names, nonetheless quickly falls back to sleep. With the butter almost gone, Reynard once again sneaks away, grabs a morsel, and then returns to grease Bruin's face with it. At the story's end, "they both woke, the sun had melted the butter, and the Bear's whiskers were all greasy; and so it was Bruin after all, and no one else, who had eaten the butter." The theme of a stupid bear losing out to a clever animal commanded little attention in a nation that more frequently embraced lovable ones or worried about vicious ones.[7]

In the first half of the nineteenth century, the German Brothers Grimm, Wilhelm and Jacob, collected and then published tales whose origins in oral traditions stretched back to the distant past and circulated into the present, including in the United States. Their stories about figures such as Sleeping Beauty, Snow White, and Cinderella provided grist for creative mills that found expression in every genre, from high-culture operas to mass-media movies and bedtime stories both vernacular and commercial. Lesser known among the Grimm tales are those featuring bears. One is "Bearskin," a complicated tale in which a soldier returning impoverished from battle strikes a deal with the Devil. In exchange for sleeping in a bearskin and presenting himself as desperately ugly for seven years, he would eventually gain access to abundant wealth. Four years into the seven, the youngest of the three daughters of an impoverished old man promises to marry him, though her older sisters were repulsed by his unattractiveness, which stemmed from his association with bears. After he returns at the end of the seven years, now a handsome gentleman, the two older sisters take their own lives when they realize their earlier mistake. The man who was once a bear marries the youngest sister—and presumably they live together, happily ever after.[8]

"Snow White and Rose Red" is another, more intriguing of the Grimm tales featuring a bear, one that also explores gendered relationships. An impoverished and lonely widow, the story goes, lives in an isolated cottage in front of which grow two rose trees, one that bears white flowers and the other red ones. They parallel her two children, Snow White and Rose Red, who live comfortably at home and safely in nature nearby. One evening, Rose Red answers a knock at the door, only to discover to her surprise a bear, who reassures the family that he means them no harm. Before long the children are playing games with "their clumsy guest." At dawn's break the bear leaves but returns every night. However, when spring comes he departs, telling his new friends that he has to protect his treasures from an evil dwarf. At one point Snow White thinks she sees a hint that under the bear's skin lies "gold shining through it."

When the girls venture into the forest, they encounter a dwarf who, surrounded by precious jewels, bristles angrily at their efforts to help him. At one point, they surprise him after he "had emptied out his bag of precious stones . . . that glittered and sparkled with all colors so beautifully." As he once again curses them, the bear suddenly appears. The dwarf offers him the girls and his jewels in exchange for sparing his life. "Come, take these two wicked girls, they are tender morsels for you, fat as young quails; for mercy's sake, eat them!" The bear instead strikes the dwarf dead and reassures the girls that they are out of harm's way. As the bear comes closer to them, suddenly "his bearskin fell off, and he stood there a handsome man, clothed all in gold." Then the man who has emerged from his identity as a bear explains what has happened. "I am a king's son," he tells the surprised young women, and "was bewitched" by the evil dwarf, who had stolen his riches. "I have had to run about the forest as a savage beast," he remarks reassuringly, and could only be freed by killing the wicked dwarf. This fairy tale, like many others, has a happy ending that reaffirms traditional relationships between men and women. Snow White marries the king's son and Rose Red weds his brother (who conveniently suddenly appears), the two couples dividing the captured riches. The mother lived on "peacefully and happily," the two rose trees remaining outside her home, where annually they "bore the most beautiful roses, white and red," perhaps, in an unspoken way, representing grandchildren.[9]

What we have in these two bear stories from the Brothers Grimm are variants of tales of beauty and the beast, in which the innocent female encounters a bear who turns out to be a marriageable man. In "Bearskin," from the beginning the key figure is a man, albeit one cloaked in a bearskin. He is also wilder and uglier than the principal bear in "Snow White and Rose Red." This first tale ends happily for one sister but tragically for the two others. In contrast, the second one is more complicated and ends happily for all, except of course for the evil dwarf. In "Bearskin," the man who earlier appears as a bear is neither fully drawn nor more exceptional than your run-of-the-mill gentleman. In "Snow White and Rose Red," the man transformed from a bear, not just one dressed like a bear, turns out to be a wealthy prince. Since in "Bearskin" the hero's association with a bear is only skin deep, so to speak, this second story more resonantly evokes themes that have characterized tales of relationships between people and bears from time immemorial.

This tale suggests that underneath the bear's skin resides a man, and an exceptional one at that. More importantly, and more significantly than is true with "Bearskin," "Snow White and Rose Red" emphasizes the possibility of deeply emotional and positive relationships between people and bears. This harkens back and points forward to an emphasis on close connections between the species. Early in the story, a friendly, nonthreatening bear enters the household and coexists with the mother and her two daughters. Later on, we learn, a girl who had played affectionately with a bear emerges as a woman who marries a prince magically transformed from his identity as a "savage beast."[10] Fairy tales are often frightening, but in "Bearskin" the bear is more ugly than menacing, while in "Snow White and Rose Red" it is the dwarf and not the bear that is evil and dangerous.

Baloo the bear, a sloth bear, is a major figure in Rudyard Kipling's *The Jungle Book* (1894) and *The Second Jungle Book* (1895), stories based in part on ancient fables from India. Kipling spent his entire life in places that were or once had been part of the British Empire, and he wrote these books in Dummerston, Vermont. He earned a well-deserved reputation as a supporter of British imperialism. Though open to varied interpretations, his 1899 poem "The White Man's Burden" encouraged its readers to

Take up the White Man's burden—
Send forth the best ye breed—
Go bind your sons to exile
To serve your captives' need;
To wait in heavy harness,
On fluttered folk and wild—
Your new-caught, sullen peoples,
Half-devil and half-child.[11]

The poem appeared in London and New York publications on February 12, 1899, six days after the US Senate ratified the Treaty of Paris, which confirmed American control over the Philippines, Guam, Puerto Rico, and Cuba.[12]

Baloo is an important figure in the story of Mowgli, a young boy in India who is raised by a pack of wolves. Baloo serves as Mowgli's mentor, teaching him the laws of the jungle, just as other bears offer instruction to children. He tells the boy that the monkeys are lawless and uneducated outcasts. "Their way is not our way," he insists. "They are without leaders. They have no remembrance." With no justification for doing so, "they boast and chatter and pretend that they are a great people about to do great affairs in the jungle."[13] So it was important for Mowgli to learn not to be like monkeys. In the process, Baloo became his wise mentor who taught him to distinguish between uncivilized monkeys and agents of civilization like Baloo himself. This reflected Kipling's emphasis on the white man's burden as understood by the imperial colonizers in India.[14]

It was Disney's version of the story, offered in a 1967 film and accompanying media, that brought the story to broader American audiences. *Jungle Book*, the last movie Walt Disney worked on, though he died before it appeared on screens, differed considerably from Kipling's rendition, including the portrayal of Baloo.[15] No longer the wise and "revered teacher" who instructs Mowgli about the jungle's laws, Baloo has become the unwise and overly permissive dad. As the popular culture scholar Greg Metcalf has perceptively noted, Baloo was now "a slob with a knack for living effortlessly in the jungle" and a "soft touch," and "a little slow on the uptake—quite a shift from Kipling's Baloo, the teacher of all the laws of the jungle."[16]

To be sure, Baloo was Mowgli's teacher, but now of very different lessons. As one book version of Disney's narrative offered up, Baloo knew that "Mowgli needed some lessons on how to survive in the jungle." So he taught him "everything he knew, like how to find delicacies," and as new friends they "spent the afternoon doing what Baloo liked best: nothing but eating and relaxing."[17] Another book version doubled down on such themes. As in the film, Baloo taught Mowgli how to "fight like a bear," yet "the bear's silly behavior soon began to amuse" the boy. Before long, "Mowgli quickly scampered onto his belly" and soon "he started to tickle him all over."[18]

If British imperialism and its accompanying racism suffused Kipling's version, Disney's echoed American racial stereotypes. At one point the film pictures a Baloo with exaggerated coconut lips redolent of racist depictions of African Americans. As Anna Waterman, at the time a rising junior at New York University, observed in 2015, "the film's producers wanted to place Louis Armstrong in the role of the musician King Louie." However, because "they anticipated controversy over a black man voicing an ape," they instead "cast the Italian-American singer and trumpeter Louis Prima," a decision, she noted, that mirrored "many of the key features in the history of minstrelsy." After all, here was a white performer taking the place of an African American musician who sang "a song in character as an orangutan king who wants to be human."[19]

We can see how in other ways depictions of Baloo changed from 1894 to the ones Disney offered. In the illustrations Kipling's father drew for the book, Baloo is more or less realistic, standing on all fours, hardly anthropomorphized and minimally threatening. In contrast, as is true of the illustrations the Disney books offered, the film contains images of Baloo as humanlike, playful, kind, and fun loving.

Also racially charged in ways parallel to Disney's Baloo is Brer Bear, or Brother Bear, brought to us by Joel Chandler Harris, a white journalist in Atlanta who called for racial reconciliation in the New South. Yet Harris is even better understood, the historian Robin Bernstein has noted, as "one of slavery's most effective and influential apologists."[20] Harris had lived some of his teen years on a plantation and beginning in the late 1870s wrote *Uncle Remus Stories*, which relied on tales based on African American folklore he had collected. He then transformed the stories into print in an 1880 book.

In them, Uncle Remus, formerly enslaved but now living as a freedman in the post–Civil War South, tells stories to the son of a plantation owner. Less prominent than the tales of Brer Wolf or Brer Fox are the few that feature Brer Bear.[21] One of them, "Brother Bear's Big House," involves a family of bears living comfortably in "de biggest an' de warmest house." Uncle Remus, in dialect, underscores his commitment to the young boy that "ef I kin he'p it I never will be deceivin' you, ner lead you inter no bad habits." Then he adds, "All er his fambly wuz fat an' had what folks calls heft—de nachal plunkness." One day the bears hear a loud knock on the door, which they soon discover is from a Polecat, who offers his services as a housekeeper. Not having enough room inside for him, Brer Bear says Polecat is welcome to keep the outside of the house in order but not work inside. Brer Polecat responds, "You may think you aint got no room, but I bet you got des ez much room ez anybody what I know. Ef you let me in dar one time, I boun' you I'll make all de room I want."

At this point, Uncle Remus looks at the boy to see if he understood what Brer Polecat said before "he saw the faint shadow of a smile on the child's face. ''Taint gwine ter hurt you fer ter laugh a little bit, honey,'" Uncle Remus remarked. "Brer Polecat come in Brer B'ar's house, an' he had sech a bad breff dat dey all hatter git out—an' he stayed an' stayed twel time stopped runnin' ag'in' him."[22] And so Brer Polecat took over the house the Bears once lived in, forcing them to live out of doors.

"Why Brother Bear Has No Tail" is a second Uncle Remus story about the same figure. In it, Brer Rabbit challenges Brer Bear to slide down a slippery rock as he notes that, unlike the smaller animals who preceded him, "Brer B'ar foot too long en he tail too long fer ter slide down dat rock." Brother Bear took

Uncle Remus paused to see what effect this statement would have on the little boy. He closed his eyes, as though he were tired, but when he opened them again, he saw the faint shadow of a smile on the child's face. "'Taint gwine ter hurt you fer ter laugh a little bit, honey. Brer Polecat come in Brer B'ar's house, an' he had sech a bad breff dat dey all hatter git out—an' he stayed an' stayed twel time stopped runnin' ag'in' him."

Illustration for "Brother Bear's Big House," in Joel Chandler Harris, *Uncle Remus and Brer Rabbit* (1907).

up the challenge, responding with "Maybe dey is, en maybe dey ain't, yit I ain't a-feared ter try." And so he slid down the rock and he "break off he tail right smick-smack-smoove, en mo'n dat, w'en he make his disappear'nce up de big road, Brer Rabbit holler out: 'Brer B'ar!—O Brer B'ar! I year tell dat flaxseed poultices is mighty good fer so' places!'" And then "Brer B'ar ain't lookin' back."[23]

With both tales Uncle Remus was offering lessons to the young boy and Harris to a broader audience. The first tale apparently warns against letting strangers into a home lest an intruder disrupt domestic tranquility. The tale of how Brother Bear lost his tail warns against unwisely imitating what others have done and might even suggest, as did "Brother Bear's Big House," the danger of crossing social boundaries involving distinctions that wisdom teaches us to maintain. After all, not following social norms threatens the well-being of both a family comfortably situated and an animal who had all his body parts. Then there is the issue of what such narratives signify in the context of late nineteenth-century race relations in the New South and earlier on plantations. After all, the view of racial reconciliation that Harris endorsed only went so far along the path to social justice. It is possible that Chandler, speaking through

Uncle Remus, is advising post-Reconstruction African Americans to remain respectful of somewhat changing but nonetheless long-standing social relationships. And perhaps in "Brother Bear's Big House," if the comfortably situated bears represent naive whites who allow a shrewd animal to take over their house without violence, the implication is that plantation owners should keep African Americans toiling in the fields, being wary of letting them work in the Big House and upsetting the social order without resorting to violence.[24]

Disney transformed the Uncle Remus stories into many texts, consistently marked by the use of demeaning dialect and reminders of racist minstrelsy. In 1946 the studio produced *Song of the South*, a film that drew on these narratives. Since then and increasingly so, observers have criticized the film as well as its use on the Splash Mountain rides in Disneyland and Disney World for its use of animal minstrels from the 1946 film. In 2020, the company announced its "reimagining" of the ride by deploying figures from the 2009 film *The Princess and the Frog*, which featured Disney's first African American princess. Disney rolled out that version, a new ride titled Tiana's Bayou Adventure, in June 2024. "It's a historic moment for Disney," wrote Brooks Barnes in the *New York Times*. "After 69 years in the theme park business, the company will have a marquee attraction based on a Black character."[25]

The closure was a delayed reaction to criticism of how Harris depicted the past, as he portrayed African Americans as dumb, gullible bit figures who play significant roles in more recent discussions of racism and cultural appropriation. Both Toni Morrison and Alice Walker earlier denounced what they saw as the racist ventriloquism.[26] When Henry Louis Gates Jr. and Maria Tatar, specialists respectively in African American studies and folklore, edited *The Annotated African American Folktales* (2018), they struggled with the issue of how to handle what Harris conveyed from Uncle Remus. Tatar insisted that "suddenly this entire tradition has been appropriated for white audiences, and made charming rather than subversive and perilous, dangerous." On the other hand, Gates noted that his father "would have us read the Uncle Remus tales but within a whole different context," as he in effect "re-breathed blackness into those folktales."[27] Yet they agreed that Harris worked within the tradition of minstrelsy, in the process both offering a "utopian depiction of Southern plantation life" and revealing "the cruel contradictions" of the system of slavery.[28]

The prominent African American writer Julius Lester transformed these stories in ways that, rather than demeaning African Americans, treated them more respectfully than Harris could accomplish or even imagine.[29] Changing the Uncle Remus stories from racist to antiracist lessons for children and transforming oral traditions into print, Lester introduced his retelling of the Uncle

Remus stories by celebrating their importance as "the largest single collection of Afro-American folktales ever collected and published," with "their place in Afro-American culture . . . singular and undisputed." He found problematic how Harris relied so heavily on racist dialect, made Uncle Remus a central figure, and used the N-word. He also took issue with how Harris, in his own words, wrote of the "faithful darky" who "had nothing but pleasant memories of the discipline of slavery." Lester noted that Harris insisted an enslaved person "identified wholly with his white master and mistress, espouses their value system, and is derisive of other blacks." Lester criticized how such characterizations were "used as a symbol of slavery and a retrospective justification," with most whites appreciating the way Uncle Remus "confirmed an image of black inferiority many whites needed." He also objected to how Harris deployed the white boy as the audience for these stories because this obscured the important role the stories played in the lives of African Americans.[30] In contrast, Lester especially appreciated the figure of Brer Rabbit as "a symbol of how black people responded to slavery. Unable to resist physically, black resistance to slavery found sublimated expression through the figure of the wily Rabbit who outsmarted those seeking to oppress him."[31]

There are at least five stories about Brer Bear that Harris offered and Lester modified.[32] Generally speaking, both versions drive home the point that as a trickster Brer Rabbit outsmarts Brer Bear. Compare Lester's "The End of Brer Bear" with the version derived from Harris and offered in Richard Chase's *Complete Tales* with a slightly different title. Both tales tell of Brer Rabbit tricking Brer Bear into getting stung by bees when he invades a beehive. Not unlike the nineteenth-century version, Lester's ends with the narrator saying, "For all anybody know, them bees are stinging him still."[33] In "Brer Rabbit, Brer Bear, and the Honey Orchard," as in the story related by Harris, Lester tells of Brer Rabbit figuring out why Brer Bear is so fat while all the other animals were famished. Conspiring with them, he tricks Brer Bear again. In both the Harris version and Lester's, all the animals "took a lot of honey for the wives and children," thus redistributing what Brer Bear had hoarded. Lester's version ended more pointedly than the original by using the remark that "all the animals came and laughed at Brer Bear." This underscored both the justifiable humiliation its community-oriented nature exacted—and, of course, as in the story of the Big House, how the disenfranchised redistributed wealth.[34]

While Lester did not include "Brother Bear's Big House" in his books, he did offer the story of Brer Bear losing his tail. In many ways similar, the versions differ significantly along lines Lester deployed elsewhere. He eliminated the racist dialect, the little white boy as listener, and Uncle Remus as narrator.

Instead, he offered himself acting as the storyteller telling tales directly to the reader. This means that Brer Rabbit, rather than the original storyteller, under-cuts the plantation owners, who are the boy's parents. The original ended with "Yit Brer B'ar ain't lookin' back," while more pointedly Lester finishes with "But Bear was sore all right, but whether he was more sore in his hindquarters or his feelings, I just don't know."[35]

If the Uncle Remus stories varied with changing times and imperatives, we can see even more variety among those in Wikipedia's "List of Fictional Bears," which focuses mainly on American examples.[36] Divided by genre, it contains well over three hundred entries, a number that a little work might easily double or triple. There are bears that express a wide range of moods, most of them lighthearted and unthreatening—the continually annoyed, grumpy Barney Bear in the series of the same name produced by the MGM Studios beginning in 1939; the neurotic Pepper from the Cartoon Network's *Summer Camp Island*; the simple-minded Barnstable Bear in Walt Kelly's *Pogo* cartoons; and Fozzie Bear in *The Muppets*, who somehow cannot perform effectively as a comic. Then there are bears with distinct identities, notably Bi-Polar Bear, a character in the *Queer Duck* series, which in the early years of the twenty-first century explored issues in the gay and lesbian communities. As is true with authors of children's books, producers in other media deploy bears to teach young-sters how to behave properly, whether it's Burble Bear, who in the PBS *Danger Rangers* series tells youngsters how to remain safe; the principal figure in Dis-ney's *Special Agent Oso*, who shows children how to clean up their rooms; or Peetie the Panda in *South Park* warning kids against sexual harassment. And of course, there is an ample number of connections with storied bears: teddy and the three associated with Goldilocks, yes, but most cleverly P. T. Bridgeport as part of Walt Kelly's *Pogo*, referencing the city where P. T. Barnum served as mayor and was laid to rest.

The vast majority of these stories feature unthreatening, comical, cuddly, and friendly bears, characteristics ideally suited as instruments of childhood education. Anthropomorphized to various extents, they blur or cross the line between human and nonhuman animals. Most of the exceptions are variously identified as distant in time or place. Pixar's 2012 *Legend of Mor'du* tells the story of how an evil prince is transformed into the title character, a violent black bear. *Tomorrow's Pioneers*, a Palestinian children's show sponsored by Hamas, well before October 7, 2024, featured a teddy bear named Nassur who promises a jihad that will "slaughter" the Jews "so they will be expelled from our land."[37] Sacha Baron Cohen's 2006 *Borat! Cultural Learnings of America for Make Benefit Glorious Nation of Kazakhstan* features a black bear. As Borat and his companion Azamat Bagatov travel across America, they protect themselves with the black bear, named after Borat's former wife Oksana, whom a bear had killed before he came to America. Cohen's use of ironic humor transforms the bear from a murderer to a friendly companion in a way that counters what *The Legend of Mor'du* and *Tomorrow's Pioneers* offer up.

It is possible to highlight similar representational issues in many forms, especially as mascots, as well as with animation, comics, film, and video games. Bears have served as mascots for hundreds of high school, college, and professional sports teams, few of them as intriguing and emblematic as those involved in the intrastate rivalry between the Bears of the University of California at Berkeley and the Bruins of the University of California at Los Angeles. For both universities, potentially ferocious grizzlies over time turned into less threatening ones as prominent symbols of athletic prowess. Until 1941, Berkeley's teams, named the Golden Bears and represented by the mascot Oski, deployed live grizzly cubs. Since they inevitably grew larger and more dangerous, something had to be done. At a rally in 1941 a student appeared on the sidelines dressed in an extra-large yellow sweater and what the university's website describes as "blue trousers, oversized shoes, large white gloves, and a *papier mâché* head caricaturing a bear." By 1946 the switch was standardized, with men of much shorter stature than grown grizzlies but possessing ample abilities as gymnasts dressed up in bear costumes to serve as mascots.[38]

Although the Berkeley bear, notes the American Football Database, "has his benign side ('patient' and 'silent'), he is more often presented as growling, fighting, rumbling, grumbling, thundering, and shaking the ground," and in Berkeley's fight songs "he is described as sturdy and mighty."[39] Yet in many pictures, such as the smiley-faced version on his seventy-fifth birthday in 2016, hardly bears this out.[40]

Downstate, the UCLA Bruin has a more complicated history and at times an even more comical visage. The institution's first mascot was Rags, a stray dog found on campus in 1917. Then for a brief period, Cubs was the mascot's name, signifying that compared with Berkeley's founding in 1868, UCLA was a youngster, a university standing on its own only in 1927. A few years earlier, students had selected a grizzly to represent the university's powerful toughness, or, as a 2010 article in the *Daily Bruin* labeled it, a "ferocious moniker."[41] That choice turned out to be short-lived. In 1926 the institution that was about to emerge as UCLA sought to join the Pacific Coast Conference, which already had the University of Montana Grizzlies, a school that has yet to abandon the ferocious symbolism. Rejecting Gorillas and Buccaneers, students at UCLA settled on

Oski the Bear, mascot of Berkeley's Golden Bears, celebrates his birthday. UC Berkeley. Photo by Brittany Hosea-Small.

Bruins when their opponents at Berkeley relinquished any claim to that variant and became Oski the Bear.

At one point in the 1930s, students at UCLA somehow deployed, of all things, a Bruin drawn in a Mickey Mouse style and then revealed a book-loving Bruin in the 1940s. Beginning in the early 1950s there was Little Joe Bear, a live bear, usually a Himalayan cub from India, soon called Joe Bruin. In 1961, to offer reassurances of normative gendered relationships—like Smokey at the National Zoo in Washington—he was joined by a female named Josephine (later Josie) Bruin. Apparently unlike the pairing in the nation's capital, the goal in Westwood was not to produce an heir but to emphasize that UCLA was a coed institution. By the middle of the 1960s, as had happened up north a quarter of a century earlier, real bears ended up in zoos, and students, in this case both male and female ones dressed up as bears, took their place at athletic events. As was true at Cal and elsewhere, it did not take long for UCLA to shift from potentially dangerous bears to humorous, nonthreatening ones.

"It's a cute sight, seeing Joe and Josephine Bruin kiss as a mass of cheerleaders steadily lift them up for all the audience to see," commented a *Daily Bruin* reporter in 2010.[42] To this day, representations of UCLA's Bruin have varied.

Joe and Josie Bruin, UCLA's mascots. Photo by UCLA 1919. Wikimedia Commons, CC BY-SA 4.0, https://creativecommons.org/licenses/by-sa/4.0/deed.en.

In 1985, alumni raised money for a new fight song, "Mighty Bruins," and for the Bruin, a six-foot-tall and ten-foot-long statue. Alums delighted to have this statue "after years of feeling frustrated by the lack of an appropriate Bruin symbol on campus," ran the accompanying notice, with the animal's "fluid forward movement symbolizing the ongoing strength and progress of UCLA." Then the intent was driven home more pointedly. "With its ferocious look," the announcement ran, "the grizzly was a departure from UCLA's friendly Joe Bruin mascot." The appropriately named Alexander Hamilton, a representative of the Alumni Association, doubled down, insisting, "You'll notice it's formidable, . . . the antithesis of fragility."[43] Despite the best efforts to return to the Bruin as a symbol of ferocity, more comforting, humorous, and loving images persist: A "real" bear, albeit a smiling one. And an iconic smiling and welcoming one. And above all, the antic, not-at-all ferocious, and loving Joe and Josie.

In the comic book world, few strips containing bears match the popularity of *Garfield*, drawn by Jim Davis. First seen in 1976 and syndicated nationally beginning two years later, at one point *Garfield* held the Guinness World Record as the most widely syndicated comic strip. The central figure is Garfield, a

Garfield and Pooky, characters created by the cartoonist Jim Davis in the 1970s.

lazy, manipulative cat who interacts with other figures, including a teddy bear named Pooky.[44] Pooky appeared for the first time in late October 1978 when Garfield discovered him in a bureau drawer. Like most teddy bears, Pooky remained both silent and his companion's best friend.

Garfield talks of how, like other cats, he is independent, needing "nobody, no time, no where, no way." And just as he asserts this, we see him proudly holding up his favorite stuffed animal as he asks, "Isn't that right, Pooky?"[45]

In another sequel Garfield celebrates two insights he has about life as he picks up an immobile Pooky, who sits in front of him. Holding Pooky in the middle panel, Garfield says lesson number one concerns the reciprocal love he and Pooky have for each other. In the last panel, Garfield has returned Pooky to his original position, this time sitting there even more passively. "Simple truths," the active cat says to an inanimate teddy in the way a parent might instruct a child. "Simple truths are the most profound truths." In another sequence, Garfield wonders why people so love their teddy bears. "It's for their dont's," he concludes, since they neither eat your food nor dance with your date. Along similar lines, this time playing on what's inside Pooky, Garfield insists that since teddy bears are always "stuffed," he loves eating with them.[46]

To be sure, Pooky is less prominent in Garfield's world than other characters. There is Garfield's owner Jon (a.k.a. Jonathan Q. Arbuckle); Odie, Jon's beagle; and Dr. Liz Wilson, the vet who takes care of both Garfield and Odie. Because these three figures are animate rather than stuffed, they are more complex, active, and on occasion adversarial than Pooky. This goes to underscore that as a teddy bear, Pooky, a cat's best friend, is of necessity cuddly and nonthreatening—or in other words, as unlike animate, larger-than-life, and rarely cuddly real bears as possible.

Like so many other productions featuring bears, such as Yogi Bear (originating in 1958) and the Gummi Bears (launched in 1985), the Garfield franchise expanded from its origin in one medium into seemingly infinite examples in others, where its varied enterprises reportedly garner income as high as $1 billion a year. Starting with Paws, Inc., which Davis launched in 1981, the resulting enterprises have thrived under the umbrellas of continually shifting corporate entities. What began as a locally published comic strip titled *Jon* in 1976, and was renamed *Garfield* in 1978, before long developed into the syndicated feature appearing in 2,600 newspapers. From there it spread into a seemingly endless number of forms that included comic and art books; movies; television shows and series (with four prime-time specials winning Emmys); an educational website (www.ProfessorGarfield.org); credit cards; and its own official website (Garfield.com). There's also a variety of webcomics such as Garfield Minus Garfield that allows you to view and play with comic strips; items for purchase or use such as toys and clothing; and even Caribbean cruises and short-lived virtual or ghost restaurants in several global locations that offered Garfield-shaped pizzas.[47]

Garfield even made it to video games, including a 2004 one, *Garfield: The Search for Pooky*. It turns out that while Garfield was sleeping, three Mafioso Mice arrived on the scene and stole Pooky. Once awake on Monday morning, Garfield is determined to find his beloved companion. Gamers then control Garfield as he sets out on a mission of recovery, in the process encountering characters from the comic strip, coming up against Garfield's characteristic foul-ups, and all the while like Garfield accumulating food along the way.

This is but one of many video games featuring bears. And what is notable is that they provide the major exception to the pattern of contemporary fabulous bears as more friendly than fierce. Bears appear prominently as figures in them, balanced more evenly than elsewhere between tame and threatening or, as a website describing some of the best ones notes, among them are "cuddly bear cubs, ruthless killing machines, and pretty much everything in between." At one end is Franklin Fizzlybear, a figure in the *Viva Piñata* series, himself a giant piñata stuffed with candy. A large, innocent, and easygoing grizzly, he belies his species by spending his days enjoying his adventures as if he has no cares in the world. At the other end is Tibbers, a teddy bear who is the favorite of Annie Hastur, a figure in the *League of Legends* franchise. With a witch and warlock as parents, at a young age Annie transformed Tibbers into her pet protector; in battle Tibbers ferociously attacks Annie's enemies, setting them on fire and placing them on the path to deadly destruction. And with ambiguity in between these two extremes is Monokuma, a key figure in the Japanese video games produced by Danganronpa. His bifurcated body—divided down the center, with white and a smile on one side and black with an evil grin on the other—reflects his dual nature. Sometimes Monokuma resembles the cuddly Garfield and at others, and more fundamentally, he is evil incarnate, angrily on the attack and taking pleasure in wreaking merciless havoc.[48]

Then there are contemporary narratives that focus on real live celebrity bears. Live celebrity bears appear during Fat Bear Week, which takes place in Katmai National Park and Preserve, with over a million people going online to vote for the heftiest bear in the region. In October 2023, the victor was Grazer, who with 108,321 votes triumphed over Chuck with a mere 23,134. The competition's website celebrated her as a successful angler who "can chase down fleeing salmon in many parts of the river or patiently scavenge dead and dying salmon after they spawn." In addition, she was "a particularly defensive mother bear who has successfully raised two litters of cubs" and who "often preemptively confronts and attacks much larger bears—even large and dominant adult males—in order to ensure her cubs are safe." A single mother, "Grazer's combination of skill and toughness makes her one of Brooks River's most formidable, successful, and adaptable bears."[49]

Friends who live in Jackson Hole, Wyoming, alerted me to the case of Grizzly 399.[50] Writing for the local newspaper in late 2021, Paul Hansen identified her as "a remarkable bear, maybe the most beloved and iconic wild animal in American history," who had "blessed" the community for fifteen years. He celebrated her as a mother who successfully raised four cubs that season, offspring who were so well behaved that they "walked past hundreds of cows and horses and did not bother one." One night, the story continued, the "mom took the brood north, walking right through the heart of the town of Jackson," with the mother and her cubs getting "a police escort through town" as they headed to where they would hibernate. This praise for their good behavior contrasted with the problematic habits of local residents. "The whole county is kind of behind the times in terms of trash storage and conflict prevention," noted Hilary Cooley of the US Fish and Wildlife Service. Some locals met to review the community's "bear-friendly rules," which county and town officials then failed to implement. "It is past time," Hansen noted, "to get the regulations, enforcement, education and cost-sharing needed to protect our wildlife," which seemed more endangered because of local poorly behaved people.[51]

Hansen's remarks remind us that even with actual bears, there is a blurring of the line between real and representational ones. Nowhere is this clearer than in the work of Thomas Mangelsen, from whose workshop you can spend $5,295 to purchase a 48-inch by 72-inch museum-mounted print of *399: Portrait of a Legend* from a Limited Edition Collection.[52] Then you can read on his website an essay from the *Mountain Journal* by the journalist Todd Wilkinson.[53]

Wilkinson's essay, not unlike Mangelsen's photographs, showcases how even though some observers celebrate experiences with real live bears in the wilderness as authentic, even the most compelling images and stories on which they rely do not come to us in pure, direct, and unmediated ways. Some of how Wilkinson and Mangelsen portray 399 underscores how they frame her in anthropomorphic terms. Wilkinson reiterates that "unbeknownst to her, she's become the most famous living wild bear on Earth" and one, moreover, that provides "delight to millions" and helps raise consciousness about the need to protect grizzlies. "399's composure," he insists, "challenged the human knee-jerk tendency people have to only see grizzlies through a lens of danger and fear, and which historically provided a justification for treating them as menaces and thus eradicating them." Wilkinson played on media-infused themes. He compared "the final chapter in a thrilling page-turning potboiler filled with twists and turns" with "the final pages in this bear biography" that "have yet to be written." He also spoke of "this single mama grizzly, whose own behavior has transformed the way people think about grizzlies and whose status has caused some to cast aspersions on her as 'a celebrity bear.'" Again and again, as is true in so many films that feature bears, both Wilkinson and Mangelsen celebrate 399 for her maternal power. "Think of 399 as both an old new mother and grandma passing through the fading twilight of senescence," Wilkinson insists. "Successfully raising four offspring would be a difficult feat for any mother, let alone a wild grizzly," he continues, "but for a matriarch to have quadruplets to feed and fend for at age 24?"—which she did, he noted, under exacting conditions. There were the times, he notes, "when she got separated from one of her cubs," and she would "call, and race around, and worry about it, only to exude motherly tenderness when they were reunited." Notably, the title of Mangelsen's 2023 book is *Grizzly 399: The World's Most Famous Mother Bear*.[54]

On June 17, 2023, almost exactly one month after Wilkinson offered his remarks, Mangelsen echoed what Wilkinson said. He criticized those "who steadfastly condemn anthropomorphizing." Celebrating 399's cognitive and emotional powers, he then proceeded to ask, "Who says a mother doesn't love her children, wouldn't do anything to give them a better life, wouldn't ardently care for them, protect them from harm, feed them, teach them and prepare them for their own journey in life?"[55]

Narratives of bears began in oral traditions, found expression in print, and then appeared in the widest possible range of modern media. Throughout, these bears that have emotions and agency are representational rather than real. In fabulous tales stretching from unwritten stories, the Bible, Native American traditional teachings, *Aesop's Fables*, Garfield's Pooky, and eventually to contemporary video games, bears vary greatly—smart and dumb; animate and as close as possible to a human being or an inanimate stuffed animal; wild and threatening or tame and friendly. Often they are unquestionably in the world of nonhuman animals, but at other times they morph from bear to human or connect with people in emotionally rich ways. Precisely because we see them as emotionally variable, their didactic deployment shifts, offering warnings about life-threatening danger or respect for private property.[56]

Strikingly, although we can identify the species of some fabled bears, in most cases such an identity does not matter. The ones in the Bible are probably the now distinct Syrian brown bears, but who knew or cared? Nor is the specific taxonomy important to most of us when it comes to those in the heavens or in tales offered by Aesop, the Brothers Grimm, or Uncle Remus—let alone when it comes to Yogi, the Gummi Bears, or bears appearing in video games. Garfield's Pooky is a teddy bear, far removed from the one Teddy Roosevelt refused to kill. Kipling's Baloo is a sloth bear, but Disney's studios transformed him into a bear of no particular type. To be sure, as mascots most bears are black, brown, or grizzlies; but what are they when they appear on the field as cartoonish figures with people inside? In the end, so many times a bear is a bear abstracted from the life of an actual animal.

Fables and folklore reveal many transformations. One is the shift from racist stories to ones that celebrate African American culture. Generally speaking, and with some notable exceptions, over time we witness a change from domination to reciprocity. Even though this happens at a time when people are endangering the lives of bears through hunting and poaching, for example, they emerge as less threatening, more like us than like real bears, and increasingly kinder, even humorous. These shifts often operate in ways that challenge the assumption of human superiority or wisdom. Yet such changes occurred unevenly. There are examples of opposing but simultaneous depictions, beginning with how the Bible contained references to bears as warlike and peaceable.

Many examples undermine simple, linear trajectories, with different genres and audiences controlling representations. For example, a group of UCLA alumni want a fierce, manly Bruin, while in most cases fans watching brutal combat on the field or court are entertained by a lovingly innocent heterosexual couple. Or take the contrast between Disney's Baloo or Garfield's Pooky and most bears in video games. Those in charge of and seeking profit from Baloo and Pooky assume that preteens (and their parents) want cartoonish and playful bears. In contrast, their peers who develop video games know that many among the customers in their audience are testosterone-driven teens and older, likely to purchase and play with Tibbers. However, even within this genre the situation is complicated, as witnessed in the popularity of Monokuma. In the end it is hard not to be struck by the shape-shifting, rollicking, border-crossing, and emotionally resonant qualities of some fabulous bears expressed in every imaginable genre. Unlike what is true with so many other nonhuman animals, humans can project onto bears, especially fabled ones, an immensely wide range of characteristics that over time both remain constant and shift significantly.

2

The Stories of Hugh Glass

THE CASE OF A DISAPPEARING
AND REAPPEARING DANGEROUS BEAR

✕

Folktale bears who are rarely threatening. Bears seen in the heavens and told of in biblical stories and Native American teachings. Narratives of bears in Reynard the Fox and the Brothers Grimm, Rudyard Kipling's Baloo, and Brer Bear from the *Uncle Remus* stories. Bears here, bears there, bears everywhere—often anthropomorphic, friendly, lovable ones that, rather than harming people, help, love, comfort, and protect them.

On the other hand, there is Old Ben in William Faulkner's story "The Bear," embedded in *Go Down, Moses* (1942). In his evocative, complicated style, Faulkner describes this legendary black bear, a seemingly immortal animal, as a beast that "had earned for himself a name, a definite designation like a living man:—the long legend of corn-cribs broken down and rifled, of shoats and grown pigs and even calves carried bodily into the woods and devoured and traps and deadfalls over-thrown and dogs mangled and slain and shotgun and even rifle shots delivered at point-blank range yet with no more effect than so many peas blown through a tube by a child." When the hunter Boon Hogganbeck and his dog Lion attack Old Ben, "the bear surged erect, raising with it the man and dog too, and turned and still carrying the man and the dog it took two or three steps toward the woods on its hind feet as a man would have walked and crashed down." Soon after, members of the hunting party looked closely at the body of Old Ben. They found "the little hard lumps under his skin which were the old bullets (there were fifty-two of them, buckshot rifle and ball) and the single almost invisible slit under his left shoulder where Boon's blade had finally found his life."[1]

There are other terrifying examples of dangerous bears. I can remember visiting a National Park decades ago. At the visitor headquarters I saw an exhibit of the car door that a grizzly ripped off so the bear could hunt for food inside. Then there are the familiar stories of a bear disturbing a suburban idyll. Edward R. Ricciuti captured this in his 2014 book, *Bears in the Backyard: Big Animals, Sprawling Suburbs and the New Urban Jungle*.[2] Dramatic and frightening stories of bears killing people also exist. "A 39-year-old woman was found dead Friday night after an apparent bear attack in Southern Colorado," CNN reported on May 1, 2021. Even though Cory Chick, the regional manager of Colorado Parks and Wildlife, noted that "bear attacks are extremely rare," with only four fatal ones in fifty years, he remarked that the incident, which involved a black bear, was "a sad reminder that bears are wild and potentially dangerous."[3] The same double response of reassurance and terror appears in David Quammen's 2003 *Monster of the God: The Man-Eating Predator in the Jungles of History and the Mind*. Buried in 437 pages of a text where he explores dangerous animals, including bears, all over the world and throughout history, there appears a short presentation of reassuring statistics. In ninety years at Glacier National Park, only nine people died from bear attacks. In the same years forty-eight drowned, twenty-three met their fate when they fell off cliffs, and twenty-six perished in car crashes.[4] Fascinated terror, as often happens, triumphs over calm reassurance.

Then there are three famous narratives of violent bears, typically more about the harm that humans do to themselves and to each other than about how dangerous bears are—highlighted in varying degrees in stories about Hugh Glass, Grizzly Adams, and Timothy Treadwell. The early ones are inextricably connected with how the pursuit of Manifest Destiny played out on the Western frontiers, and all of them pit men against ursine opponents, the tales often revealing more about humans than bears. Centuries before white trappers and traders arrived in the region, Indigenous peoples from many different nations had settled there, living in villages, trading what they captured in hunts, and eventually farming the land. The United States had acquired vast territory as part of the

Louisiana Purchase of 1803, a mere score of years before a bear mauled Glass. Fourteen years later the federal government established its first trading post in the region. This marked the beginning of continuous settlement by whites, initially in scant numbers. It served as a base for the area's dominant activities by these whites—conflicts with some Native Americans and cooperation with others, as well as the slaughter of animals as part of fur trapping and trading.

The story of Hugh Glass begins with his near death at the paws of a grizzly bear (*Ursus arctos horribilis*), followed by heroic recovery and revenge-driven resolution, told and retold since the 1823 incident that began in what is now South Dakota. Influentially recorded by James Hall in 1825 in a short narrative in Philadelphia's *The Port Folio*, it was then elaborated around campfires and in saloons. Soon after, other versions followed suit as they relied on first, second, and thirdhand information as well as wholly invented details. The story quickly morphed and became part of regional folklore reinterpreted more broadly, ranging from tales told by vernacular storytellers to skilled literary practitioners and then to the historian Jon T. Coleman. Ninety years after Hall's rendering, the first major version appeared in *The Song of Hugh Glass* by John G. Neihardt, an amateur historian and ethnographer best known for bringing into print *Black Elk Speaks* (1932), the story of an Oglala Lakota medicine man. In 1915 he published an epic poem more than one hundred pages long, one better known for its narrative than for its literary quality.[5] In postwar America, a growing series of explorations proliferated. Three-dimensionally, a sculpture by John Lopez is now on display at the Grand River Museum in Lemmon, South Dakota, where the bear looms more prominently than in almost any other genre. In print, there is Frederick Manfred's *Lord Grizzly* (1954), *The Saga of Hugh Glass: Pirate, Pawnee, and Mountain Man* (1963) by John Myers Myers, and Michael Punke's *The Revenant* (2002).[6] On-screen renditions begin with a 1966 TV episode in *Death Valley Days* titled "Hugh Glass Meets the Bear." Then comes the 1971 *Man in the Wilderness*, a movie with a very modest budget of less than $2 million and the first significant version of the saga of Hugh Glass to jump from print to the big screen. Despite or because of its box office success, critics deemed it full of pretention and lacking in subtlety. Most readers will know the story of Hugh Glass from the 2015 film version of Punke's novel *The Revenant* that grossed over half a billion dollars and won three Oscars—for the director Alejandro G. Iñárritu, actor Leonardo DiCaprio as Hugh Glass, and the cinematographer Emmanuel Lubezki. A version of the story even appears in the video game *World of Warcraft*, sold by Blizzard Entertainment.[7] Glass himself never tried to monetize his story, but in the late twentieth and early twenty-first centuries others did, turning Hugh Glass, more than the bear that attacked him, into a celebrity.

Americans had first learned of grizzlies from reports by Lewis and Clark. "Here was an animal," the Western historian Robert Righter wrote me, "who did not fear human beings and even attacked and killed them." In a way, they "changed how we saw the wilderness," since the encounters with what Meriwether Lewis called "a very large and turrible animal" forced observers to realize that humans were "not necessarily the most threatening predator." As Lewis and Clark had noted, grizzlies were "said more frequently to attack a man on meeting with him than to flee from him." Only implicitly, however, did Hall connect the story of Hugh Glass with the Western wilderness, the nation's transformation, or with Christian traditions, as some later versions did.[8]

To a greater or lesser extent all versions of the life of Hugh Glass (ca. 1783–1833) rely on what James Hall wrote in 1825. "He was employed by Major Henry as a *trapper* and was attached to his command before the Arickara towns," Hall wrote. He was referring to Andrew Henry, who with William H. Ashley owned the Rocky Mountain Fur Company, and to the Akiara Indigenous peoples, today part of the Mandan, Hidatsa, and Arikara Nation. Glass was a part of a small group of "adventurers," Hall noted, who "usually draw their food, as well as their raiment, from Nature's spacious warehouse." Because Glass was such a skilled shooter, he preceded the party and soon encountered a grizzly bear who "arose within three yards" of him. Before Glass could retreat, "he was seized by the throat and raised from the ground. Casting him again upon the earth, his grim adversary tore a mouthful of the cannibal food," and then moved away to give her cubs some of what she had torn from the body of Glass. He tried to escape, but the bear "seized him again at the shoulder" and then "lacerated his left arm very much, and inflicted a severe wound on the back of his head."

His fellow trappers arrived and shot the attacker, "dispatching the bear as she stood over her victim." Though being "snatched from the grasp of the ferocious animal," whose appearance now ends in this narration but not in versions that followed, Glass was in terrible shape. Having "received several dangerous wounds, his whole body was bruised and mangled, and he lay weltering in blood, in exquisite torment." He could not be moved, there was no medical help nearby, and danger lurked since the mountain men were "now in the country of hostile Indians." Major Henry offered rewards to the two men (correctly identified elsewhere as Jim Bridger and Fitz Fitzgerald) who would stay with Glass until he died or recovered and could be moved. After these men remained by Glass's side for five days, they became convinced he could not recover and so they abandoned him—leaving him with little, not his rifle nor nearly any of the equipment he would need to survive. When "these unprincipled wretches" caught up with

Illustration from an unidentifiable nineteenth-century newspaper of a huge bear attacking Hugh Glass. Source: https://en.wikipedia.org/wiki/Hugh_Glass.

Major Henry, they told him Glass had died of his wounds and that they had buried him.

Gradually recovering, Glass left for Fort Kiowa (named Kiawa in Hall's document and also known as Fort Lookout), and "with indefatigable industry, he continued to crawl," supposedly (though it is not entirely clear in Hall's depiction) for three hundred miles until he reached that destination. Before he could fully heal while there, he resumed his journey. "The primary object of this voyage was declared to be the recovery of his arms and vengeance on the recreant," now identified in the singular, who "had robbed and abandoned him in his hour of peril." After unidentified Native Americans killed his five companions, Glass arrived at a fort, which he realized Arikaras had captured, but rival Mandan members rescued him and delivered him to another fort. Always on the move, Glass and members of his party snuck away and traveled thirty-eight miles to where Major Henry was stationed. He discovered that the trappers who abandoned him had gone onward. On the last day of February 1824, he headed for Fort Atkinson, located on the Missouri River just north of what is now Omaha, Nebraska, to find those men.

Glass and his companions came to where the Arikaras were and the Native Americans welcomed them to other lodges, though Glass and his compatriots were suspicious of their intentions. When they realized they were in danger, they escaped, "pursued by their treacherous entertainers:—the whites ran for life; the red warriors for blood," Hall noted, using typically racist language. With several in his party killed by the Arikaras, Glass (because he was "versed in all the arts of border warfare") was able "to baffle his blood-thirsty enemies," and they abandoned their search for him "in despair." Now he continued on, along the way surviving, as he often did, on berries and on the meat of wild animals he killed with a knife he had devised. At last, he arrived at Fort Atkinson, "where he found his old traitorous acquaintance [Fitzgerald] in the garb of a private soldier." Because Fitzgerald was a soldier, the officer in command "shielded the delinquent from chastisement." The commanding officer "ordered his rifle to be restored," Hall wrote, and gave Glass other equipment. "This appeased the wrath of Hugh Glass, whom my informant left," Hall noted, "astounding, with his wonderful narration, the gaping rank and file of the garrison."

Like others who followed, Hall wrote didactically. To him, the story revealed multiple dangers in the West and admirable characteristics of the mountain man who was forced by circumstances to rely not on civilization but on his own skills and talents. As a "trapper whose erratic steps lead him continually into new toils and dangers," Glass sustained himself on shrewdness, fearlessness, resourcefulness, "skill and perseverance," and "indefatigable industry." Hall insisted that "the hardships voluntarily encountered, the privations manfully endured by this hardy race in the exercise of their perilous calling, present abundant proofs of those peculiar characteristics which distinguish the American woodsmen."[9]

In retrospect, several things are striking about Hall's narrative. The violent bear makes the briefest of appearances. As others have noted but Hall only hinted at, when Glass finally found the man who had abandoned him, he achieved not revenge or vengeance but a version of lawful and chivalrous frontier justice, all of these imperatives following codes infused with manly strengths. Regaining his possessions was enough to "appease his wrath." What would have happened if being in the military had not shielded the miscreant from Hall's wrath remained unclear in this telling. And Hall's rendering is not without complications. When he notes that "the primary object of this voyage was declared to be the recovery of his arms and vengeance," he used the passive voice, leaving it unclear who saw the mission involving vengeance and whether getting his equipment back would have necessarily sufficed to satisfy Glass. In addition, though some of the post-1825 versions of the story of Hugh Glass focused on the predatory behavior of bears, in Hall's telling the more serious threats came from humans—not only from the men who abandoned Glass but more fatally from Native Americans, whom Hall described in racist terms as "treacherous" and "blood-thirsty." Though Mandans helped save him, we know (as Hall could not) that ten years later, in the early spring of 1833, some Arikaras killed Glass. At some points Hall identifies specific Indigenous peoples but at others leaves them unnamed.[10]

As a scholar who still believes it is possible to approximate reality, I nonetheless understand how stories in so many media offer multiple versions of the elusive truth. "What occurred on this expedition is historically true" appears on-screen close to the beginning of the movie *Man in the Wilderness*. In a "Historical Note," Punke acknowledged that, as with other versions, "some legend no doubt has invaded the history of Hugh Glass." Though he "took literary and historical liberties in a couple of places," he tried "to stay true to history in the main events of the story."[11] Yet the scant and scattered amount of information about the life of Hugh Glass enabled storytellers to tell tall tales that connected one life with the nation's history. As Coleman put it in his 2012 *Here Lies Hugh Glass: A Mountain Man, a Bear, and the Rise of the American Nation*, "Hugh Glass was an undocumented nobody, an empty vessel" that authors could fill as they projected their own aspirations and their culture's imperatives onto someone about whom so little is accurately known, or if known could be disregarded for any number of reasons.[12] As with so many bear narratives, the story of Hugh Glass begins with an incident told at the time, soon recorded in a local newspaper, and retold where people gathered. Derivative narratives continue orally and in print for a long stretch of time before expanding into other media.

Tracing the multiple stories of Glass reveals three issues, the third of which is most relevant to the history of human encounters with bears: variations in the core narrative, changing interpretations of Native Americans, and the shifting attention given to the bear that attacked him.

Some narratives offered versions of a past that Hall never mentioned. Manfred tells how the prehistory of the life of Hugh Glass in Lancaster, Pennsylvania, tempered his search for vengeance. *Man in the Wilderness* also invents a past. At one point we see Glass back East dreaming of family reconciliation as he feels his child growing inside his wife. In the film we also witness a young Hugh Glass being physically punished by his Sunday school teacher for refusing to affirm biblical teachings. As the story develops, the adult Glass gets religion, something accentuated by symbolic scenes of baptism and resurrection. "It's my apocalypse. It's a very special and very personal statement about a man struggling for personal identity, looking for God and discovering Him in the wilderness, in leaves and trees," remarked the film's star who played Hugh Glass. "It's all the things that the young people, and we, are missing today."[13] The film version of *The Revenant* also connects the rebirth of Glass with Christian resurrection. When Glass has a vision of where his wife was killed, the movie captures the image of the church the marauders destroyed, and we see a fresco on the wall that depicts Christ on the cross juxtaposed with Glass dreaming of hugging his very much alive son. Later, as the credits roll, we see Glass, breathing laboriously and barely surviving, eyeing the specter of his dead wife—thus ending the film uncertainly without acknowledging that Glass survived for a decade. Instead, viewers are left to wonder if the real resolution has more to do with Glass joining his deceased wife and son than with exacting revenge on those who abandoned him. In addition, every story has a different take on what kind of justice—military or frontier—he exacted on the men who abandoned him, variously but not always identified as Bridger and Fitzgerald. What motivates Glass shifts from the very mild (involving reconciliation) to severe expressions of revenge, with Glass sometimes distinguishing between what the two men deserved.

Over time, versions of the story of Hugh Glass reflect shifts in the depictions of Native Americans, from often racist and essentializing ones to more sympathetic and complicated renditions. In the urtext, Hall described the Arikaras as "treacherous" and "blood-thirsty," whereas the Mandans were friendly and protective. Manfred has Glass remark, "Maybe we palefaces can't shine with the red devil," and Major Henry saying, "Some [unidentified] Indians" see grizzlies as "some sort of god" before Major Henry went on to claim it reminded him "of the way the white man, the civilized man, has treated his Lord and Master, Jesus Christ. Civilized man had to kill him too, crucify him even, before he could become their giver of life."[14] Though at moments essentialized Indigenous peoples also appear menacing in *Man in the Wilderness*, this film offers a positive sense of the impact their religion has on frontiersmen. Near the film's culmination, we listen to the chief, speaking in a native language English speakers cannot understand, with no subtitles below. He makes clear he wants peace with the party of whites with whom his comrades have just recently had a deadly and stereotypical shoot-em-up. If *Little Big Man* of 1970 represented an important step in the exchange of sympathetic treatments of Indigenous peoples for earlier hostile ones, *Man in the Wilderness* offered up peace-loving and peacemaking Native peoples. Nonetheless, as is true in other instances of racial disguise, such as the 1971 "Crying Indian" advertisement (which deployed the Italian American Espera Oscar DeCorti), the filmmakers chose not an authentic member of an Indigenous group but Henry Wilcoxon, who had begun his Hollywood career in 1934 as Mark Antony in Cecil B. DeMille's *Cleopatra.*[15]

The film version of *The Revenant* did its best to meet contemporary demands for respect for Native Americans and their traditions, in the process reflecting major cultural imperatives that counter earlier, often racist tropes. Iñárritu hired Native American experts and deployed others as actors. To be sure, there are some bad Native Americans, but central to the movie's story is the presence and prominence of good ones who represent honor and spirituality rather than the crass commerce of whites. The story inventively goes that Glass had married a Pawnee wife whom whites had murdered, leaving him with a son to care for—someone a super-evil and racist Fitzgerald murders. This means Glass seeks revenge against Fitzgerald much more for the murder of his son than for his abandonment and the theft of Glass's rifle. The key Indigenous figure is Hikuc, a Pawnee played by the Navajo (or Diné) Arthur Redcloud, a decision that did not fully respect distinctive Native cultures. Hikuc helps Glass survive, at one point building a sweat lodge where Glass recovers. Soon after, Glass finds Hikuc lynched by French-speaking hunters who have also hung a sign that reads in French "We are all savages." Glass then enters their camp and in one of a series of wholly invented scenes saves the Native woman Powaqa, the daughter of an Arikara chief, from a rapist. She castrates her rapist, and Glass rides off on Hikuc's horse. At a crucial moment Glass does not finish Fitzgerald off because he recalls that Hikuc said, "Revenge is in the creator's hands." Glass, speaking in Arikara, remarks, "Revenge is in God's hands . . . not mine," and turns Fitzgerald over to a group of Arikaras, even though they are not God. Elk Dog (played by the Nuu-chah-nulth Duane Howard) then scalps Fitzgerald, a cinematic tradition that, despite the film's best intentions, draws on earlier racist tropes.[16]

As much as the stories of Hugh Glass morph over almost two centuries in terms of what motivates Glass and how Indigenous people are represented, what is especially striking are the disappearance and then reappearances of bears, especially the one that attacked Glass in 1823. James Hall and Frederick Manfred paid remarkably little attention to the animal that mauled Hugh Glass. Offering a sometimes confusing mixture of mystical dreams and storytelling, Neihardt's version represents almost no emphasis on the bear. Yet the cover of one edition of the book features not one but four of them, more playful than threatening, even though the original story itself featured a bear that viciously attacked and almost killed Glass. *Man in the Wilderness*, filmed not in the American West but in provincial Spain, relied on a stuffed bear that pretends to be vicious, even though the cover of a paperback highlights a vicious grizzly. As novel and film, *The Revenant* deployed different strategies. At one point in Punke's version

Cover of the Bybliotech edition of *The Song of Hugh Glass* by John G. Neihardt.

Glass looks skyward and sees the bears around the North Star, which leads him to envision the swan Cygnus and the Northern Cross. This image is more prominent as a reference to imagined bears than to the live ones at the novel's beginning, where we read of how a sow determined to protect her cubs attacks Hugh Glass. We see her alive very briefly but vividly as she charges, "roaring with the focused hate of protective maternal rage."[17]

If in the novel *The Revenant* bears are barely present, in the film version as in other texts they appear more prominently, in heaven and on earth, not only as spiritually transcendent lodestars but also as vicious animals. Early on the film offers a brief but dramatically compelling scene of the bear attacking Hugh Glass. The film's reliance on powerful cinematic techniques not possible either in print or in a movie of the early 1970s heightens the drama. Compared with almost any other version, in the *Revenant* film Glass endures harsh brutality, including in a more extensive scene than usual when the bear ravenously attacks him. Of course, not an actual bear but one performed by stuntman Glenn Ennis, produced courtesy of Industrial Light & Magic. Yet this contrasts with

Scene from the film *The Revenant* (2015) of a grizzly bear attacking Hugh Glass. © 20th Century Fox.

how later Glass draws strength from the bear he killed—as the bear's fur he wears keeps him warm and as his caressing the remnants of the bear's claws strengthens his resolve.

Responding to an interviewer's questions about whether "you and the bear discussed" the scene before or "you've talked since," DiCaprio described the scene as "almost like virtual reality." Iñárritu spoke of the "painstaking" months of research that involved his interviewing more than a hundred people who witnessed or survived bear attacks and his reading a book on the subject, presumably the exhaustively researched *Bear Attacks: Their Causes and Avoidance* by Stephen Herrero.[18] There followed weeks of rehearsals and then the filming itself. "I tried to not do a Hollywood thing," he insisted, in ways that overly simplified and even mocked the emotional lives of bears, "where animals have sensations attached, where they are *scared* or they are *mad* or feel empathy for us. No, they are just feeding their cubs." Without revealing the artistic and technological wizardry involved in presenting a bear, he mentioned CEI, which to the unanointed refers to Cinema Entertainment Immersion.[19]

At least for this historian, the best rendition of the story of Hugh Glass comes from another historian as we shift from a historical film to more reliable scholarship. Coleman's *Here Lies Hugh Glass* appeared in 2012 between Punke's novel *The Revenant* and Hollywood's loosely adapted version. Coleman focused extensively on actual bears as he offered incisive interpretations of the stories about Hugh Glass, ones that the lack of factual data made it possible to imagine and reinvent again and again. He well understood the impact of changing literary conventions that took advantage of how little we actually know of the life of Hugh Glass. He also offered richly suggestive explorations of the many contexts that inform these tales. More so than what others had done until then, he made clear that the West Glass inhabited in the 1820s was "a region defined by the diversity of its multicultural, multinational, multilingual, multiracial, and multigendered cast of human beings"—"men, women, Indians, French Canadians, free blacks, slaves, mulattos, Germans, Spaniards, and Britons."[20]

Moreover, he explored the interactions between the activities of the federal government, frontier capitalism, Indigenous peoples, and working-class white men. He understood changes in the West that shaped history between James Hall's 1825 story and Frederick Jackson Turner's 1893 talk about the end of the frontier. Among them were the tragically changing fortunes of Native groups; the implications of the demise of the trade in furs for the lives of the mountain men specifically and the nation more broadly; the waning presence of beavers and bears; and the growing power of the federal government, railroads, and capitalist enterprises.

Above all, Coleman connects the stories of Hugh Glass with two themes. The first was how his "journey from anonymity to minor celebrity opens new sightlines on the interplay of culture, labor, nationalism, and nature in the American conquest of the West"—with stories told and reinvented playing critical roles in how Americans understood their nation's history. How little we know of Glass, Coleman writes, "created an opening for poets, novelists, screenwriters, and actors to fill him with whatever imaginative content they liked." Over time, Americans "used the violently altered bodies of working-class hunters out West to define their nation" and in the process "marginal people laboring in far-off places and the rise of American exceptionalism." Second, the myths that emanated from fragments of the life of Hugh Glass played a crucial role in fostering what Coleman calls not American environmentalism but "Environmental Americanism." This involved the creation of "a race of men who absorbed punishment, recasting catastrophe as progress, infirmity as toughness, terror as resolve," and in the process "their physical transformations naturalized collective power and exceptionalism." If that was what was necessary to foster national identity, as storied literary expressions the results were more mixed—not simply individual heroes but also freaks, con men, and most recently for Glass, modern survivalists.[21]

Looking back at all these stories of Hugh Glass from 1823 to the present reveals striking changes. In the original versions, and many ensuing ones, the attacking bears hardly make any appearances except in accompanying visual renditions. Only with Coleman's book is there more than minimal focus on actual bears. The most dangerous and extensively presented grizzly appears not early on but most recently, thanks to modern cinematic technology, in the film version of *The Revenant*. Otherwise, having largely disappeared from dangerous earthly roles, bears sometimes reappear in inspiring heavenly ones, most notably when a dead one in Punke's novel gives Glass emotional strength. Oddly enough, most versions emphasize threats coming not from bears but from the troubled relationships between humans—both the two men who abandoned him and between whites and Native Americans. This is so even if, over time, Indigenous peoples become less hostile, less essentialized, and more helpful.[22]

Like other tales of threatening bears, many renditions picture bears as known for their viciousness rather than through their complex cognitive and emotional lives. Thus these stories, having little to do with bears, are often less about dangerous ones and more about the threats humans pose to each other. They remind us that not all cross-species interactions end well. In some ways they also tell us how, over the long course of history, Americans have shifted their understanding of their relationships to animals. Initially highlighted for how they threatened people, animals needed to be killed in order to protect humans. Eventually they came to represent opportunities from which people could draw spiritual strength (albeit, in the film version of *The Revenant*, only through remnants of a dead bear) as understandings minimized or erased a sharp division between humans and nonhumans.[23] Yet fascination with bears as dangerous predators persisted even as the narratives also reveal the importance of transcendence and affection in the relationships between humans and bears. With stories about Grizzly Adams and Timothy Treadwell—two other prominent examples of bears attacking men who became very well known—actual bears emerged as famous and dangerous while they competed for celebrity status with their human counterparts.

3

Out of Hibernation and Into
Children's Literature

✕

From time immemorial bears have played central roles in tales adults tell children. While such stories are prominent in folklore, this has also been and continues to be true of English-language children's books published for almost two centuries. From the story of Goldilocks's three bears in the 1830s to the most popular books today, bears have been more conspicuous in children's literature than any other animal.[1] In America the tale of Goldilocks was among the most influential, and the earliest to emerge, of all fabulous bear stories that found full expression in books that are read to children and that children read to themselves.[2] What followed were stories about Winnie-the-Pooh, Paddington, and the Berenstain Bears, in all their iterations and in every conceivable medium, from oral traditions to video games. Stories of bears were ever changing, albeit within formulaic boundaries. And they reveal how useful bears are as educational instruments, as well as how they became such famous celebrities, their lives closely intertwined with people's.

With *The Story of Three Bears*, the English Romantic poet Robert Southey in 1837 offered the first well-known published version of this narrative. Drawing on oral traditions, he wrote of three bachelor bears who lived together in a house in the woods—Little, Small, Wee Bear; Middle-Sized Bear; and Great Huge Bear. Each of them has appropriately sized pots of porridge, chairs, and beds. One day, waiting for their porridge to cool, they go out for a walk. While they are gone, "a little old woman," who "could not have been a good, honest" one, enters their home. Of course, the three bears would have invited her in had she asked and probably would have let her share their breakfast. After all, "they were good bears—a little rough or so, as the manner of bears is, but for all that good natured and hospitable," Southey writes reassuringly. Yet the uninvited, "impudent, bad old woman" goes ahead. She rejects the porridge of the Great Huge Bear as too hot and the portion of the Middle-Sized Bear as too cold. Then, finding that of the Little, Small, Wee Bear just right, she eats it all up. Trying the chairs of each of the three bears, when she sits in the chair of the smallest one, she breaks it and "down she came, plump upon the ground." Going upstairs, she repeats this pattern with the beds, this time falling into a deep sleep in the smallest of them.

When the bears return home, they discover what the old woman has done. "Someone has been at my porridge," they repeat in turn, each in their distinctive voices, ranging from gruff to moderate to quiet, with Little, Small, Wee Bear adding, "and has eaten it all up!" One by one they repeat this pattern as they see that the old woman had sat in their respective chairs, with the smallest member of the family emphatically noting that she "has sat the bottom out of it!" In turn each of them responds to what has happened to their beds, shouting, "Somebody has been lying in my bed!" The smallest of the three sees that "upon the pillow was the woman's ugly, dirty head which was not in place, for she had no business there." He exclaims, "Somebody has been lying in my bed—and here she is!" Awakened, the old woman "tumble[s]" out of bed and runs toward the window, which is open because "the Bears, like good, tidy bears as they were, always opened their bedchamber window when they got up in the morning." The woman "broke her neck" when she falls to the ground and then runs into the woods, where she ends up lost. Whether she escapes or is "taken up by the constable and sent to the House of Correction for a vagrant as she was" is impossible to know. Yet we are comforted with this: "The three Bears never saw anything more of her."[3] In this original version the intruder is an ugly and disrespectful old woman whose fate is uncertain but surely not propitious. Her presence is bothersome but not especially frightening. In the ensuing years several changes occurred that over time produced the stories we know.

In the nineteenth century, whether the three bears were frightening or kindly remained up for grabs. In some renderings the intruder remains an ugly old woman who meets a terrible fate. Shortly came one notable change: The unwanted visitor emerges as a beautiful, young, and often innocent girl, someone with golden locks. The fate she suffers when she leaves the bears' home varies, albeit one that rarely involves danger. The bears remain three in number, initially in some instances identified as bachelors, but well before the twentieth century they are written of in familial terms as Papa Bear, Mama Bear, and Baby Bear—the last one more like a cub than an infant. In most cases, Goldilocks is the evil villain and the bears are reasonably well behaved, often dressed in human clothes and living domestic lives. Some instances feature the message that Goldilocks must learn good manners. She should not behave irresponsibly by straying from her family's home. Once in the home of the bears, she should have been respectful of their property and way of life. From an oral tradition in which the visitor can be frightening, it transitions into a child in a way that suggests a minimal hint of danger. Rather than being an ugly woman who intentionally disrupts where the bears live, she is innocent, less a problematic intruder and more a curious visitor. The bears themselves become more like human beings, friendly and increasingly domesticated. In all cases, compared with the intruder, the three bears are benevolent. In some instances, the lesson was clear: People and bears could get along.[4]

Scores or more of contemporary versions have Goldilocks and her bears appearing in a wide range of texts. An exploration of selected examples gives some indication of the robustness and diversity that have made these bears such famous celebrities. Many stories follow the basic narrative of Goldilocks entering the home of the bears when they are away. Once inside, she samples three bowls of porridge, sits in each of the three chairs, and tests each of the three beds before falling asleep in Baby Bear's. The three bears return home and discover what had happened: some porridge eaten, a chair broken, and a bed slept in. Goldilocks flees. However, within that framework variations abound, some of them minor or subtle and others more significant, even inventive, in the liberties they take and the narratives they offer.

Many children's books I borrowed from the public library illustrate how differences play out. In one published in 2003, the front cover depicts three well-dressed bears who look down at Goldilocks with kindly affection and curiosity rather than with wildness in their eyes or threats in their hearts. The dust jacket informs readers that this is a "tale about a feisty little girl whose irrepressible curiosity leads her into more trouble than she's bargained for." Reading between the covers, we learn that the story is less about danger and more about appealing to mothers who want to make sure their children obey them. On occasion, Goldilocks "forgot to do things her mother told her to do," most of them minor, such as "forgetting to wipe her mouth after eating bread and jam." Yet at least this one time her not following her mother's advice "would lead to much more serious trouble." But after all, it's not very much trouble, thanks to the benevolence of the bears.

The girl's mother had agreed to let her go into a meadow so she could pick flowers but warned her not to enter the woods because, ominously, she had "heard that a family of bears lived there." Goldilocks leaves the meadow and enters the woods because she is chasing lovely birds. Even though "her mother has often told her not to be nosy about other people's private business," out of curiosity she enters the bears' home and then goes through the three usual steps. Awakened from Baby Bear's bed, Goldilocks remembers "that her mother had told her not to talk to strangers," so, risking less than Southey's old woman did when she jumps out of the window, Goldilocks runs down the stairs and exits through the front door. Safely at home, her "scary experiences" (which do not sound scary to me) meant she "never, ever forgot not to do what her mother told her not to do." Indeed, as if to underscore the importance of domesticity, which the three bears also represent, on the book's back cover is "Mama Bear's Porridge Cookies," notable because "Baby Bear loves to help Mama Bear bake cookies!"[5]

Other didactic tales abound, mostly about teaching children how to behave properly. Parents can rely on some versions to help with potty training or nutritious eating. In *Goldilocks Returns* (2000), remorseful over having broken into the bears' home earlier, she develops a business selling locks and keys. Even though she continues to intrude unwanted, she does so to add a padlock to their front door, improve the quality of their food, and redecorate their home. In *Goldi Socks and the Three Libearians* (2007), she enters a house constructed of books where three librarians live. She ends up comfortably looking at a book in Little Bear's reading tent. *Goatilocks and the Three Bears* (2014) follows a goat who eats Baby Bear's porridge, chair, and bed. Back home the next day, she realizes she must make amends, so she gives the three bears some flowers that they promptly eat up.[6] Some versions draw on the standard genre and break the mold in other ways. *Goldie and the Three Hares* (2011) tells of Goldie falling down a rabbit hole when trying to escape from three bears pursuing her. In *Goldi Rocks and the Three Bears* (2014), Goldi falls asleep on the piano in the home of a rock n' roll family of bears that has gone out to find a singer who can join their band. When they return, they awaken Goldi and she screams in a high c so perfectly that it earns her a job as the band's lead singer.

In *Goldilocks and the Three Dinosaurs* (2012), the award-winning author of children's books Mo Willems deploys humor as he goes farther than almost all other books in exploring an alternative narrative. Not three bears but three dinosaurs, the youngest of which is visiting from Norway and all of whom "for no particular reason" cook not porridge but yummy chocolate pudding. They leave the house, with Mama Dinosaur hoping "NO INNOCENT LITTLE SUC-CULENT CHILD HAPPENS BY OUR HOME" while they are away. Soon Goldilocks, "a poorly supervised little girl," enters their home, having "never listened to warnings about the dangers of barging into strange, enormous houses." Hearing a dinosaur remark that a "DELICIOUS CHOCOLATE-FILLED-LITTLE GIRL" who had consumed not one but three bowls of the confection was "YUMMIER," she realizes she faces danger. "Say what you like about Goldilocks, but she was no fool"—and so she rushes out of the home. The dinosaurs quickly return, sadly to realize they are too late: What is left in the house are three disappointed dinosaurs. The moral, Willems notes at the end, is "If you ever find yourself in the wrong story, leave." Willems's book uses wit, humor, and surprises as he plays with the tried-and-true genre—offering alternatives to the usual simple morality tales.[7]

Other narratives push hard against boundaries established by tradition and the preference for simple moral lessons. A notable example is the book *Leola and the Honeybears: An African-American Retelling of Goldilocks and the Three Bears* (1999) by Melodye Benson Rosales. In important ways this rendition is distinctive, beginning with a different family for Leola, the stand-in for Goldilocks. Rosales dedicates the book to "all the grandmothers who have loved and cared for their grandchildren" and notes that the story she offers reflects "memories of growing up with old-fashioned values in a family filled to the brim with love and understanding."[8]

As in other versions, the child's elder warns the young girl not to stray. Bored and "as stubborn as Grandmama's old mule," Leola wanders off, gets lost, and encounters Ol' Mister Weasel. "Now, now child, I don't mean to scare you none," he says. "I'm jus' wantin' to *eat you whole*!" She runs and, despite her grandmother's warning, enters "a stranger's house" where Papa Honeybear, Mama Honeybear, and Lil' Honeybear live. This is not a single-family residence but a "charming little inn" where "woodland folks from far and near came to visit." Despite her grandmother's insistence on good manners, Leola enters the house, tastes the food (which includes grits but no porridge), sits in a series of chairs, tries out a series of beds, and falls asleep in the smallest of the three. Upon returning, the three Honeybears find everything in disarray.

When they wake Leola up, she sees "three angry-looking bears leaning over her!" She begs them not to eat her. No, we won't, Mama Honeybear responds, "but didn't your folks teach you any manners?" Yes, Leola responds, but so

Illustration from *Leola and the Honeybears: An African-American Retelling of Goldilocks and the Three Bears* (1999) by Melodye Benson Rosales.

frightened by Ol' Mister Weasel's threat, she answers, "I didn't think anyone would mind, *just this time.*" Responding with kind understanding, Mama gives Leola "a tender good-bye bear hug" and insists, "Your Grandmama told you right. She must love you very much." The Honeybears send Leola off, guided by Miss Blackbird. Back home with her grandmother, Leola has learned her lesson and "she never strayed too far from home again." As seen in this illustration from *Leola*, African American culture suffuses the story of a girl with an African American grandmother, Black hair, and a Black doll whom a blackbird guides home. Once again, the girl fails to follow an elder's advice, in this case about the danger of straying, which leads to the threat not of dangerous bears but of an evil weasel. The more prominent point concerns the importance of politeness, a lesson that the initially frightening but eventually kindly Honeybears drive home.[9]

Of the scores of Goldilocks versions on film and video, several stand out for their playful reconfigurations of the familiar story. If more generally mass media did not spread the fame about bears until after World War II, in 1934, Paul Terry and his associates at Terrytoons produced "The Three Bears," an episode

Bears gamboling in *The Three Bears*, Terrytoons, 1939.

redone in 1939.[10] In just under seven minutes, this zany tale cleverly explores the possibilities of melding two genres, cartoon and jazz. Yet, perhaps inevitably when creative license is in play, any resemblance to the traditional narrative is purely coincidental. Papa, Mama, and Baby Bears leave their house while their plates of spaghetti rather than porridge cool off. The quarreling parents yell at each other using distinct and rough Italian accents, while Baby displays musical talent. Walking through an open door rather than breaking in, Goldilocks provides evidence of her own musical skills as a violinist and songstress. When the bears return and wake Goldilocks from her sleep in Baby's bed, she politely says she "just dropped in." Ordered by Papa to leave, she plays "Santa Lucia" on the violin, bringing Papa and Mama to tears and leading Papa to invite her to stay on. Soon Goldilocks and Baby Bear play a jazz duet as the adults dance to the music. A hunter and his dog break into the bears' home, and a clever Goldilocks distracts the hunter from harming the frightened bears by cooking him a dish of spaghetti, placing his gun in the fireplace and handing him a broom instead. Once his pasta is consumed, she orders the bears to take off their fur coats, which reveals that Papa and Baby, perhaps not bears after all, are dressed in pajamas. Given a code of decency, Mama remains fully clothed in her bear costume. When the gun explodes in the fireplace, Goldilocks whacks the hunter with the broom and the three bears attack him. The hunter and his dog retreat in hasty disgrace. This gives Goldilocks and the three bears cause to celebrate, with Mama, Baby, and Goldilocks playing music while Papa dances. Earlier on the hunter laughs and says, "Well, I guess this ain't in the book." Indeed true, for here instead of the usual cast we have a well-behaved and musically talented Goldilocks who saves the no-longer-fighting parents and their musically talented offspring from the real but subsequently overcome danger a hunter poses.

As with other bear stories, it is really in the postwar period that mass-media depictions proliferated on a grand scale. The television series *Fractured Fairy Tales* (1959–64) include a slightly shorter *Goldilocks*, with no mention of three bears in the title. The story opens with a "pretty girl" combing her hair in her home. We learn that though her name is Tusinelda Water Pickle, because of her beautiful hair she is called Goldilocks. As a child her only fault is that "she was very careless with things that belonged to other people." When she plays with other children who have toys, "they always wished they hadn't." One day, after a walk in the deep and dark woods she finds herself lost. She lies down for the night near a house where Papa Bear, Mama Bear, and little Oswald Bear lived. When they leave so their porridge can cool off, the scent wafts out and attracts Goldilocks. Not bothered by the fact that no one answers the door when she knocks, she enters. The usual incidents follow as she eats Oswald's breakfast and breaks his chair, not caring about what she has done because, after all, it isn't hers. Awakened from her sleep in Oswald's bed and hearing the three bears discovering what she has done, she trembles fearfully in bed.

A frantic chase within the house ensues until she rushes out and returns home. "Now, now," Mama Bear tells her husband, "she's only a people, she doesn't know any better." Oswald doubles down with "and I'll bet she sure learned a good lesson." Then the narrator, Edward Everett Horton, triples down, remarking, "And from that time on Goldilocks was as careful as can be of everybody's things." We of course learn she "lived happily ever after" as we see her playing reciprocally with a friend, a scene that stands in contrast with an earlier one, when she had yet to learn her lesson about respecting other people's property. The story closes with the three bears sitting in front of a television set and "after a little house cleaning and ending, so did the three bears" learn theirs.[11]

Sesame Street experimented with the themes inspired by *Goldilocks and the Three Bears* in multiple media and with widely varied stories.[12] The best-known version explores how Goldilocks changes from being Baby Bear's nemesis to a friend, but my favorite is something else.[13] In the 1985–86 season, Kermit the Frog tries, unsuccessfully it turns out, to direct an episode based on the classic story. What frustrates his directorial skills are both the inability of Goldilocks to express feelings genuinely and how Irving, a stage manager who speaks with what I take to be a German or Yiddish accent, doesn't follow directions. Initially the curtain opens to reveal three chairs. Having urged Irving to listen more carefully and Goldilocks to express more surprise and fear, Kermit tries again, only to have the curtain open revealing three identically sized squares. Goldilocks expresses fearful surprise, to which Kermit responds by mistakenly acknowledging her skills as an actor. Before walking off the stage, a truly frightened Goldilocks shouts at Kermit, reminding him that her contract states she does not have to work with children and bears. At last, Kermit tells Irving to call the playwright and ask for a revised version, titled "Goldilocks and the Three Chairs." "There's no business like show business," he tells Irving, who responds with "That rhymes, Mr. Boss."

Many were the online responses to the episode, some of them playing on themes from Goldilocks variations—noticing that in the stories there are three chairs, albeit of different sizes, and that the writers are teaching children about shapes and rhymes. "Somebody's Toucha My Spaghet!" we hear. Which returns us to the Terrytoons version of Goldilocks in the 1930s and thus underscores how audience members, like producers of *Sesame Street*, playfully play upon plays.[14]

There is nothing quite like the stories of Goldilocks and her three bears in their richness, inventiveness, power to both persist and morph, emphasis on crossing the color line, and ability to inspire widely varied versions over almost two centuries. The multiple and often wildly different versions remind us that there is no simple trajectory of depictions of bears over time, that different genres and audiences demand disparate depictions, and that celebrity bears have no fixed emotional meanings.

These narratives in all their variety paved the way for other bear stories that, like Robert Southey's, started in print and migrated into myriad media—and did so in ways that offer us assorted images of bears. We can begin with three popular and historically important tales—from *Winnie-the-Pooh* in 1926 to the Berenstain series launched in 1962, with *Paddington Bear* of 1958 in between. *Après ceux, le déluge*, what with thousands if not tens of thousands of bear stories for children. And like the ones that originated with folklore and in other media that became multi, they spread like the wildfires that Smokey was supposed to prevent: A bear whose first name derived from the Canadian province of Winnipeg that a young boy visited in the London Zoo. One whose second name represented a swan named Pooh from a book that the father of a five-year-old had recently published, in which his son feeds the majestic bird. Toy animals about which the author's sons imagined fanciful stories, as well as real animals near the family's farm that served as inspiration. Illustrations based on a Steiff teddy bear growler that slept in the bed of a book illustrator's son.

Winnie-the-Pooh appeared in print in the fall of 1926 after it emerged from the imagination of the English author A. A. Milne and his longtime artist collaborator E. H. Shepard. Then in his mid-forties, Milne had already established himself as a prolific author of poems, children's stories, novels, mysteries, short stories, and plays for theater and screen. Unlike most authors of children's books that feature bears, Milne produced only two in which his bear was a major character—*The House at Pooh Corner* followed the first in 1928. After that, although later corporations including Disney greatly expanded the franchise, no more Winnie-the-Pooh books appeared from Milne. His son Christopher Robin Milne, whose stuffed animals included one named Pooh, grew up, and his father wanted to protect his son's privacy from publicity as best he could. Milne also had too passionate a commitment to producing original works in many genres to soldier on with more featuring Winnie-the-Pooh.

In *Winnie-the-Pooh* Milne tells the story of many by-now-familiar friends of the bear, the main character named in the book's title—among them Piglet, Christopher Robin, Roo, Kanga, and Eeyore. The book brings together a series of ten short stories, many of them adapted from what Milne had previously published in leading English periodicals. Accompanying them are simple black-and-white drawings, which made the 1926 book longer and less lavishly illustrated than what became standard in America in the post–World War II period. And as such it was more likely to be read to a child by an adult than read by your average or even above-average youngster.

Inside the covers are the charming stories of the adventures and misadventures of Winnie-the-Pooh and his friends. In his lighthearted introduction, Milne stops short of pretending to tell fully how the book came to be—but not before he offers a more or less true story of how when Christopher Robin goes to the London Zoo, he walks "to where the Polar Bears are, and he whispers something to the third keeper from the left" before wandering "through dark passages and up steep stairs, until at last we come to the special cage." With the cage opened, "out trots something brown and furry, and with a happy cry of 'Oh, Bear!' Christopher Robin rushes into his arms."[15] But of course what follows are stories not of a real, live bear but of an anthropomorphized teddy bear and his friends—animate toys in the menagerie of Christopher Robin and the imagination of A. A. Milne.

At the book's beginning we see Christopher Robin dragging Winnie-the-Pooh down the stairs and, at the end, up them. In between, however, he comes alive. Early stories reveal a too inquisitive and innocent bear getting into trouble as he chases after more honey than he should be eating, "Silly Old Bear" or "Bear of Very Little Brain" that he is. As Piglet says to himself, "'Pooh hasn't much Brain, but he never comes to any harm. He does silly things and they turn out right.'" Then comes a turn of events in which Pooh reveals that, rather than being stupid, he exhibits simple common sense. To rescue Piglet when he is dangerously surrounded by water, Pooh suggests to Christopher that they use the boy's upside-down umbrella as a boat. Pooh, Milne writes, recommends "something so clever that Christopher Robin could only look at him with mouth open and eyes staring, wondering if this was really the Bear of Very Little Brain whom he had known and loved so long." So moved by this realization and by Pooh having saved Piglet, Christopher Robin decides to give him a party. In a dream, Pooh imagines that he is "a Bear of Enormous Brain." At the party Christopher presents Pooh with a "Special Pencil Case," and in it are instruments "marked 'HB' for Helping Bear, and pencils marked 'BB' for Brave Bear."[16] It turns out that Pooh is not so silly or stupid after all.

Milne's book was an immediate commercial success that added to the long list of celebrity bears. Published in London in mid-October 1926 and in New York not long after, it had sold 150,000 copies by the end of the year. Over time it has been translated into more than fifty languages, driven by its combination of innocence and sophistication and its charming original illustrations. Its 1958 Latin version, *Winnie-ille-Pu*, was the first foreign-language book to appear in the *New York Times* list of bestsellers. An exhibition of Pooh and his friends attracted 750,000 visitors a year when hosted in a Manhattan library beginning in 1987. Since then, books featuring Pooh have sold more than fifty million copies.

Milne quickly turned his attention as a writer elsewhere. Four years after the book's publication, the American popular culture entrepreneur Stephen Slesinger acquired the Canadian and US rights, which allowed him to transform the stuffed bear into a golden one through the development of phonograph records, board games, toys, a film, and a radio show. The commercial floodgates burst further open in the 1960s when the estates of Milne and Slesinger licensed some of the rights to profit from Winnie-the-Pooh to the Walt Disney Company. What ensued were Disney versions of Winnie-the-Pooh in multiple media, including short and feature films, television shows, books, and a role in Fantasyland in Disney theme parks. Outside the multimedia Disney universe, Winnie-the-Pooh has had robust and often intriguing lives. For example, YouTube offers a satirical video developed by an African American man with the handle manlikeissac and more than three million followers. "If Winnie the Pooh Was Black" featured Winnigha the Poo and a pig named Niglet.[17]

More so than with most famous bears, Winnie-the-Pooh has engaged the talents of scholars. Carol A. Stanger has explored what it means to read what Milne wrote from a feminist perspective. "Milne creates, in effect," she writes, "an all-male Eden" through which women could learn "about the difficulty of coming to terms with a patriarchal society."[18] Yet the story most intriguingly reverberated elsewhere in three bestselling books—*The Pooh Perplex: A Freshman Casebook* (1963) and *Postmodern Pooh* (2001), two critical spoofs by the scholar Frederick Crews, and *The Tao of Pooh* (1982), in which Benjamin Hoff uses Milne's figures to explain Taoism.[19]

In his two wickedly funny books, Crews offers parodies of a full range of approaches to literary criticism, complete with imagined but authentic and outrageous footnotes and penetrating biographies.[20] As one of Crews's pseudo-authors notes, these essays reveal how subtle is Milne's technique, one that "has beguiled three generations of fools into imagining that the book is nothing more than a group of children's stories."[21] In the first of his two books, which turned out to be an unexpected bestseller, Crews is the editor of a casebook that first-year college students use to understand different approaches to literature, offered up as a series of essays he authored that nonetheless capture how others might interpret Pooh. For example, he channels the immensely influential Cambridge University professor F. R. Leavis, in the book identified as Simon Lacerous, "perhaps the most feared and respected critic in England," who is "an implacable foe of sentimentality, flabby aestheticism, and inflated reputations."[22] For Lacerous as Leavis, "This Sir Edward Bear, Sir Pooh de Bear" evokes "the very image of a fat old Tory who passes all his time pampering his depraved tastes and reminiscing about his imaginary exploits." Then Lacerous/Crews continues, "And you will recognize the likeness at once. He is a *flabby* bear, and flabbiness in literature is the thing I detest above all else."[23] Other essays offer up analyses that reflect a wide range of ideological commitments, Marxist, Freudian, and New Criticism among them.

Almost four decades after his first book, Crews brought up to date his tongue-in-cheek analysis of the latest in literary criticism. With *The Postmodern Pooh* he published papers presented at a fictitious panel at the 2000 meeting of the Modern Language Association. The session focuses on what he identifies as the current rage in English department offerings, Teaching the Conflict. Once again, he caustically captures the contours of contemporary criticism. Among my favorites is the essay by Felicia Marronnez, University of California at Irvine's Sea and Ski Professor of English, who arrived there from Yale "with the specific aim of helping to narrow the sophistication gap between our two coasts." Her award-winning dissertation—"Heidegger Reading *Pooh* Reading Hegel Reading Husserl: Or Isn't It Punny How a Hun Likes Beary?"—makes clear how she could apply what she had learned about deconstruction from Jacques Derrida. In her MLA talk she carefully deconstructs Pooh: a "Man stripped of all striving, truly attuned, for once, to that discursive impossibility, a Nature without cultural excess or archive," and a bear who once deconstructed is "just a mouth and a digestive tract in charge of some rudimentary powers of rationalization." Looking at both the text and character who give it its name, she insists, "Not only Pooh in the flesh but *Pooh* as a text habitually concretizes social constructs, reversing the sinister process whereby mere things were once promoted to signifiers."[24] The other authors vary in what they offer up: this time revivified Marxism, feminism, postcolonialism, and an overly hip analysis of popular culture. Among what Crews accomplishes in both books is revealing how Pooh, like other bears, can represent the widest range of possibilities—from cuddly to vicious.[25]

If Crews skewered literary critics with satirical sharpness, Hoff relies on a lighter kind of humor as he links Pooh with ancient Chinese wisdom. The back cover of the paperback version of *The Tao of Pooh*, which remained on the *New York Times* bestseller list for forty-nine weeks, insists that the book "revealed that one of the world's greatest Taoist masters isn't Chinese or a venerable philosopher but is in fact none other than the calm, still, reflective" Winnie-the-Pooh. Hoff set out to "write a book that explained the principles of Taoism through Winnie-the-Pooh, and explained Winnie-the-Pooh through the principles of Taoism." He did so by weaving together exchanges between the well-informed and patient narrator and a skeptical bear with the wisdom of classical Taoism. Pooh, he notes, is able to accomplish all that he does precisely "because he *is* simple minded." Hoff, like any well-informed Taoist, knows this is not the same as being stupid. Rather than being clever or arrogant, in his childlike way Pooh offers "Simplicity" or "useful wisdom, the what-is-there-to-eat variety—wisdom you can get at." Committed to "recognize Inner Nature work with Things As They Are," Pooh, a good Taoist, is not "confused by Knowledge, Cleverness, and Abstract Ideas" but achieves what he does by "seeing, appreciating, and making use of what is right in front [of] it." In the end, it turns out that because sophisticated intelligence leads people to chase after useless goals, more than Owl, Rabbit, or Eeyore, "a Bear of Little Brain" achieves what he does by relying on contentment and wisdom.[26]

If we count the three bears into whose lives Goldilocks intruded and Winnie-the-Pooh, then Paddington Bear is the fifth of the species who, crossing the Atlantic from Britain to America, provided the basis for more than ample cultural productions of immense popularity in which bears are central. Paddington is an Andean or spectacled bear from "darkest Peru" found abandoned by an English family in London's Paddington Station, dressed in his now familiar squashed hat, holding an empty jar of marmalade, and with a tag hanging around his neck saying, "Please Look After This Bear, Thank You." The man behind this bear (A. A. Milne's successor) was Michael Bond. Born in 1926, conveniently for me the year Milne published his first Winnie-the-Pooh book, Bond left school at age fourteen even though his parents hoped he would go to university. He started working at the BBC when he was fifteen years old, employment interrupted during World War II so he could serve in the military. Around the war's end, he resumed working at the BBC, eventually as a cameraman, and began to write short stories and plays. He published *A Bear Called Paddington* in 1958. He had not intended to write for children, and it "started life as a doodle," he later recalled. "I was looking around the room and we had this small bear, which" he had purchased at a shop near Paddington and then "had been a kind of stocking filler for my first wife, and I wondered, idly, what it would be like if it was a real bear that landed on Paddington station and I typed the first words down."[27] Well over one hundred books featuring Paddington eventually appeared, with five more in the series in print between 1959 and 1964 while Bond continued working at BBC. They were so successful that he could quit his BBC job to devote himself full-time to writing.

The dust jacket of *A Bear Called Paddington* describes him as "an earnest, gentle, and well-meaning bear" with "an absolute talent for getting into trouble" despite his good intentions. Inside, Bond introduces us to Paddington, a stowaway who has emigrated from Peru. (Bond originally described Paddington as having come from "darkest Africa" but switched to Peru when his literary agent told him there were no bears in Africa.) Paddington used to live in Lima with his Aunt Lucy, who taught him to speak English because she wanted him to emigrate. He had to do so because she knew that eventually she would have to enter a home for retired bears. At the London railroad station, the bear eagerly accepts the offer of Mr. and Mrs. Brown to come and stay in their house, something they know their children Judy and Jonathan will enjoy. The bear announces that he has a Peruvian name no one could possibly understand, so the Browns name him after the railroad station where they found him.

Polite and well mannered, Paddington speaks proper English. Yet ironically, chapters tell stories of how he continually gets into trouble when he tries to right what he sees as a moral wrong because the rules and customs of his new world are so unfamiliar. When necessary or when he cares to use it, he has "a very powerful stare" that "he kept for special occasions." Otherwise, he is preternaturally well meaning and kind. Nonetheless, he frequently causes chaos—at the Underground, the department store, the theater, and the seaside. Yet if Paddington is troublesome, it is not because he is a large and wild animal but a small and civilized one who makes mistakes because of innocence and not malice. Indeed, at key moments the mishaps he causes end up benefiting those in his host society.

Queen Elizabeth II and Paddington Bear having tea to celebrate her Silver Jubilee in June 2022. Buckingham Palace/Studio Canal/BBC Studios/Heyday Films/PA Wire/Shutterstock.

This happens, for example, when he stumbles into the window of a department store and brings it additional business; when he turns Mr. Brown's canvas into a prize-winning painting; or when he unintentionally wins accolades as an actor.[28]

Paddington, an observer remarked in 2014, three years before Bond's death, represented "an extraordinary level of success for a British children's book character who doesn't play quidditch—one matched only perhaps by that other endearingly bumbling bear, Pooh."[29] And as was true with Winnie-the-Pooh, Paddington became a celebrity, with a capacious and long-standing franchise. As with other bear characters, the brand was licensed to a series of corporations around the world, including as a book translated into forty languages and selling more than thirty million copies—to say nothing of theater productions, postage stamps, cartoon strips, a cookbook, feature-length films on the big screen and television sets, and special shops with merchandise for Paddington and friends. *Paddington's Guide to London* would take you to a statue of the bear himself in Leicester Square. And of course there were stuffed animals galore. Three months before she died, Queen Elizabeth II had tea with Paddington as part of the way the palace promoted her jubilee.

Race and gender are prominent when it comes to thinking of other children's books that feature bears. With Paddington those could be appropriate categories, but immigration is uniquely relevant to Bond's creation. Attending school in Redding in his early teens, Bond had seen children at the train station, evacuees from London who, he recalled, "all had their labels round their necks with their names and addresses on them and a little case or package containing all their treasured possessions. So Paddington, in a sense, was a refugee." Also inspiring him was knowledge of the Jewish refugees on the Kindertransport, beginning in late 1938, as well as mid-1950s refugees from Hungary. Paddington's dear friend Mr. Gruber was an antiques dealer and Hungarian refugee. Bond based Gruber on Harvey Unna, his first literary agent, someone who had left Hamburg to escape the grip of the Nazis. Gruber, Bond later remarked, was "a lovely man, a German Jew, who was in line to be the youngest judge in Germany when he was warned his name was on a list. So, he got out and came to England with just a suitcase and £25 to his name."[30]

In the late 1950s, before restrictive policies took hold with the 1962 Commonwealth Immigrants Act, as many as 100,000 immigrants arrived in Great Britain annually, mostly from the West Indies, Africa, and Pakistan. In 1958, a few weeks before Bond's first Paddington book appeared, racist anti-immigrant youths using the slogan "Keep Britain White" attacked West Indian residents in Notting Hill, less than two miles from Paddington Station and where Bond lived. Many who supported immigrants who came to England during and after World War II deployed Paddington as a symbol in the fight for their acceptance. Bond and social justice advocates used Paddington to represent sympathy for refugees, immigrants, and asylum seekers, with Paddington's Aunt Lucy insisting, "London will not have forgotten how to treat a stranger."[31]

Inevitably scholars saw issues in more complicated ways, arguing as they did about whether Bond's stories amplified imperialism, complicated issues such as identity and foreignness, and challenged racism. The scholar Philip Smith shows how Paddington films released in the second decade of the twenty-first century provided Brits with a sympathetically multicultural narrative that stood in opposition to anti-immigrant discourse. This was because Bond's stories depict Paddington as a bear who presents no threat to Britain's social and cultural orders. After all, although physically he is marked as non-white, Paddington dresses, acts, and speaks in ways marking him as truly English. "Paddington reads as 'ours,'" Smith observes, "because he is an immigrant whose manners and outlook express, and upon whom audiences can project, qualities of Englishness." In addition, he notes with both the early books and later films in mind that

"English cultural praxis can tolerate difference in terms of race but demands homogeneity in language, habits, mannerisms, taste, and beliefs."[32]

Looking at *A Bear Called Paddington* with conditions that obtained more than half a century after its publication, Kyle Grayson recently offered a more complicated assessment. Bond's first Paddington book, he asserts, "is both complicit in and critical of contemporary understandings of foreignness, liberalism and migrants." In some instances, the emphasis is on how his "hygiene, poverty and education" mark him as a problematic immigrant and foreigner. In contrast, the portrayal of Paddington reassures natives of England about the meaning of being "a good host and a good foreigner in a liberal society."[33]

If Paddington and those who welcomed him came to epitomize one aspect of Britishness, perhaps the most quintessential of American cartoon bears are the Berenstain Bears. The more than three hundred books about the Berenstain Bears printed in more than 260 million copies since 1962 provide an important marker in the history of children's books that feature bears.[34] Though there had been many published on this side of the Atlantic Ocean before, there was no American blockbuster precedent. Teddy bears were already everywhere but not part of a franchised empire that emerged from a book. Yogi Bear debuted in 1958 but on-screen, not in print. Given that Goldilocks and the Three Bears, Winnie-the-Pooh, and Paddington originated in Great Britain, the Berenstain imprints were the first homegrown American books for children whose franchise achieved such heft.[35]

In 1941 Stan Berenstain and Janice Grant met on their first day at the Philadelphia Museum School of Industrial Art. After going their separate ways during World War II to support the war effort, they married in 1946. In the next year their work as artists took off when the first of more than a dozen drawings appeared on the cover of the prominent weekly magazine *Collier's*. They had "zoomed into the higher reaches of American cartooning," they later noted.[36] In 1951 they published their first of over twenty cartoon-laden books that taught parents how to navigate the challenges of bringing up their baby boomer children. Among them were *Have a Baby, My Wife Just Had a Cigar!* (1960) and *How to Teach Your Children About Sex Without Making a Complete Fool of Yourself* (1970). However, these were books without bears and ones adults could read for themselves rather than ones they could read to their children.

In 1962, the Berenstains published their first bestselling bear book, *The Big Honey Hunt*. They had already tried their hands at producing a bear book for children when they worked on *Freddy Bear's Spanking*, the story of a boy who tries but fails to negotiate alternative punishments with his parents. What happened next set them off in a more promising direction. They met with Theodor Geisel, who was serving as editor-in-chief of a division at Random House seeking new properties and not as the author of books featuring Dr. Seuss. Geisel played a key role in the development of the Berenstains' successful venture into books for children. At one point he urged them to think about the Uncle Remus stories as providing some aspects of a model to follow. "And, yeah," they later wrote, "the Br'er Rabbit idea was sort of what we had in mind." A series of bear books, Geisel remarked insistently, "would be a millstone around your neck." Besides "there are already too many bears," Geisel told them. "Sendak's got some kind of a bear. There's Yogi Bear, the Three Bears, Smokey Bear, the Chicago Bears. No, for your next book you should do something as different from bears as possible."[37]

On the train back from Manhattan to Philadelphia, they saw an ad for Kool menthol cigarettes that featured a penguin. If they abandoned the crowded markets for bear books for ones that featured penguins, they told themselves, "We'd have the whole penguin market to ourselves."[38] Yet soon after, having witnessed the remarkable success of *The Big Honey Hunt*, Geisel told them excitedly, "We're selling the hell out of the bear book." So the Berenstains abandoned penguins and returned to bears. Without asking their permission, Geisel changed their names as authors from Stanley and Janice Berenstain to Stan and Jan Berenstain and inaugurated the series as Berenstain Bear books.[39]

Berenstain sons Leo and Mike appeared in 1948 and 1951, respectively. Additions to the family meant they were living in cramped quarters in Philly not far from where Stan and Jan had themselves grown up. So they moved to exurban Philadelphia. Residing "in the affluent serenity of Bucks County," the journalist Elizabeth Mehren reported, "about 40 miles and a million light-years from their old address in downtown Philly, they live in a house replete with wood and stones, and blessed with an endless view of thickets and meadows. They emanate coziness, built on 50-plus years of sharing an easel and finishing each other's sentences."[40] Over time their sons joined the family business and produced bear books for older children. When the parents died, Stan in 2005 and Jan seven years later, the operations turned fully over to their sons, Mike as writer and illustrator and Leo taking care of the business operations.

In the series that began with *The Big Honey Hunt*, Papa Bear works as a carpenter, loves the outdoors, and, though well-intentioned, too often is more bumbling than productive. That frequently means that to the more homebound Mama Bear falls the task of raising the children, which she does by gently and effectively acting as the family's disciplinarian. She usually uses household obligations to inculcate a sense of responsibility in her offspring. In the early books, there is only one child, Small Bear, whose name eventually changed to Brother

Bear and who prototypically loves playing with dinosaurs and building model airplanes. Eventually along comes Sister Bear. Both following and departing from traditional gender norms, she loves playing with dolls and playing baseball. The last member of the family is Honey Bear.

Using simple rhymes and colorful illustrations appropriate for preschool-age children, *The Big Honey Hunt* tells the story of Small Bear following Papa Bear as he looks for honey. Mama Bear suggests they go to the Honey Store, but Papa Bear insists on looking for honey in the woods, with Small Bear tagging along.

> If a bear is smart,
> If a bear knows how,
> He goes on a honey hunt.
> Watch me now!

So off they go, and at every turn Papa Bear staggers into danger as he fails in his quest, both to find honey and to prove to his son how smart he is. At the end, we see Mama Bear smiling as she looks on Papa Bear purchasing the honey at the Honey Store because "the best sort of honey. It comes from a Store."[41] The lessons, perhaps clearer to this historian than to a four-year-old, are that persistence can be important, mother knows best, and it is safer to purchase a product in a store than to court danger by looking for it in the woods.

Ensuing Berenstain Bears books drove home other lessons. Some of them focus on helping children learn from new situations in a type they called a "family experience book." *The Berenstain Bears' New Baby* (1974) helps Brother Bear overcome his fears as Sister Bear joins the family. When Mama Bear insists on turning off the television set for a week in *The Berenstain Bears and Too Much TV* (1984), the children learn not only that they can thrive without that distraction but that there are other, better, and less commercial ways to entertain themselves. *The Berenstain Bears Go to Camp* (1982) teaches Brother and Sister Bear (and the children listening to their parents read the book to them) not to fear going off to a place like Grizzly Bob's Day Camp—and more broadly to accept changes in their routine and location. *The Berenstain Bears and the Bully* (1993) teaches kids not only how to counter a hostile peer but also how to solve problems and learn to communicate. Others dramatize that Mama Bear is wiser than Papa Bear, in what the Berenstains later called stories of "our Papa-Bear-as-lovable screwup."[42] In *The Berenstain Bears Learn About Strangers* (1985), Mama Bear gives nuance to Papa Bear's blanket warning about never talking to people they do not know. When in *The Berenstain Bears' New Neighbors* (1994) the notably black-and-white Panda family moves in next door, Mama Bear and the new neighbors teach the children tolerance and that under the fur all creatures are alike, thus countering Papa Bear's distancing himself from them because they seem different.

As is true of other bear empires, one that started with a story offered in a print book expanded slowly and then dramatically, and not just in the millions of books sold. For about sixteen years after the publication of *The Big Honey Hunt* in 1962, it was mainly twenty-two books that carried the Berenstains' messages to children. In the time since, franchising and synergy brought in revenues well in excess of $50 million as more than two score of companies hawked more than 150 different products. The spread from old-fashioned print to other media began in 1979 when *The Berenstain Bears' Christmas Tree* aired as the first of five animated features on NBC. Computer games featuring the family first appeared in 1983. Animated cartoon shows programmed for weekend mornings started two years later. Other appearances followed, including a stage show, museum exhibits, and play areas in theme parks. There were even stuffed animals and books sent to the offices of every pediatrician in the United States as part of a campaign by Lederle Laboratories to get children vaccinated. As far as I can determine, all this and more happened with little to no marketing power of empires like Disney. Yet the imprint of the Berenstain Bears appeared on food products, toys, puzzles, clothing, and thirty-five figurines of Berenstain Bears that accompanied Happy Meals at McDonald's. Nonetheless, the Berenstains insisted what really mattered amid "the mad multitudinousness of it all" were the simple pleasures of drawing and narrating stories about "a family of bears who live down a sunny dirt road deep in Bear Country."[43]

If with other series under consideration criticism focused on how authors handled issues such as race, gender, and immigration, with those featuring the Berenstain Bears, the focus has been on the problems of morally laden didacticism in repetitive cultural productions. Citing a range of stories, critics find their books "syrupy, sexist, simplistic and unsatisfying," "infuriatingly formulaic," "hokey," and "little more than stern lectures dressed up as children's stories."[44] Yet defenders insist that parents want their children to learn lessons that convey a moral imperative. As Margaret Coughlin from the Children's Literature Center at the Library of Congress notes, because the Berenstains dealt "with first-time experiences and many of the ordinary, yet vexing, issues of family life," they "'meet current concerns, and they do it well. They are supportive and nonthreatening. They offer parents a sense of assurance.'"[45]

Even though the robust book sales suggest that in the marketplace the wholesome vision of the Berenstains triumphs for many admirers, the critics seem to have won the day. Writing in British Columbia's *Vancouver Sun*, a mother insists that "reading Berenstain Bears for moral content is like feeding your kids Fruit Shaped Sugar Snax and thinking you've covered one of the food groups."[46] Some deride the Berenstain version of family values in an antifeminist, safe, and old-fashioned world where Mama Bear stays at home and Papa Bear works outside. These stories offer homilies about personal virtues and social morality. And to underscore this, they emphasize that well-behaved children play jacks and hopscotch rather than watch television. The Berenstains maintain that, as a reporter in 1996 noted in the *Washington Post*, "children should be sheltered from, not barraged by, madness and mayhem," especially that conveyed by television and new media. The Berenstains proudly insist "that the familial harmony in the Bear books is a reflection of their home life."[47] Or as another writer noted more critically twenty years later, the books "were intentional throwbacks, reflecting not the tumultuous America of their time—we never saw 'The Berenstain Bears Turn On, Tune In and Drop Out'—but of an imagined, idyllic past."[48]

Despite how the Berenstains claim the mantle of traditional values, the sharpest criticism comes from the conservative Charles Krauthammer. Writing in the *Washington Post* seven years before the appearance of their defense of their values, Krauthammer assumed there were "thousands, perhaps millions of other parents who share my hostility to these lumbering cuddlies but who cannot say no to a child who begs for just one more dose." Referring to Bruno Bettelheim's *The Uses of Enchantment: The Meaning and Importance of Fairy Tales* (1976), he acknowledges that its author "has quite eloquently elucidated how these parables—by not flinching from the great existential terrors of life: death, betrayal, abandonment—enrich the moral imagination of kids in a way that their insipid modern variants never do." And yet he confesses that he found it troubling to read these stories to children because they are "too gory. In some, it seems, every other character is either eating or being eaten, a cannibal's feast."

Krauthammer critiqued "the smugness and complacency" of the Berenstain stories. "The raging offense of the Berenstains is the post-feminist Papa Bear, the Alan Alda of grizzlies, a wimp so passive and fumbling he makes Dagwood Bumstead look like Batman." *The Berenstains Forgot Their Manners* (1985) features Mama Bear, "the final flowering of the grade-school prissy," laying down "a new set of family rules of conduct." Papa Bear appears to acquiesce but "continues his slovenly, craven ways, spending much of this tome mopping up around the house to pay off his doltishness."[49]

Immune to such criticism, eventually Mike Berenstain added decidedly Christian messages to his parents' legacy series. His father had grown up in a secular Jewish household and his mother in an Episcopalian one. But their sons, like many children of mixed parentage, absorbed what the writer Stan

Austerlitz in 2016 described as a version of "stolid, universalist postwar morality." Converting to Presbyterianism, Mike found religion, which he deployed to enhance markets for the family's books. In 2006, not long after his father died but with his mother in agreement, he began talks with HarperCollins about an additional venture. After all, he had watched the significant flow of letters from committed Christian readers who expressed appreciation for the values the series had long conveyed. The result was scores of books that appeared in the Living Lights series published by Zondervan, a powerful Christian media company. Among those titles are *The Berenstain Bears: God Loves You!* (2008), *The Berenstain Bears: Do Not Fear, God Is Near* (2013), and *The Berenstain Bears Go to Sunday School* (2010).

Austerlitz, an observant Jew who read Berenstain books to his four-year-old son, found this religious turn "particularly jarring." Having always taken it "for granted that the moral framework of contemporary children's books . . . would remain disengaged from any actual dogma," he had to wonder when and why "the Berenstain Bears found Christ." He laments that the books had "abandoned their universalist appeal. Their stories were no longer about milestones and stumbling blocks in every young child's life but took a more narrowly targeted approach that left some out even as it pulled others in." Just as books in the original series provide suburban "refuge from tumult," the new ones offer religion as "a cloak for the bears' deliberate and unfashionable fustiness." Yet in the end, Austerlitz had to admit that books in the new series serve a familiar purpose. To his son they provide the usual dose of entertainment. As a father, his "discomfort with its Christian themes" is "outweighed by its uncanny ability to speed the progress from bath to bed." His son, he notes, "could not have cared less that the Berenstain Bears were quoting from the Bible, any more than he would have noticed references to the Quran or 'The Communist Manifesto.' He was just glad that the Bears had found a place to have their picnic—and that they always would."[50]

The writer Rebecca Onion doubled down on what Austerlitz had to say. Writing in 2021 about *Thanksgiving Blessings*, which appeared eight years earlier in the Living Lights series, she remembers appreciatively lessons she had learned from reading Berenstain books as a child. As an example, she points to how "the labeled shoeboxes in the closet in *The Messy Room* (1983) have translated into my obsession with organization." Now, however, Michael Berenstain has transformed his parents' franchise into problematic products. "Steer ye clear of *Thanksgiving Blessings*," Onion warns, "unless you like breaking your brain every autumn trying to explain toxic patriotism to a little person who just likes Sister Bear's polka-dot blouse." Not unlike Austerlitz's son, her four-year-old daughter liked the bears but seemed unaware of the lessons the tale taught. She simply loved "this universe of upright quadrupeds who wear the same outfits every day (but—as she, who loves going barefoot, tends to point out—'no shoes')."[51]

Since the arrival of the first Berenstain book, and even before, in the United States there have been an almost uncountable number of children's books that feature bears.[52] Almost all of them, but especially those with young children as the intended audience, focus on gentle, lovable, cuddly, and often bumbling members of the species. To be sure, there are some ominous outliers, such as *I Want My Hat Back* (2011) by Jon Klassen and *His Dark Materials* (1997) by Philip Pullman. And of course, there are books for children that use polar bears to teach about climate change, perhaps less ominously than warranted.[53]

Yet most of today's top bear books for youngsters feature endearing and lovable creatures. Nowhere is this clearer than with books on recent Amazon lists of bestselling children's books that feature bears, some of them old-timers and classics.[54] Among the bestsellers is Amelia Hepworth's *I Love You to the Moon and Back* (2015), which tells the story of a bear and cub who "splash in the water, climb mountains, watch the colorful lights in the shimmering sky, and play with friends. They show their love for each other by touching noses, chasing each other, and, of course, hugging and snuggling before bed." This is "a sweet, gentle rhyme, perfect for sharing with a special little one," we are told.[55] Or there is Lisa Tawn Bergren's *God Gave Us You* (2011). This is the story of how when Mama Bear tucks her youngest offspring into bed, "she gently, tenderly, and reassuringly communicates the message loving parents everywhere (bears and non-bears alike) want their children to hear: 'We wanted you very, very much, and we are so very glad because—God gave us you.'" This book, the promotional copy continues, "provides a valuable opportunity to build children's self-esteem every day and assure each one that he or she is a truly welcomed, precious, and treasured gift from the Lord."[56]

Reading such hype, it is hard not to be struck by its rhetorical reassurances. At a time when so many people sense families and childhood in peril, authors and publishers use the relationships between young children and bears to enable parents to reassure their offspring that they are wanted and loved—not only by their parents but also by God. And so they feel welcomed and special in ways that even at age two will increase their self-esteem. Yet in the end, one wonders if the reassurances are aimed less at a child going to sleep than at a parent wondering if they have brought an innocent being into a haven in a heartless world.[57]

From *The Story of Three Bears* in 1837, through proliferating and myriad versions of *Goldilocks and the Three Bears*, and to the present day of bestselling children's books in which bears figure prominently, several things are striking. Even more so than with folklore bears, specific species matter little. The bears whose home Goldilocks invades are identified as Papa, Mama, and Baby. Winnie-the-Pooh seems connected with a classic teddy bear, a polar bear, or a black bear. Paddington may have originated as an Andean bear, but once out of Peru his species identity does not matter. The Berenstain Bears may have been grizzlies, but that identity seems irrelevant.

What began with oral traditions and short stories grew, especially after World War II, into expansive expressions in a wide range of media, with the Disney empire playing an outsize role. In the process, intimacy was lost and bold amplification triumphed. In the genre of children's books and elsewhere, especially those for young children, the trajectory is one that has moved resolutely toward reassuring relationships between youngsters and anthropomorphized bears. The contemporary exceptions can be found in genres such as video games and books for older children. Otherwise, most books featuring bears offer lessons adults want to convey to children—including warnings about dangers to avoid and reassurances of comforts that can be attained. They hype stories of bears who, whatever their innocent shortcomings, are kind and smart, capable of teaching their readers important lessons. They provide reassurance that all is peacefully well in the relationships between children and bears (as well as between parents and their children) because these animals offer not danger but friendship, love, and humor.

It is easy to figure out why bear books have been so popular from the viewpoint of the producers of their wide-ranging expressions. When talking of the Berenstain Bears and Care Bears, Charles Krauthammer noted that they "are mere subsidiaries of larger conglomerates . . . just part of a much larger universe of movies, videos, audio cassettes and little cuddly things that you are encouraged to buy. These conglomerates, by the way, put in question my most basic political principles, since I cannot deny that socialism, whatever its faults, does not permit such things."[58]

Yet it is more difficult, absent access to data developed by major participants in the Bear Industrial Complex, to know what all this means to consumers, both parents and children. Austerlitz perceptively offers some answers. On the one hand, as noted above from his observations, however ideologically ambitious writers and scholars may be, reading a bear book to children speeds the process of getting them from bath to bed and then to sleep. That way their parents can have some time to themselves at the end of a long day. Yet he also understands, based on his experience with his own son, that "young children are continually concerned about changes to their perceived order: Where is Mommy tonight? Why is there no school today? Where did my toy go?" In that context, like their Winnie-the-Pooh and Paddington peers, the lives of the Berenstain Bears change little despite facing different challenges every day in every book. "This familiarity is essential to the books' sitcom-like appeal," he notes, and "the stories start with a necessarily brief outburst of chaos, but order is always restored to Bear Country by the end. Parents know best, children always heed their lessons and everything is in its right place. Family values literally reign triumphant, with the books an ongoing celebration of the value of family."[59] Every series of bear stories presents its own lessons that authors, publishers, and parents hope children will learn. And in that context bears (cuddly, nonthreatening, bumbling, anthropomorphic, and cute) offer abundant reassurance. That is a task that other species in popular books for children—pigs, spiders, horses, foxes, rabbits, toads, and caterpillars—cannot perform as well.[60]

The dramas of famous bears in folklore and children's literature underscore the necessity to question the widely accepted story of linear progression from threatening bears to cuddly ones. The standard interpretation is that as wild animals disappeared from people's lives, what with modern conditions, bears appeared as not dangerous but innocent and lovable. This understanding hardly explains why, in 1850, Joseph Cundall's *A Treasury of Pleasure Books for Young Children* could picture three bears strolling, the wife and mother dressed as if participating in an Easter parade, but forty years later Raphael Tuck's *Combined Expanding Toy and Painting Book Series* (1890) contained an image of an angry bear ready to pounce on an innocent Goldilocks. In the nineteenth century, whether the bears were threatening or kindly remained up for grabs, as seen in the contrasting images for Goldilocks books sampled in this chapter.

Depictions of bears hardly develop in a simple and historically linear way. It may well be that as people experienced wild bears less frequently or not at all it was easier for them to become imagined as cuddly. Yet in describing relationships between humans and bears, it is important to consider the genre of a story, the traditions on which it relies, and its intended audience. More than is true of children's literature, folklore and fables operate within a tradition that offers up frightening images. Books for young children are apt to be more reassuring than those for young adults. The demands of video games meant that in the early twenty-first century there were more ferocious than friendly bears. More recently, as we have seen in the discussion of bears as contemporary mascots, at UCLA one Bruin has a "ferocious look" at the same time others appear comically portrayed. Meanwhile, at Berkeley, its beloved bear is "growling, fighting,

Illustration from
Joseph Cundall's
*A Treasury of
Pleasure Books for
Young Children* (1850).

Illustration from
Raphael Tuck's
*Combined Expanding
Toy and Painting Book
Series* (1890). Smith
College Archives/
Alamy Stock Photo.

rumbling, grumbling, thundering, and shaking the ground" at one moment and at another stands there with a silly smile. All of this is to say that celebrity bears remind us that they appeal, including as educational instruments, not just because they resemble humans but because they also evoke a wide range of emotions, including conflicting ones. Bears in children's books may have wise and complex emotional lives, but in the end they are bears represented and not real. Children's stories about bears are more about what people believe than about bears' experiences.

4

Grizzly Adams

BEARS HE TAMED, THOSE HE DISPLAYED,
AND THOSE RESPONSIBLE FOR HIS DEATH

✕

Like Hugh Glass stories, those about Grizzly Adams offer dramatic and violent tales told and retold that involve bear attacks, in this case not one but many. Adams was a mid-nineteenth-century mountain man who traveled throughout the West, collecting and training grizzly bears and other wild animals so he could display them in zoos, menageries, and circuses. He has entered into American culture in so many ways, not only in print and on-screen but also on the flag of the state of California, where Samson, the most ferocious bear Adams captured, appears, based on a drawing of Charles Nahl. Compared with the paucity and elusiveness of reliable information on Glass, all versions of the life of Adams draw on somewhat accurate though problematic sources. On the surface, the story of his life is straightforward; however, from 1860 until now observers have offered their own interpretations in which grizzly bears play varying roles.

As shape-shifting as were the narratives about him (though more consistent and reliable than those about Hugh Glass), he was variously known by many

Samson, a bear Grizzly Adams captured and trained, served as the model for the bear on the flag of the State of California. Wikimedia Commons.

CALIFORNIA REPUBLIC

names, including John "Grizzly" Adams, James Capen Adams, Grizzly Adams, Old Grizzly, the Hunter, Bruin Adams, and the Wild Yankee Hunter.[1] As was true with tales of Glass, those about Adams vividly remind us that not all relationships between people and bears involve cuddly animals. Unlike with Glass, with Adams they could be both seemingly domesticated friends and dangerous enemies.

Born in 1812 in Medway, twenty-five miles southwest of Boston, into a family that provided the nation with patriots in the American Revolution and two presidents in the new nation, Adams was a cobbler from age fourteen until twenty-one and then again from twenty-four to thirty-seven.[2] In between, for three years he lit out for the wilds of northern New England. There he worked as part of a commercial enterprise that hunted animals for display in the urban menageries organized by a zoological institute. Among them was a Bengal tiger that severely injured Adams, one of the first of attacks (including later ones by grizzly bears) that played a role in his death in 1860. In 1849, lured by the possibilities the California Gold Rush opened, he headed West. Those who chart his life claim that by the time he left New England he had saved $6,000, an unlikely figure since that would be almost $200,000 today. On the way to California, where he hoped to make money by selling boots and shoes, he stopped first in Saint Louis, where a fire destroyed his stock. He continued to California via Mexico, where, like many who preceded and followed him, he gained and lost minor fortunes as he shifted from one pursuit to another—provisioner, investor in mining enterprises, hunter, trapper, farmer, and rancher. By 1852 he had established himself in the California foothills of the Sierra Nevada. From that base camp he traveled widely—north and east to what are now Montana and Wyoming, west to inland valleys, south to the Tejon Pass.

Everywhere he went, he captured hundreds of wild animals, grizzlies included. The first of that species was a young female he caught in 1853 and named Lady Washington. Over time he trained her to accompany him unleashed, carry a pack, pull a sled, and allow him to ride on her. He even slept next to her when it was cold outside. A year later he took possession of two baby male grizzlies—the one he named Ben Franklin saved his life when a grown female grizzly attacked Adams, giving him a wound to his head and neck that would later contribute to his death. Lady Washington, having mated with another grizzly, gave birth to a cub Adams named after the famed explorer and one of the first US senators from California, John C. Frémont. Later on, Frémont injured Adams during a training session, reopening the wound that in 1855 had dislodged his scalp and neck so seriously that at times his brain tissue was supposedly exposed.

By 1855, Adams had begun to display his animals, initially on a spot south of San Francisco and eventually in the city itself. There he showed his menagerie in a series of locations—in 1856 at the Mountaineering Museum in a basement on Clay Street and briefly at some performances at the Union Theater. Soon, with the help of a business partner, George Washington Call, he moved to the California Exchange. He named his exhibit the Pacific Museum, which some called the California Menagerie, where his animals could entertain larger audiences.

Yet all was not well. Evicted from his museum by creditors, his health threatened as the result of long-standing injuries, and yearning to return to the wife and children he had left behind in Massachusetts (whom he now wanted to leave financially secure), Adams lit out for a different frontier. On January 18, 1858, a newspaper had called Adams the "Barnum of the Pacific."[3] Almost exactly two years later, in the expectation of joining P. T. Barnum's show, he boarded a clipper ship, appropriately named *Golden Fleece*, to begin a fifteen-week voyage to New York. Once in Manhattan, he reconnected with his wife for the first time in ten years and joined forces with Barnum. His California Menagerie, which opened on the last day of April 1860, was located in a tent on the corner of Fourth Street and Broadway before moving to Wallach's Theater on Thirteenth Street and Fourth Avenue. Barnum provided the venue and managed the shows, while Adams handled the animals, even though the financial arrangements between them were often in doubt. Despite a doctor warning him that his life was in danger (probably because his brain was allegedly visible), Adams nonetheless kept performing, even when he moved the show from Manhattan to locations in southern New England. Unable to continue when complications from long-standing injuries intensified, he died in late

Grizzly Adams with his bear Ben Franklin, as depicted in Theodore H. Hittell's *The Adventures of James Capen Adams* (1860).

Of all his bears, Ben Franklin was Adams's favorite.

October 1860, five days after returning to the home his wife had established. He had made sure the arrangements with Barnum provided financial security for his family.

That is the basic story. In renderings of the life of Adams, the relationship between attacks that may have killed him, often mentioned almost in passing, and his death several years later is not entirely clear.[4] Moreover, where for Glass one grizzly early on almost killed him and later on he killed others that supplied sustenance, for Adams bears play many roles. He writes of them as attackers, noble animals, domesticated workers, pets, and commodities that he violently trained and then displayed and sold for profit. Again and again, he refers to his favorites, Lady Washington and Ben Franklin especially, with praiseful words like "a most faithful and affectionate servant" and "faithful friend and constant companion."[5]

The connection between Barnum and Adams is historically significant. As Susan J. Douglas and Andrea McDonnell have noted, Barnum "was one of the earliest and most wildly successful creators of celebrities who were featured in his museums, his circus, or on their own tours." To become that, he "capitalized on print technology and the power of mass distribution, using newspaper advertisements, pamphlets, press releases, and provocative broadsides, complete with detailed illustrations of his wondrous collection, splashed across metropolitan centers to publicize his shows." He heralded the process of celebrity creation by persuading people to pay for entertainment as members of an impersonalized audience while they witnessed spectacles.[6] Before he left the West Coast, Adams had already accomplished much of what Barnum amplified—the combination of famous beings and instruments of commercialization. Relocated to New York, he had a bigger stage. When he left San Francisco, it had a population of 56,802. He arrived in a Manhattan that contained 814,000 people.

Across the decades, the story of Grizzly Adams was retold in multiple versions and media, offered beginning in 1860 in contemporary narratives and later in books and eventually on film. There were two dominant narratives, sometimes offered by themselves and sometimes in tandem, but in both cases grizzlies played important though distinct roles. One pictured Adams as a mountain man who killed, captured, and domesticated wild animals—an individualist who embodied frontier virtues and whose life was best understood through the trope of the conflict between civilization and wilderness. The other one emphasized that he domesticated grizzlies and other beasts using the knowledge he gained about animal behavior as well as the skills of an entrepreneur and/or flimflam man. In both narratives the wounds Adams suffered from grizzly attacks resulted in his demise years later.

The skein of stories all begins with two primal urtexts. The first is by Theodore H. Hittell, who, since Adams had little formal education, was responsible for the words early on the scene in print. Hittell was a San Francisco–based politician, lawyer, and writer who for two and a half years beginning in July 1857 took down notes from conversations with Adams. He soon turned them into a first-person, 378-page book published in 1860—*The Adventures of James Capen Adams, Mountaineer and Grizzly Bear Hunter, of California*. "Before long," a chronicler of Adams's life wrote over a century later, Hittell "was an unpaid public relations man for the Mountaineer Museum and the Mountaineer himself." The book, he noted, was "Hittell's biography—or Adams's autobiography via Theodore Hittell."[7] It featured Adams and a tamed grizzly.

Near the beginning of the book, through Hittell's prose, Adams speaks of a major turning point in his life. After talking of making and losing fortunes over a period of three years, in the fall of 1852 Adams apparently told Hittell that "disgusted with the world and dissatisfied with myself, I abandoned all my schemes for the accumulation of wealth, turned my back upon the society of my fellows, and took the road towards the wildest and most unfrequented parts of the Sierra Nevada, resolved thenceforth to make the wilderness my home and wild beasts my companions." Once resettled, "the new and romantic scenes into which I was advancing, enchanted my imagination, and seemed to inspire me with a new life. . . . I seemed to be a part of the vast landscape, a kind of demigod in the glorious and magnificent creation."[8]

Yet the long narrative that followed revealed something other than the story of what inspired Adams's new life. What dominated the vast majority of the pages were discussions of Indigenous peoples of unspecified allegiances and his experiences with wild animals and the spectacular and challenging landscapes of the American West. Hardly alone, Adams relied on the help of Native Americans, about whom he drew both racially negative and relatively sympathetic pictures. There were no identifying markers other than a few individual names and words such as "the Indians"—with one notable exception: his pejorative reference to "Diggers," a term white settlers at the time often used to refer to members of several groups.[9]

Grizzlies were among the animals he hunted, killed, trapped, and trained. More so than is the case with Hugh Glass or Timothy Treadwell, or indeed with so many other discussions, Adams (speaking through Hittell) extensively described actual bears and gave them intelligence and power. A grizzly, he observed, was "the monarch of American beasts, the most formidable animal in the world to be encountered." Compared with the lion and tiger, "the grizzly is not second in courage and excels them in power." The California grizzly, "in the consciousness of strength and the magnanimity of courage, alone of all animals stands unappalled in the face of any enemy, and turns not from the sight of man." And "when roused and particularly when wounded, there is no end to his courage. . . . It is to him that the appellations of science, *ursus ferox* and *ursus horribilis*, are peculiarly applicable."[10]

Yet Adams remained convinced that a grizzly "may be made the perfection of animal goodness" and if properly trained can grow "up a devoted friend, exhibiting such remarkable qualities of domestication as to almost lead one to suppose that he was intended, as well as the dog, for the companionship of man." And train them he did, with a studied combination of force, violence, and positive reinforcement. He commented extensively on how he tamed Lady Washington, using a lasso to capture her as a cub, chaining her to tree, and then lashing her to a cart that he trained her to pull. "It is with bears as it is with children," he noted, as he called them "his pets," that "if the right course be taken, their natural characters may be modified and improved to such a degree as to be a subject of wonder. . . . I myself have changed savage natures to affection and gentleness." He slept with them by his side, albeit tying them to a peg driven into the ground, and "felt as responsible and proud as any *pater familias* in the abodes of civilization."[11]

Yet no kindly head of a family was he, underscoring the combination of affection and violence he deployed. He boxed their ears and kept them chained, because "they did not show any disposition whatever to acknowledge a master. Lady Washington, whom I had treated with the greatest kindness," he insisted, "was particularly violent, and invariably would jump and snap at me." At least once she seriously injured Adams, after which he "came to the determination to give her a castigation that would make her recollect me." So he "continued trouncing her back" with a cudgel until she was exhausted. It was, "beyond question, a cruel spectacle, to see a man thus taking an animal and whipping it into subjection; but when a bear has grown up, untutored, as large as Lady was, this is the only way to lay the foundation of an education,—and the result proved the judiciousness of my course." After he patted her, she became milder, "which satisfied me that the lesson had been beneficial, and that she would not soon forget it." Over time he allowed her more freedom once "she gave good promise of what she afterward became," even though he had to give her "a few raps on the back" that "reminded her of the duties she owed."[12]

At several moments, Adams emphasized the importance of the values a frontier mountain man embraced more generally. Although initially, Adams remarked early on, he was a "misanthrope," before long he realized he "had duties and obligations to fulfill towards others." Albeit "far removed, as it were, from the laws and jurisdictions of government," Adams nonetheless knew he had responsibility to his fellow man. "I was a kind of sovereign," he continued, "amenable in that remote quarter to no laws except those of God and nature; but so well was I imbued with the spirit of my country's free institutions, that no right was violated and no liberty infringed." He denigrated the work of "the most nicely-adjusted legal tribunals, which are too much bound up and hampered by antiquated dicta and decisions." Instead, he celebrated how even though Westerners disregarded social and legal norms, they relied on informal rules to arrive at proper decisions on how to behave. Drawn to how Nature provided access to the magnificent and the sublime, he turned his back on "the abuses of civilization." Again and again, he balanced pictures of himself "alone in the mountains, far from my fellows, far from what are usually considered the pleasures and comforts of society, with none to think of but myself," with acknowledgment of how "the feelings of humanity in my breast" prepared his "mind for a complete reconciliation with my fellows." So he celebrated his individualism born in situations where he was alone, along with lengthy discussions of his relationships with so many others—Indigenous companions he relied on, those he negotiated with, investors he bargained with, and teamsters he hired.[13]

Yet what remained largely in the background or was mentioned only briefly was why he put his life in danger and worked so arduously. He used the words *gold* and *money* only five and two times respectively. In contrast, *bear* appeared seventy-eight, *hunt* eighty-four, *mountain* seventy-six, and *danger* thirty-eight. Nonetheless, it is possible to piece together from fragments what he was up to even if he did not, perhaps, initially understand his own mission. Near the narrative's beginning he asserted, "Upon entering the mountains, indeed, it was without any idea of devoting attention to bear hunting as a business." Perhaps so, but soon after he referred to an event in the spring of 1858 that "gave a direction and purpose to my mountain life." He entered into a business partnership with his wealthy brother William, who would fund him as he collected animals, though the passage in question did not make clear the purpose of such a collection.[14]

This pattern of scattered hints left unexplored or hanging in midair continued. Threaded throughout the book were very brief references to trading, settling accounts, dealing with agents or teamsters, striking bargains, and agreeing on reasonable prices.[15] He referred to shipping "animals, skins, oil, and curiosities" from Portland, Oregon, to Boston. After the animals arrived, he continued, they would be "sold to different persons,—some placed in museums, others carried about the country,—all contributing more or less, to spread a knowledge of the natural history of the Pacific Coast of the United States." A little over one hundred pages later he mentioned, without elaboration, that he helped his brother fulfill a contract to send some bears to Lima, Peru, without telling us what would happen once they arrived there. He discussed bargaining with Native Americans. He talked of a camp that "resembled a sort of bazaar," including "the wild animals, which formed quite a menagerie," the only time in almost four hundred pages when that word appeared. On occasion, the book mentioned how he and his business partners would divide "the prizes and profits" of an "expedition." He talked of the "laborious earnings of so many small proprietors, myself among the number."[16]

Only in the last six pages do we begin to get an idea of what he was up to, whether or not he initially realized the goal toward which he worked so long and hard. The first hint comes as he describes leaving the wilderness and beginning his trip to San Francisco. "The people viewed my curiosities, and particularly the bears, with the liveliest of interest," he observes, even as he contrasts his own "unpresentable" manner as a shabbily dressed wilderness man with having to turn down an invitation to a "civilized dinner." Neither he nor we can reconcile his statement that in San Jose "I began to give exhibitions" with his aw-shucks comment that "playing the hero" of "the hydra-slaying Hercules type . . . is out of fashion now-a-days, and, to use a homely but expressive Americanism, 'will not pay.'"[17]

As he approaches his destination of San Francisco, we reach the book's two final paragraphs. There, he remarks that he "established the Pacific Museum. I have by degrees gathered all my animals together," which included bears, panthers, wolves, foxes, elk, and deer. "As I look upon them," he continued, "I am reminded of the freshness and freedom of the forest and live over again in imagination the golden days when I trod, in pleasure and in joy, on the mountain side." Yet freshness, freedom, pleasure, and joy inadequately describe the danger, toil, and uncertainty that we have just read about at length. In the final paragraph, Hittell presumably transcribed what Adams had told him. Perhaps knowing that he might die soon (though he could not know how soon), he talked of meeting death when it came. He hoped it was his destiny "to become a mountaineer and grizzly bear hunter in California." Yet even as he was planning to return to Boston and join forces with Barnum, he mentioned returning to the Sierra Nevada, where he "would fain lay down with" three of his favorite bears by his side. "There, surely, I could find rest through the long future, among the eternal rocks and evergreen pines."[18] Just as throughout the book he hid his entrepreneurial ambitions by focusing on the life of a mountain man, so at the end he emphasized being a mountaineer at rest and not a showman with keen business instincts.

The second foundational but contrasting narrative was variously titled *The Hair-Breadth Escapes and Adventures of "Grizzly Adams" in Catching and Conquering the Wild Animals Included in His California Menagerie* or *The Life of J.C. Adams, Known as Old Adams, Grizzly Adams.*[19] It was a fifty-three-page pamphlet published in 1860 as "Written By Himself" but in fact commissioned by Barnum, who probably connected Adams with a ghostwriter. Hittell's version of the life of Grizzly Adams, which relied on prolonged interviews with his subject plus his lawyer-like carefulness, was very different from the humbug-laden tales Barnum told. A side-by-side reading accentuates the differences between the picture of Adams as a mountain man with little interest in financial gain or showmanship and the one that emphasizes his skillful pursuit of fame and fortune. If Hittell, writing in San Francisco but looking no further east than Salt Lake City, celebrated Adams as a West Coast frontiersman, from his perch in Manhattan Barnum was providing promotional copy for his subject's East Coast tour. Moreover, unlike Hittell, Barnum never went beyond describing Indigenous individuals with any words other than their names. And if Hittell's descriptions of the relationships between Adams and bears included

P. T. Barnum flyer advertising a show of Grizzly Adams and his bears in Manhattan, 1860.

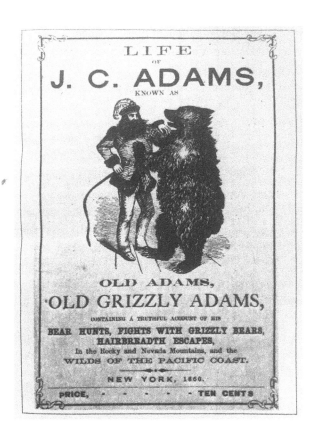

violence, affection, and servitude, by and large Barnum highlighted only the violent and ferocious struggles of the encounters.[20] Yet the most significant difference is that Hittell located his story within the reach of frontier savagery and Barnum his amid urban civilization.

Davy Crockett may have been "born on a mountain top in Tennessee," been "raised in the woods so he knew every tree," "killed him a bear when he was only three," been "King of the Wild Frontier," and "made himself a legend forevermore."[21] Similarly, Barnum created a legend he hoped would last, if not forevermore, at least for the time being. Adams was "born under a great pine tree," and his mother predicted as he lay in his "rude cradle" that he would "be in love with a wild life, and find happiness only away from the haunts and vestiges of civilization," even though he may not have killed a bear until he was in his early forties. Indeed, at several points Barnum let slip what *he* was up to. Thus, he revealed how well he understood the fables that undergirded showmanship. At one point, referring to the cubs Adams had captured as his "little trophies of war," he had him say, "No millionaire could have contemplated his property with more secret joy than I did those little creatures." Yet when Barnum reported Adams telling a story to three men who accompanied him, "they laughed at it as a gross invention" that implied "a generous sense of my ability to manufacture an exciting tale without being too particular to put all the facts in." Later on, Barnum remarks that, like other Gold Rush stories, he realized one "to be pretty much a humbug."[22]

Barnum's story of the life of Grizzly Adams connected the specifics of his subject's life to a compelling if highly fictionalized narrative. He hardly shied away from using commercial terms to describe what he thought motivated Adams. In the very first sentence he wrote of "the collection of wild animals" that "has excited the curiosity of thousands, and may yet excite that of thousands more." What followed was a cascade of pecuniary terms that referenced transactions, prices, profits, markets, money, merchandise, and menageries— the last a term Hittell used only once but Barnum employed three times in his much shorter text and once in the pamphlet's title. At first, "disgusted with the companionship of my fellow-creatures, and heartily sick of everything like the hypocrisy of social being," Adams achieved happiness by turning his back on "white settlements," so that he had "no deceitful heart to take advantage of my unsuspiciousness in order to defraud me." However, before long, though he "wanted neither male nor female company," he hired helpers Tuolumne and Stanislaus as a "bargain" and on "reasonable terms."[23]

At other times, Barnum wrote of how Adams made money from his grizzlies. He had Adams say of four grizzlies that once he had "rendered them comparatively docile and obedient, my next thought was how to make money by their exhibition." Once he delivered a bear to the town of Mariposa in inland central California, he "fought him handsomely in public, and not only gained considerable notoriety, but netted about $800." Along somewhat similar lines, if Hittell was silent on why Adams shipped bears to Lima, Barnum was quite specific. He wrote that Adams "agreed to deliver, at Stockton, to two gentlemen, named McSheer and Robinson, who proposed to take them to Golina, South America, to exhibit and fight them there, and pay one-half the proceeds." Barnum had Adams talk of turning bear cubs into "my property," which meant he and his "companions" were "charmed with the prosperity with which we were favored.... We felt that we were growing comparatively rich, and by honest labor." Hittell stopped short of moving his story beyond when Adams set up shop in San Francisco, but Barnum makes clear the extent of Adams's further ambition. He wrote of his plan to introduce a buffalo to "New York society" and more generally to make his "collection" available "for Atlantic observation."[24]

There were many prominent retellings of the story of Grizzly Adams in the decades after Hittell and Barnum spun their tales—initially in melodramas and popular novels.[25] Eventually the Bear Industrial Complex kicked in. Among the versions that entered the arena was 1966's *The Legend of Grizzly Adams: California's Greatest Mountain Man* by Richard Dillon, a prominent and widely read author of books on Western history. His version of the life of Adams is closer to Hittell's than Barnum's, emphasizing as it does the savagery of a mountain man in the wilderness rather than the crafty ambitions of an entrepreneur in the city. Dillon presents the tale of a man who initially rejects civilization and then roams the West as he encountered Native Americans, Mexican Americans, and mixed-race peoples. Despite using a derogatory word to describe them, at times Dillon offered a positive picture of how Adams viewed Native Americans: using racist language, he lay "blame for all Indian troubles" on "whites" and "not with the redmen who were his friends." Even though Adams surrounded himself and interacted with many others, Dillon often called his subject a loner, "probably the greatest individualist that California ever produced," who "turned his back on civilization." Smart, cagey, and skilled, he lived in the true wild—capturing a few bear cubs but killing scores of them and other wild animals and then eating or selling the meat.[26]

In Dillon's telling, the bears Adams encountered ranged from the savage to the civilized. He talked of Adams training Lady Washington by beating her into submission but also of him sleeping with her and others under his blanket. He called Lady Washington and Ben Franklin "Adams's closest friends" and immediately said this was "largely because of the perfect control in which their keeper held them." At the far end of the civilization/savagery continuum stood tales of how dangerously vicious bears could be. He mentioned "a fight which Adams would never forget and which would, eventually, be the death of him," when an "antagonist, a huge female, . . . punched a hole the size of a silver dollar near the top of his [*sic*] master's forehead"—details that Hittell failed to mention. Even on the ship from San Francisco to New York, Adams was not safe. En route, Adams killed a bear but not before it had seriously wounded him when "the she-bear had bitten him deeply in the neck. . . . Worse, she had ripped his scalp dreadfully."[27]

Dillon generally emphasized Adams as a man drawn to the wilderness. Yet without connecting the dots, he threaded his narrative with examples of Adams's financial ambitions and acumen. "As he rode into the wilderness," Dillon observed early on, "Adams resolved that from now on, he would forsake the accumulation of money" and become like Robinson Crusoe, but in the Sierra Nevada. Yet as the narrative continued, Dillon provided grist for the mill of a business historian. He talked of Adams earning money by selling the hides and meat of animals he killed "for excellent prices." He used the word *menagerie* at least five times, at one point claiming that Adams, while still in the wild, "was thinking of removing to San Francisco, or some city, to show his menagerie of animals for pay. He had a hunch that he could make a living at it."[28]

At moments, Dillon hints at the transformation of Adams into an urban entertainer, as when he mentions his "three solid years of showmanship" during his final years in San Francisco. Yet he threads the needle by insisting that Adams kept dressing "in rough frontier garb," which he never traded "for serge and broadcloth," but that he would rather dine "at one or another of San Francisco's many excellent restaurants" than cook for himself. At the end of the book and of the life of Grizzly Adams, Dillon placed him in wild nature and not urban civilization. He "died far away from his truest friends—Lady Washington, Frémont, Funny Joe, even Samson and the other 'critters' of his Happy Family at the California Menagerie."[29] In the end what dominates is Great Nature, not tamed and business-oriented civilization.

In 1985 a book much like Dillon's appeared: *The True Adventures of Grizzly Adams: A Biography by Robert M. McClung.* A zoologist and author of books on wildlife, McClung pictured Grizzly Adams as an individualistic mountain man who preferred wilderness to civilization. The book's cover features a large bear hovering over Adams. McClung asserts that Adams "genuinely loved and appreciated wildlife and unspoiled nature, and decried the encroachments made on it by civilized man"—except of course, I must add, when he himself killed, trapped, traded, and forcibly trained animals. Like Hittell, McClung saw Adams as a misanthrope at the same time he told of how he lived among and relied on people. This included Native Americans, whom he usually identified only as "Indians," though at one point he used the same derogatory term as Hittell to describe Native peoples who worked in mines and lived in earthen homes as "a tribe of California Indians—'Diggers,' the prospectors called them." McClung claimed that Adams saw Native Americans as "little better than animals," though most of their troubles "were due to the way white men" took advantage of them.[30]

Without necessarily realizing he was doing so, McClung described Adams's relationships to bears as contradictory. On the one hand, some of them were his protectors, companions, comrades, and friends, whom he trained so that he could sleep with them at night. On the other hand, it was clear that Adams placed himself in a superior position; as McClung states, "Grizzly Adams was their god," a divine being who could in so many ways assert his dominance.[31]

McClung left the reader in the dark about how early, if at all, his subject was collecting and training wild animals, bears included, as part of an effort to make

Featured on the cover for Robert M. McClung's *The True Adventures of Grizzly Adams* (1985) is a huge, ferocious bear—its mouth wide open as if it is about to attack Adams.

The True Adventures of
Grizzly Adams

Robert M.
McCLUNG

The life behind the legend

money displaying them on the East or West Coast. He provided scattered evidence of how crafty and skilled Adams was as a showman. Only toward the end of the book did McClung begin to mention with some focus and consistency what Adams was doing. More fully than Dillon, McClung told of how Adams developed his shows in San Francisco as he raised his fees and hired a band to promote his exhibits. Once in New York, Adams, he reported, paraded bears down Broadway. On each side were two grizzlies, "held only by chain leashes in the Wild Yankee's hands." Those paying to enter the menagerie watched as "some bears danced and some sang, while others turned somersaults or wrestled with Adams."[32] Yet Grizzly Adams knew how bear attacks imperiled his life. "I have been beaten to Jelly," he supposedly told Barnum in his waning days, using the adjective "treacherous" to describe them, unlike any he had deployed earlier.[33]

The obituary for Adams in *Harper's Weekly* captured many of the dimensions of the relationships between Adams and grizzlies, only hinting at the ultimately

The Life and Times of Grizzly Adams (1974), Sunn Classic Pictures. Screenshot.

fatal ones and not even mentioning their roles in his commercial entertainments. "His tastes," it read, "led him to cultivate the society of bears, which he did at great personal risk, but with remarkable success, using them as pack horses by day, as blankets by night, as companions at all times."[34] However, it was Adams who had the last word. Several months before his death, "How I Came to Be a Showman with After Reflections" appeared in the *New York Weekly*. "I have labored and made myself a slave to collect a menagerie of American animals, with a hope of enjoying the exhibition and realizing a fortune from it; but now I find myself a slave to the thing designed to serve me, which does little else but exhibit me and demonstrate my own weaknesses and follies."[35] So in the end, in his sort of posthumous statement, wilderness was better than civilization.

The story of Grizzly Adams had at least one more major rebirth, the 1974 film *The Life and Times of Grizzly Adams*, which drew on and underscored the importance of contemporary environmentalism.[36] A very-low-budget, independent film directed by Richard Friedenberg and starring Dan Haggerty, it grossed more than four hundred times what it cost to produce. Almost any similarity between the film and what we know of Adams is purely coincidental, although again what we see is Adams affectionately relating to a companion bear.

The film's plot is simple enough. It begins in 1853 with James Adams holding the hand of his daughter Peg in front of a simple home as he tells her he is leaving "forever" because he has been accused of a murder he did not commit. The scene soon shifts to a deer approaching him, then him feeding it and it nuzzling up to him. This was just one of scores of scenes to come of evocative and sentimental human/animal interactions that reinforce the film's major theme, that the wilderness is a peaceful place where all beings can get along with one another. "Slowly," Adams says, "I began to understand I was going to be a part" of the wilderness, as he remembers times early in his life "when animals would come to me when they wouldn't come to any other human." Soon he rescues a grizzly cub that its mother abandoned, one that hugs him and licks his face. In return, Adams promises to get it to a safe place. He decides to call the cub Benjamin Franklin, places a leather collar around his neck connected to a leash, likens him to a child, and begins the process of teaching him the ways of the world.

Before long begins a story that is more central to the life of Adams than to that of any grizzly. It involves the twists and turns in his relationship with a Native American named Nakoma, played by Cherokee and Choctaw Hollywood stuntman Don Shanks. What shapes their reciprocal connections are a series of scenes where they rescue each other. They do their best to communicate with one another, even though they do not understand each other's languages. As they part for the first time, Nakoma draws blood from Adams's arm and from his own and then binds their wounded arms together. So now they are "blood brothers," Adams claims as Nakoma leaves "to go back to his people," whom we never see or learn about.

In parallel scenes that emphasize reciprocity, we follow Adams and Ben interacting. Adams teaches the cub the ways of the world. In exchange Ben comforts Adams when he is glum. And together they play hide and seek and cuddle, while Adams often talks to Ben as if Ben understands him. Alone except for Nakoma, who at key moments is always "keeping an eye on me," Adams decides to leave his camp because he senses there are men out there looking for him. He decides to go "so deep into the mountains no one would ever see me again." Then, suddenly (presumably because the local zoo has substituted a trained adult grizzly for a young one) Ben appears as an adult. Together they settle in a beautiful valley where Adams builds a cabin. Careless for a moment as he does so, Adams is injured by a falling tree, but this time Ben comes to the rescue, rolling the fallen log off his leg. This example of Ben helping Adams is echoed when he scares off a big cat and again when Ben once again snaps Adams out of a gloomy mood. In another parallel scene of rescue and reciprocity, Nakoma miraculously appears, this time to save Adams from an attack by a black bear. "I tried to explain to Nakoma that we were even now," Adams says. Ben gets into the act and scares off the black bear while the narrator comments that "nothing in the mountains can stand up to a grizzly for very long."

Following this comes the film's final turn, when out of nowhere Nakoma arrives with Peg, now a beautiful young woman who has come to bring her father home because the real murderer had been captured. When Adams asks his daughter how she found him, she replies that it was because he was now famous as the man who tamed a grizzly bear. As we watch Ben, Grizzly Adams, and Peg play peacefully, we learn that she loves animals "and all the animals loved her right back." Yet danger still lurks. This time Peg wanders off and plays with a baby wolf, only aware of how dangerous this is when the mother wolf comes and attacks her. Once more comes a magically timed rescue scene: Ben and Grizzly Adams arrive and Ben frightens the wolf away. Despite his daughter's hope that he will leave the wilderness and return home with her, he insists he will stay where he is. Nakoma and Peg ride off into the distance, leaving Adams with his beloved but now fully grown Ben. However, because he realizes that if Peg could find him, others might do so, Adams decides to move to another wilderness home. We see him and Ben amble away as off-screen a man sings, "This is my home; I mean, the mountains. It's where I belong," followed by "We are staying here forever in the beauty of this place . . . living free in harmony. . . . Take me home. Take me home."

The Life and Times of Grizzly Adams is remarkably different from the life and times of the real Grizzly Adams, however varied are the more accurate renditions that more or less closely reflect what is reliably known of his life. In this film version we almost never see Adams hunting. Though a black bear does attack, and at one point Adams chases a grizzly away by throwing objects at it, grizzlies are invariably friendly and Ben especially so. There are no groups of Native Americans or discussions of them as uncivilized, just one, Nakoma, who is always watching over Adams, engaging in reciprocal rescue missions, and becoming his blood brother literally and figuratively. Only once is there explicit mention of civilization. When Adams is nursing Nakoma back to health, he says there is not much he could do for him "this far from civilization." In this case, that key word stands not unfavorably for temptation and corruption but favorably for where one can get better medical attention. Here Adams is more alone than in any other versions of the story. A low-budget film meant keeping personnel costs down, so we have only the invented figures of Nakoma and Peg—no brother, bankers, traders, companions, and above all no P. T. Barnum as the final goal of an Adams driven by dreams of financial gains.

To my sophisticated mind, as someone more comfortable in cities than in nature, this film seems mawkishly sentimental. Yet it obviously appealed to those who drove its global box office receipts above $60 million and the more than 200,000 people who have since viewed it on YouTube. As a film, *The Life and Times of Grizzly Adams* resonates with some powerfully and with others as entertainment. Part of its attraction in an age of dazzling productions, its low-budget qualities had a certain comforting appeal. Then there is how it offers a story of reciprocity between its hero and Nakoma. The film also fully conveys qualities of nature we'd presumably like to embrace: scenes of stunning waterfalls, valleys, and mountains; flowers in bloom; animals gamboling by themselves and often with humans—part adventure film, part nature film.

⚜   ⚜   ⚜

The lives of Hugh Glass and the narratives for which they provide material illuminate changing depictions of the relationships between bears and humans. With Glass, bears could be unalloyed adversaries, even if twentieth-century storytellers bestowed on them more benign and transcendent roles. The narratives of the interactions between Adams and grizzlies point to a major transition in the long story of the relationships of humans to animals, one best symbolized by the fact that his most commonly used first name is Grizzly. At one point or another and sometimes simultaneously, grizzlies were his friends, companions, servants, and enemies—to be loved and feared, domesticated and eaten, lain down with and hunted, displayed for commercial gain in American cities and sold to far-off lands. Sometimes he beat them into submission, yet as Brett Mizelle has written, Grizzly Adams was "a liminal figure who seemed to straddle human and animal worlds," with his both "going native and becoming animal" a key to his enduring appeal.[37] He treated bears as having personalities and agency. And at moments Adams interacted with them in ways that suggested some semblance of kindly cross-species relationships. Yet Adams always tried to maintain the dominant position, even though ultimately the bear strikes back, turning dominance on its head (and his head) in a deadly way. Adams projected onto his bears all sorts of human qualities, at times minimizing those that proved fatal. In the end, however varied and ambiguous his relationship to his bears, Adams forgot he was James Capen Adams and they were not Ben Franklin or Lady Washington but rather wild bears he apparently both loved and violently trained. Above all, the difference between the stories of Glass and Adams concerns what we know of the bears in their lives. We know almost nothing of the unnamed one that attacked Glass but a good deal about those Adams encountered, perhaps loved, and more surely dominated.

Strikingly, over time the depictions of the bears of Grizzly Adams changed little, as they mainly remained humanlike, perhaps more in names than in reality. What did vary was the nature of the stories of Adams himself, especially as they shifted in emphasis between wild man and entrepreneur. The most significant change from tales of Hugh Glass to those of Grizzly Adams was that by 1860 bears had begun to emerge as celebrities—both in the name of Grizzly Adams and of his bears, which carried the names of famous human celebrities and were themselves celebrities. With the help of Barnum, the stories of Grizzly Adams may well offer the first example of bears as popular culture celebrities. When Grizzly Adams joined P. T. Barnum, they formed a team that well understood how humans exalted nonhumans into the stratosphere of fame.

5

Captive Bears and
Their Captors as Workers

✕

April 10, 1871, is the date of P. T. Barnum's first circus venture, which in 1919 became part of Ringling Bros. and Barnum & Bailey. Six weeks later, on May 22, 1871, the American Museum of Natural History opened in Manhattan. It was in these years that bears appeared in captivity in zoos—New York City's Central Park in 1860, followed in 1874 by one in Philadelphia, the National Zoological Park in Washington, DC, in 1889, and then the New York Zoological Society's Bronx Zoo in 1898. The late nineteenth century was also a time when Americans hosted more and more domesticated large animals in their homes (bears on rare occasions), while fewer and fewer non-domesticated ones lived close to their homes as stockyards and dairies moved farther from the city center. Over a much longer period of time, especially after World War II, films and later video games displayed captured bears. In almost every instance people controlled and to varying extents anthropomorphized bears that achieved fame in institutions and on screens. Over more than a century and a half, in many media bears provided rich visual representations that varied in their approach from love to cruelty. The history of bears in captivity is intricately intertwined with their work as captives and with the labor of their captors, who control both real and imagined animals.

In natural history museums, visitors can view bears that were once alive. Beginning in the late nineteenth century, Americans displayed them as the trophies wealthy men brought back from their hunts; bears' heads also appeared in clubs and homes inhabited by members of elite society. Before the century's end, scientists began to collaborate with exhibition designers to elevate displays of bears by developing habitat dioramas that relied on taxonomy, offered static visuals, and involved a limited ability to convey sophisticated scientific knowledge. Then, starting in the late 1930s, developments at institutions variously called museums of natural history or museums of science began to change the static and traditional approaches to representing bears. In 1937 Franz Boas warned the director of Manhattan's American Museum of Natural History that such exhibits had armored "the Museum, like a dinosaur, against change," making "it almost impossible for it to respond to changing scientific interests."[1]

In the postwar period, scientific interests, as well as educational imperatives, drove improvements at museums of natural history. Scientific advances compelled the attention of those who displayed bears in museums and elsewhere, as did the appeal of dynamic and interactive exhibits. Yet by and large dioramas remained problematic. Since it was easier to educate and excite audiences with live insects, birds, or snakes than with dead bears, continued reliance on exhibits of stuffed ones made relevant, interactive, and immersive experiences difficult if not impossible.[2] The result was tellingly clear in Karen A. Rader and Victoria E. M. Cain's 2014 *Life on Display: Revolutionizing U.S. Museums of Science and Natural History in the Twentieth Century*. In this comprehensive history, there were five references to Donna Haraway's pathbreaking postmodernist essay "Teddy Bear Patriarchy" but only two to bears on display. One mentioned how those designing exhibits in the late nineteenth and early twentieth centuries "frequently incorporated family dynamics that visitors could easily recognize." The other described an "almost comically minimalist" exhibit that opened in 1979 at the Smithsonian's National Museum of Natural History featuring "a brown bear mounted on a base designed to look like a forest landscape next to a polar bear on a simulated ice cap."[3]

The current exhibit of brown bears at the American Museum of Natural History exemplifies how static representations persist. In 2018 Kara Blond, who had directed exhibits at the National Museum of Natural History, noted that a recent restoration and updating of the dioramas doubled "down on the powerful, visceral visitor response to standing alongside scenes of grizzly bears on the prowl." Though designers are using new technologies to modernize such exhibits to make them more compelling, she adds, so far "the craft of diorama has remained relatively static."[4]

In the late twentieth century and into the twenty-first, museum trustees and professionals faced many challenges that significantly sidelined the importance of traditional ways of displaying bears. The ascendant importance of science; the tension between science and entertainment; the lure of blockbuster exhibits; the challenges from newer institutions, such as science and theme parks; and controversies over the sources and display of Indigenous materials meant it was hard to move beyond the usual ways of focusing on bears in museum exhibits. One way out of this apparent dead end is through an emphasis on how climate change threatens polar bears. This has led to temporary exhibitions at major museums, including Peabody Essex and the American Museum of Natural History in ways that attract crowds by highlighting the dynamic relationships between these bears and their environments.[5]

Museums of art have also offered visions of bears. Not unlike what the story of Hugh Glass suggested decades earlier is one by Arthur Fitzwilliam Tait, who had emigrated in 1850 from Britain to America, where his art was widely on view in Manhattan and in Currier and Ives lithographs. His 1856 *A Tight Fix—Bear Hunting, Early Winter* is an oil painting depicting a struggle between a man and a bear. Then there is the somewhat later work of William Holbrook Beard, who playfully and satirically anthropomorphized bears. *The Bear Dance*, ca. 1870, also known as *The Bears of Wall Street Celebrating a Drop in the Stock Market* and *The Wall Street Jubilee*, contrasts sharply with another one from 1879, *The Bulls and Bears in the Market*. An art critic pointed out how "the severity of the battle is relieved by touches of humor, such as a bear tossed in the air or a bull with a tuft of wool on his horns," and elsewhere "a bear is observed busily engaged in studying his account book."[6] More contemporary but also playful is Claes Oldenburg's 1965 drawing for a proposal of a huge teddy bear monument in Manhattan's Central Park, one that pictures a lovable bear sitting on the green lawn.

If natural history museums display stuffed bears and artists offer varied representational ones, zoos present live ones, albeit often reminding us of how limited is their freedom in captivity.[7] In Europe, zoos had their origins in royal households, but in America they developed from private and public menageries and from the imperialistic adventures of elite male big game hunters, who brought wild animals back from out West and abroad. The Boone and Crockett Club, for which Teddy Roosevelt served as cofounder and first president,

William Holbrook Beard, *The Bear Dance*, ca. 1870. New York Historical Society and Museum.

played a critical role in the development of the Bronx Zoo, in the process connecting vigorous masculinity, the preservation of animals native to America, and a vision of a nation free of recent immigrants.[8]

Initially zoos presented animals in unadorned cages, separated from people by metal bars. Over time in both Europe and America, zoo masters worked to display animals in more "natural" settings. They did so even as, like the menageries from which defenders problematically claimed zoos were clearly distinguishable, they mixed education and science with entertainment. A major turning point in how zoos displayed animals occurred in 1907, when Carl Hagenbeck—a second-generation entrepreneur engaged in the capturing, buying, and selling of wild animals—displayed them outside Hamburg in Stellingen's Tierpark, or Animal Park. He used carefully designed rocks, moats, pools, and dramatic panoramas to create what the historian Nigel Rothfels calls "a theatrical illusion of freedom for the animals." This made visitors feel that animals (including bears), rather than being penned up, were free to roam as they might in their native habitats. In his authoritative book on Hagenbeck, Rothfels notes that he called his creation "an 'animal paradise'" as he connected it with the biblical one, "a place where 'animals would live besides each other in harmony and where the fight for survival would be eliminated.'" With modifications American zoos soon followed Hagenbeck's model. Yet in the end, Rothfels said, "Hagenbeck's revolution was precisely the narratives of freedom and happiness." He wanted the public to learn that "animals have been put in zoos increasingly because they are nice, healthy, safe places to be because the animals, we are told, might be better off there than in the real 'wild.'"[9]

The emphasis on immersion of audiences in the world of animals intensified in places like the San Diego Zoo Safari Park (originally named the San Diego Wild Animal Park) and the Arizona-Sonora Desert Museum. These both used considerable acreage and innovative designs to help give paying visitors the illusion of actual experiences of the natural world. As a result, they emphasized a promise of authenticity. Then there is Disney's Animal Kingdom Theme Park. It opened on Earth Day in 1998 on 580 acres near Orlando, planned with the help of zoo experts and with ample attention to previous Disney explorations of nature.[10] Disney's magic, writes the scholar Randy Malamud, was adept at beating "zookeepers at their own game; taking the display of captive animals into the realm of hyperreality; accelerating the technology and discourse of representation up to the speed limit of turbocharged American commercialism; . . . in a ritual anointed with the mantle of vintage Disney style, consummately canonical mass/pop culture."[11] Like Hagenbeck's Tierpark, notes Rothfels, the enterprises outside San Diego and Orlando are "'managing eloquence'" as they try "to redirect the audience from seeing and imagining an animal's fate in captivity" by relocating them into an imaginary storybook.[12]

The Walt Disney Corporation's portrayal of bears and other wild animals points to the complications and contradictions involved in our understanding of how designers labor so that we can work as tourists who witness bears as unwitting performers. Its "commitment to protect the environment dates back to its origins and founder, Walt Disney," insist the authors of copy on the company website. "Care for the environment was evident early on with the production of nature films, Walt's support of wildlife and its preservation, and his idea to incorporate conservation in the Walt Disney World Resort master plan."[13] Yet though places that exhibit captive animals have always juggled commitments to science, education, conservation, recreation, and entertainment, the balance shifted, toward entertainment in Disney's case.[14] And in 1993 the New York Zoological Society, founded almost a century before, changed its name to the Wildlife Conservation Society. Informed by advances in science, relying on the professionalizing of staff, responding to federal legislation and international agreements as well as pressure from environmentalists and animal activists, it increasingly emphasized conservation and improved conditions of captivity that would help preserve endangered species, as was true at other zoos as well. Nonetheless, to draw crowds the Bronx Zoo persisted in keeping wild animals in tamed captivity.

Among other forces, what challenged zoos to rethink how they presented animals were dramatic scenes of animals that people saw on television, many of which pictured some combination of pristine nature and threats to its existence. As time passed, zoos intensified their emphases on immersion. They attempted to make visitors feel as if they were actually in nature when they viewed animals. Yet more sophisticated exhibit designs had less to do with pleasing animals than with appealing to the public by providing a believable and reassuring vision of what is, after all, still captivity.[15] So this approach also involved trickster skills as zoos increasingly took on the political task of alerting the public to the threats animals faced—not the creatures they saw in zoos but the ones out in the wild, endangered by forces such as deforestation and climate change.

There were limits to how successfully zoos could convince skeptics that wild animals were better off in captivity than in the wild. Critics of new, conservation-oriented methods of displaying animals invoke the contradictions inherent in such efforts. Animals in zoos, bears among them, remain prisoners in settings that are far from truly natural at a time when capitalism and climate change are destroying their native habitats. And studies reveal that those who visit zoos, rather than gaining meaningful and empathetic education about what they see, often return home with their belief in human superiority confirmed.[16] Try as zoos might to emphasize science and preservation, two things were inescapable. Visitors were there as tourists mainly for recreational entertainment. And however captivating were the animals they saw, they were nonetheless captive. Malamud trenchantly explicates this problematic nature of zoos. "Zoo spectatorship," he notes, "is passive, minimally imaginative, cheaply vicarious, at least slightly distasteful, conducive to a range of socially inappropriate or undesirable behavior, and inhibitive, rather than generative, of creative experience and appreciation of nature." Moreover, he insists, "rather than fostering an appreciation for animals' attributes, zoos convince people that we are the imperial species—that we are entitled to trap animals, remove them from their worlds and imprison them within ours, simply because we are able to do so by virtue of our power and ingenuity."[17]

Eventually and inevitably, criticism of zoos led to calls for their abolition, a movement with a long history that started gaining momentum in the 1960s. Activists deny that most animals are endangered and assert that the efforts of zoos to protect them are problematic. They emphasize that alternative ways exist for people to experience wildlife.[18] Above all, as the British Captive Animals' Protection Society stated, "We believe all animals should live free from exploitation, harm and captivity."[19]

Bears make their appearances in zoos less commonly than some other animals but as performers in some distinctive ways that deny or minimize their agency. Bear pits, which were common in royal menageries, found their way into American zoos until such displays became unacceptable. And with good reason, for they enabled spectators to look down into a deep chasm in the middle of which was placed a pole or a tall tree trunk that bears climbed up so they could capture food people threw at them. People would taunt and torment them, replicating but making more respectable a tradition of bearbaiting, where dogs attacked chained bears, a practice outlawed in England in 1911.[20] More recently bears have been on display under less dire circumstances that nonetheless persist in treating them as captive performers. We will see how Smokey the Bear became a major attraction in the Smithsonian's National Zoological Park. Similarly, children of all ages living anywhere could see that same zoo's pandas, Tian Tian, Mei Xiang, and Xiao Qi Ji, on the Giant Panda Cams sponsored by Boeing. And the website of New York's Bronx Zoo announces that "brown bears are a fan favorite" because we love to "watch them splash around in the shallow water."[21] Zoo bears are there for us to look at rather than for them to live as they would in the wild.

Circuses also have long histories of exhibiting captive bears as performers. At one time or another there were hundreds of circuses across America, but one came to dominate. The year 1871 is the date often given to mark the birth of the classic American circus, when Barnum joined forces with other entertainment entrepreneurs to form what would eventually become, despite a seemingly unending tangle of business arrangements and name changes, Ringling Bros. and Barnum & Bailey Circus. Fueled by and reflecting the transformation of the United States into a powerful and vast nation with imperial ambitions, the American circus in its heyday was a huge commercial and itinerant enterprise that operated both in the United States and abroad. Although other circuses existed locally and on a smaller scale, for millions and millions of family-oriented Americans this one provided their most important encounter with living popular culture, featuring grandiose spectacles and abundant thrills at the expense of captive animals. Their promotional, patriotic pageants celebrated the triumphal march of white citizens across the nation and its history by sidelining or denigrating foreigners, African and Native Americans, and what they called freaks.

At its height, the iconic Greatest Show on Earth was a vast and complicated enterprise that relied on managerial and financial talents of human and nonhuman performers. For decades two separate operations traveled on the nation's railroads in sixty cars. They went to scores and scores of cities in which an

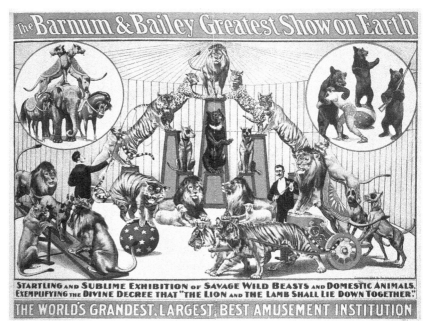

"Startling and Sublime Exhibition of Savage Wild Beasts and Domestic Animals," an 1894 Barnum & Bailey poster showing bears in three poses.

immense entourage paraded through cheering crowds gathering on streets along the way to a location where, for several days, the circus set up its Big Top, a huge tent that could be more than 250 feet long and where multiple performances took place simultaneously. Brilliant posters heralded this arrival. Features came and went, especially in sideshows, but at its core several persisted. Trapeze and high-wire artists danced dangerously in the air. As the historian Janet M. Davis has shown, with censorious ministers eyeing women performing suggestively on the high wire and on the backs of horses, as well as on terra firma, the circus offered carefully balanced "dialectics of sexual titillation and propriety."[22] On the ground clowns gamboled and horses pranced while carefully and painfully trained animals—including bears—followed the commands of their trainers.[23]

Challenges to the popularity, finances, and staying power of circuses came as the result of two world wars; the Depression of the 1930s between them; a disastrous fire in Hartford, Connecticut, in 1944; increased costs of land, transportation, and labor; changes in ownership and technology; and competition from others forms of entertainment, especially television, the World Wide Web, and theme parks. In 1952 more Americans probably saw Cecil B. DeMille's star-studded and Academy Award–winning *The Greatest Show on Earth* than they did the live production, though both included performances by the world-renowned bear trainer Albert Rix's bears. The circus soon stopped traveling to scores of cities to draw audiences to its big tent. Instead, beginning in 1957, the actual Greatest Show on Earth appeared for somewhat longer stretches of time in established indoor arenas and outdoor stadiums. Its belated swan song performance took place in 2017. Then, in the spring of 2022, CBS News announced, "Ringling Brothers circus to relaunch—without animal acts" the following year, with shows in fifty cities. Thus ended performances by bears in America's most important circus. "Word of the animal-free comeback tour drew a positive review from one animal rights group," noted the journalist Kate Gibson, as she quoted remarks by the head of captive animal law enforcement for People for the Ethical Treatment of Animals (PETA), Rachel Mathers: "Ringling is returning with a bang, transforming the saddest show on Earth into a dazzling display of human ingenuity after 146 years of animal abuse."[24]

Well before the 1960s, those interested in animal welfare had protested conditions in zoos and circuses, but with scant results. Beginning in the 1960s, philosophers including Peter Singer and Tom Regan, along with organizations such as ASPCA, PETA, In Defense of Animals, the Animal Liberation Front, and the Performing Animal Welfare Society (PAWS), pressured circuses to improve the conditions under which circus animals worked—or better yet, stop using them altogether. In addition, on-scene activists and action by courts, legislatures, and government agencies increasingly came together to challenge how cruelly circuses used and abused animals. Circuses mounted vigorous defenses, with their claims of commitment to animal welfare facing greater odds than those faced by conservation-minded zoos. What the historian Susan Nance said of one captive set of animals applies to others, bears included: "Hands-on training and rigorous travel and performance schedules of mobile circuses make elephants miserable and represent a frivolous misuse of endangered and threatened species."[25]

As the popularity of the traditional circus featuring animals waned, alternative circuses gained prominence, though bear-free ones. After offering a trenchant and passionate critique of circuses that featured many captive animals, Nance quoted a 2001 *Time* magazine article that called them out as "the interspecies version of a minstrel show." In contrast, she observed, the new versions offered "more abstract performances" that served "a broad, if wealthier and less family oriented, audience while avoiding the scrutiny of the many animal reform organizations."[26] Animal-free except for humans and sometimes horses (very rarely other species), they were artistically inventive, were smaller in scale, and relied on one ring rather than three. Among the myriads of the circus reborn are ones that offer performances locally or regionally: the Pickle Family Circus of San Francisco (1975), Big Apple Circus in New York City (1977), and Circus Smirkus in Greensboro, Vermont (1987). More recent is Montreal's Les 7 Doigts—7 Fingers—(2002), an artist collective that offers tours of highly imaginative productions. Its performances are, to put it mildly, unlike those of the Greatest Show on Earth. As the circus historian Linda Simon notes, they can focus "on the mind and the heart: how people behave when facing disaster, experiencing grief, aspiring for success or feeling thwarted in love."[27] Not to be deterred, however, bears have reappeared in at least one instance. In Manhattan during the fall of 2023, Big Apple Circus, in collaboration with the German troupe Circus Theater Roncalli, brought bears back in—sort of. At one point, the *New York Times* reported, there was "a puzzling routine in which three performers in fur suits pretended to be trained polar bears."[28] In early March 2022, the journalist Jonathan Abrams, noting that with the reappearance of Ringling Bros. and Barnum & Bailey Circus for the first time in seven years, "there are no tigers and elephants; in fact, the only 'animal' is an electric dog named Bailey."[29]

More extensive in its reach is the Cirque du Soleil, also bear-free, founded by two Canadian street performers. Its first season took place in Montreal 1984, with its first show in the United States three years later. To save money, Cirque du Soleil did not take out costly permits that would have allowed it to use animals, which meant it incorporated no bears or other species. Eventually, it relied on support from a shifting combination of private, government, and international investors. In addition to a permanent location in Las Vegas and monthlong stints in other cities, multiple troupes have traveled to hundreds of cities on all six continents, appearing before more than 100 million people. It draws on new technologies such as music synthesizers and on the international talents of jugglers, gymnasts, bicycle riders, magicians, clowns, and aerialists. Featuring theatrical spectacles, it has developed dozens of versions, each with its own series of ever-changing storylines and focal points.[30]

If contemporary circuses do not count real bears among their performers, the presence of bears in old-fashioned circuses was more prominent that what obtained in zoos. To be sure, in circuses bears never gained the celebrity status of big cats and elephants—for example, no captive bear achieved the fame that Jumbo the Elephant did.[31] Bears being captured, forced to fight with other animals, and trained to perform as if they were dancing go back at least to ancient Rome, where on the opening day in the Coliseum the Romans slaughtered nine thousand animals. Performing bears made their appearances in royal households. For centuries and continuing today in some nations, bears perform on city streets, trained to beg and dance. As with zoos, so with circuses: from ancient times on, bearbaiting was common. In 1830 a circus offered news that "a Full Grown Bear will be chained out once, at liberty for any person to set their dogs on him; he will be so secured, that any person may view the fight with perfect safety."[32] By the 1830s in traveling menageries (such as that of Grizzly Adams in the 1850s) and then in circuses, trainers like Adams were using a combination of rewards, conditioned responses, and cruelty to deploy bears. They served humans as entertainers not only by dancing but also by standing on a barrel, a ball, a horse's back, a tightrope, roller skates, a bicycle, or a motorcycle.[33] The goal was, as Janet Davis notes more generally, to force bears "to replicate human movement and behavior" in a way that metaphorically challenged Charles Darwin's hierarchical view of the natural order.[34]

Sometimes circus bears, like other animals, resisted the conditions of their captivity. Trainers would then double down on their punishing training. Bears also tried and even succeeded in escaping. Occasionally they attacked or killed their handlers and might be killed in response.[35] Their escapes were more likely to have a happy ending on-screen than in reality: in 1947 and reappearing in many media later, Disney's enterprises told the story of Bongo the Wonder Bear, whose circus skills riding on a unicycle upon a tightrope while juggling cups and saucers made him famous. Yet seeking freedom and companionship, he escapes into the wilderness, where he falls in love with Lulubelle and then wards off a bully bear by relying on the business skills he developed in shows.[36]

As happened with animals in zoos, including bears, eventually action by activists and governments (along with changes in taste and media) worked to end the use of bears in circuses. Along with other animal welfare organizations, PETA played a prominent role in this campaign. Its "6 Heartbreaking Reasons Why Bears Shouldn't Be in Circuses" emphasized that "bears don't choose to perform, and they're treated just as terribly as other animals." If under command they could not stand on their hind legs, they might well die by choking or hanging. Keeping them "in a constant state of distress when 'performing,'" trainers used fear to "make them perform mindless, uncomfortable tricks." Ripped away from their families, they lived in "cramped cages," one of many conditions that made them suffer, including from depression. Making it clear that bears deserved respect, PETA described them as "sentient beings." Finally, PETA urged people to support their efforts by boycotting circuses that relied on captive bears and instead patronize the "so many marvelous circuses with only willing human performers—who *choose* to learn stunts."[37]

Revelations about the impact of circus captivity on bears come in an intriguing and disturbing study, the Polish journalist Witold Szablowski's 2014 *Dancing*

Bears: True Stories of People Nostalgic for Life Under Tyranny. Tracking the parallel experiences of people released from the clutches of life in the former Soviet Union and bears freed from circus captivity as working performers, he emphasized how difficult it was for both groups to live under freedom rather than captivity. For generations, Roma people in Bulgaria had trained bears to perform by dancing. However, with the fall of the Soviet Union, these bears were placed in wildlife refuges, where handlers instructed them in how to hibernate, copulate, and get food so they could "teach freedom to animals that had never been free." After all, the bears' owners had trained them by beating them when they were young, made sure they'd remember they could not challenge their keepers, and used alcohol to placate them. "And then they made them perform tricks for tourists—dancing, imitating various celebrities, and giving massages."

Visiting Dancing Bears Park near Sofia, Bulgaria, Szablowski realized, "It is very difficult for bears to get used to a life in which they have to care for themselves." He "learned that for every retired dancing bear, the moment comes when freedom starts to cause it pain," so it "gets up on its hind legs and starts to dance." Returning to how they behaved when captive, they act as if they'd prefer their keepers "to come back and take responsibility for its life again. 'Let him beat me, let him treat me badly, but let him relieve me of this goddammed need to deal with my own life,' the bear seems to be saying."[38] Szablowski's work powerfully underscores the problems with the harsh practices people deploy and the reassuring tales they tell themselves to justify captivity. Trainers had used whips, electrical shocks, and beatings to train bears to ride bicycles and dance in circuses.

And then there are bears as companion animals, to be sure not as common as pets as are cats, dogs, and parrots. In the late nineteenth century, as undomesticated animals increasingly disappeared from the lives of most Americans, domesticated and representational ones increasingly entered the homes of millions.[39] As we have already seen, pets as simulacrums of live bears abound as cartoon characters and stuffed animals. Indeed, in 1990 Stan and Jan Berenstain published *Trouble with Pets*, the story of how Brother and Sister Bear persuade their parents to adopt a pet. "A pet is a big responsibility," Mama Bear remarks as she and Papa Bear suggest they might agree to get the young bears a dog. As the children dream of what they might do with a puppy, the narrator notes, "A puppy isn't a toy to be dressed in doll's clothes. It's a living creature with a mind and nature of its own." At the book's end, we learn that the dog had become more than a pet. She had become "another member of the family, to love and enjoy."[40]

Enough of fictional stories of a dog and its companion bear. In contrast, what characterizes true stories of how people have tried to turn real bears into pets echoes the title of Yi-Fu Tuan's 1984 book, *Dominance and Affection: The Making of Pets*. As the anthrozoologist James A. Serpell writes, pets allow us the "unique opportunity to bridge the conceptual and moral gulf that separates human from other animals." Yet, "instead of accepting and appreciating companion animals for what they are, we seem more inclined to abduct them across the animal-human divide, render them in our own 'image,' and transform them in the process into a motley collection of deformed or mutilated cultural artifacts."[41]

If the Berenstains provide a story of fictional bears adopting a pet dog, there are a few true stories of humans adopting live ones. To be precise, bears do not qualify as pets—they are not bred purposely to become companion animals, are difficult to tame, and do not have personalities easily amenable to living with humans. And of course, having one as a pet is hardly as common as having a dog, never mind a stuffed teddy or Winnie-the-Pooh asleep on a child's bed.

Still there are a few examples. One is *Molly and Me: The Story of a Bear* (1997), written and photographed by Daniel Samuels. The tale begins with its author fondly remembering visiting a zoo as a child, followed by reading books and watching movies about bears. On his honeymoon in East Africa, "seeing the animals living free in the wild" profoundly affected him. "You like them and quixotically want them to like you back, but you know animals well enough to know that this is fantasizing." Eventually he decides to add one to his suburban New York household, which already contained a wife and three children, by purchasing a Malayan sun bear, who eventually grew to weigh 125 pounds. He experienced conflicting emotions, not only "the great anticipation of the child-hood dream of living close to a wild animal, studying it, trying to befriend it," but also "the cold, sober intellectual awareness that no one should own a bear or any wild animal." Yet proceed he did, "determined to mitigate this sacrilege against nature by making sure that my bear would be spared, in every possible way, the usual miseries of confinement. No bars would ever imprison her, no chain or leash relegate her to a lackluster, sedentary non-existence." Hoping no one would "contemplate a similar dream," he acknowledged "the cold, harsh reality of unfairly kidnapping a wild creature away from the world in which it belongs, for the sake of human needs, ego-related or otherwise."[42]

What followed were tales of how over two years Molly and members of the Samuels family, including other pets, learned to live together. Stories abounded about challenges, including when Molly tore up a newly laid linoleum floor or destroyed the house's plumbing. Yet overall things went relatively well, Samuels insisted. Molly rarely strayed from the family's two acres and inflicted only minor injuries on family members. They came to understand what a Malayan sun bear needed, even though they also anthropomorphized her, as they did when they captioned pictures that referenced Goldilocks's three bears or a teddy bear. After all, they understood that idealized endings, such as the hope that their dog and bear could become playmates, "are associated with human desires and not so relevant in the animal world."[43]

In the end, Samuels decided that even though Molly's presence satisfied his own yearnings, ultimately her "long-term welfare had to come first." After all, he denounced how hunters and zoos endangered the lives and well-being of animals, made clear that he preferred calling grizzlies *Ursus magnificus* rather than *Ursus arctos horribilis*, and remarked that "each purchase of an exotic animal just serves to perpetuate the abuses of the 'pet' industry." So after two years together, he sent Molly off to an animal farm in the American South. Yet just as at the outset, so at the book's end Samuel focused much more on his own needs rather than those of his pet bear. When Molly departed on April 21, 1969, he wrote, it "was the worst day of my life. . . . Molly tormented me when I looked up into the trees in twilight hours. I couldn't believe she was really gone." It took him ten years to write the book "because of the painful recollection of wonderful times and then eventual parting as such a terrible ordeal." Bites from what he called her "self-righteous jaws . . . wouldn't hurt as much as the memory of her."[44]

Google points to scores or more videos and stories of bears as pets, though it turns out that they usually concern ones deployed for commercial purposes, earning money for their captors. As I reviewed them, I came to realize that in most cases these were in some ways like a dog performing at the Westminster Kennel Club Dog Show on steroids, although a grizzly bear is much more dangerous than a champion springer spaniel.[45] One example is the Montana naturalist Casey Anderson, who adopted "Brutus, the Pet Grizzly Bear" as a newborn cub in 2002. He raised him, and then Brutus served as Anderson's "cohost" on the Nat Geo Wild series and in National Geographic films before he died at age nineteen. On a video, Anderson called Brutus "my best friend" who had served as the best man in his wedding. Brutus came into the house for Thanksgiving, where he was served his own turkey, and for his birthday, where he opened presents and gobbled down a cake.[46]

Then there is the story of the Canadian Mark Dumas. Dumas "has the world's only pet polar bear," Agee, whom he trained "to star in high-budget TV advertisements." Dumas, we are told, is "the only person in the world who has this kind of bond with a fully grown polar bear," an animal who "can be very adoringly possessive of her owner" and "jealous of other women." We see Agee clamping her jaws around Mark's neck "in an amazing demonstration of just

Mark Dumas swimming with his pet polar bear. YouTube video, "The Only Man in the World Who Can Swim with a Polar Bear: Grizzly Man." Barcroft TV (USA), April 11, 2012.

how much he trusts the huge bear," and in another scene the two of them are relaxing in a pool.[47]

Among the more than one hundred responses to an online short video of Dumas and Agee are some from people who assert that more than jealousy was in the future. Jackycook64 warned that "they had better rethink their decision to keep a pet polar bear unless they want to end up as bear kibble!" Adarsh, using the words of David Attenborough and combining fear and fascination, reminded innocent viewers that "Polar Bears are currently the largest land carnivores on Earth and the only animal who thinks of humans as their food! But also very cute!😍."[48]

For good reason, caution abounds, as friendship can turn into fright and remind us that reciprocal, cross-species relationships are not always risk-free. Writing more generally about bears as pets in December 2020 on Wide Open Media's Pets site, Crystal Long noted, "Pet bears exist, but we're curious how possible it really is." As children, she said, we learned how cute teddy was and how Smokey helped prevent forest fires. Yet, she insisted, "no, bears are not good pets." Aside from legal issues, as cute as bear cubs were, they grow up to be huge and potentially dangerous and even lethal adults, something even experienced trainers and handlers recognized. Bears, Long reminded readers, will always be "wild animals" that you cannot domesticate like a dog and "that won't hesitate to attack in an instant if they become moody or angry." In the end, she advised, "better stick to seeing these omnivores in bear country and stop fantasizing that pet bears can be like cute and cuddly pet teddy bears."[49]

There may be a few examples of bears making their appearances in homes as pets but a seemingly unending number of them on films. At least as far back as the studies of animal locomotion by Eadweard Muybridge in the late 1870s, filmmakers have relied on the moving image to capture the lives of animals.[50] Most of his photographs were of domesticated animals, but by the early twentieth century movies of wildlife, often developed in tandem with imperialism's interest in the exotic, appeared on movie screens.[51] Before the end of World War II bears rarely appeared in such films, but soon after, such representations were abundant.[52] We've already seen (and will see later on) examples of postwar animals on film that featured bears—ranging from cartoons such as those about Goldilocks and the Three Bears, the Werner Herzog documentary *Grizzly Man* (2005), and Hollywood's capture of the story of Hugh Glass in *The Revenant* (2015). However, what flooded the market starting in the 1940s began with what the media studies scholar Cynthia Chris calls "The Disneyfication of Nature."[53] That may have included the animated feature *Bambi* in 1942, but the avalanche of wild nature documentaries really started with the award-winning *True-Life Adventures* series launched in 1948. With it, the historian Gregg Mitman notes, "Walt Disney Studios succeeded in capturing and monopolizing a mass market for nature on the big screen throughout the 1950s."[54]

And in that series the Academy Award–winning *Bear Country* of 1953 stands out as the best ursine example.[55] Directed by James Algar, who had previously worked on *Fantasia* and *Bambi*, this thirty-three-minute documentary had no on-screen roles for humans, even though we listen to the voice of the omniscient narrator. Chris perceptively notes, as with other episodes in the *True-Life Adventures* series, "the classic form of the wildlife film shifted from that of a travelogue to that of a coming-of-age movie, using animals as allegorical ciphers in place of human actors." With humans rarely on-screen, viewers would focus on animals, in the process anthropomorphizing them.[56] The film used powerful visuals to picture nature as awe-inspiring and pristinely beautiful. To be sure, we watch a bird swoop down to catch a mouse and a mountain lion ready to pounce on bear cubs, but in the end a reassuring natural order is restored.

The central narrative revolved around the story of two cubs born during their mother's hibernation. She spent two years teaching them the ways of the world before abandoning them so she could repeat the cycle that began with new births. Anthropomorphism suffuses the story, with the narrator talking of "lunch time," falsely claiming that a "diet of bears is much like that of humans" and included a "salad course of a lavish banquet," picturing of the cubs playing "their version of the old-fashioned game of tag," and calling the dens where bears hibernate "dormitories." However, the most pervasive and important way the film imposed human values and experiences on the lives of bears lies elsewhere. Many wildlife films offered a comforting vision of 1950s family life that involves the nurturing mother educating and protecting children before launching them into independent lives.[57] When her cubs court danger by climbing up a tree and "think nothing of performing their stunts at dizzying heights," we hear that their mother "decides enough is enough and calls them down. In bear country what mother says goes. She lets them off with a mild scolding this time." But a closer look points elsewhere—away from suburban togetherness and how mama bear relied on motherhood to overcome what Betty Friedan ten years later could have called a very different "problem that has no name." Here that challenge is twofold. We learn that, "oddly enough," the cubs' "worst enemy is the adult male," who "will kill the cubs if he finds them unattended." And though the mother does protect them from the male bear and launch them into the world, she eventually abandons them.

The mother deserts her offspring when she mates again; in order "to make way for her new family she must first get rid of the old." When "she literally leaves them, out on a limb," at "first the cubs wonder if she's made some mistake." Soon the mother "simply turns and walks out of their lives," and the two-year-old orphaned cubs suddenly feel "bewildered." With music appropriate to the mood, the camera pans over two sad and lonely youngsters. Of course, this means "they enter adulthood" abandoned, appropriate to two-year-old bears but not to suburban sons and daughters at any age. Yet at the film's end we can rest assured because, with winter coming, unlike other animals who might starve, the cubs have learned to store fat and look for a den where they can sleep for the winter, part of "the True-Life Adventure . . . until the time of easy living comes again to the bear country."[58]

Faced with the challenges of producing films for the big screen and competition from the small one, the *True-Life Adventures* series fizzled and then ended in 1964. A year before, *Mutual of Omaha's Wild Kingdom* with Marlin Perkins, a mostly self-taught zoologist and at the time the director of the St. Louis Zoological Park, began its twelve-year run. He made, Mitman noted, "more effective use of television in domesticating nature on screen."[59] Even earlier, while serving as director of Chicago's Lincoln Park Zoo in the mid-1940s, Perkins pioneered made-for-television animal shows that became popular nationwide, including *Zoo Parade*. By the late 1950s he was making the crucial shift from programs offered live from the studio in a show-and-tell format to something more compelling, stories filmed in presumably wild nature. To an audience in excess of thirty million people a week who watched the Emmy-winning shows, Perkins and his sidekicks Jim Fowler and Stan Brock worked to combine emphases on science, education, entertainment, and conservation in half-hour shows that began and ended in an indoor set. With an insurance company sponsoring his program, he made sure he underscored the parallels between caring for human family members and nonhuman animals caring for theirs. "Just as the mother lion protects her cubs," he insisted on one show, "you can protect your children with" a Mutual of Omaha insurance policy.[60] At another moment, Perkins insisted that if "trapping mountain goats takes the skill of an expert," so "planning your health insurance needs" requires "the skill of an expert from Mutual of Omaha."[61] The shows also connected conservation of nature and of family resources. Not protecting our natural resources, listeners learned, "can do great harm to our environmental security," just as inadequate insurance coverage "can ruin our financial security."[62]

"Bears of High Country," which appeared in season five of *Wild Kingdom*, followed Disney's *Bear Country* in its emphasis on how the black bear mother protects her two cubs, albeit here without the threat of the murderous male or the abandoning female.[63] Unlike the Disney episode people are very much present—not only Perkins (who at the beginning and end appears in a library) but also his cohost Jim Fowler, as well as Peter Gros, added later to introduce the episode. The drama of the show's first half involves Perkins and Fowler virtually and awkwardly hunting their prey amid pristine nature, with their voices ever present and omniscient. "If we can keep them under observation without them knowing it," we hear, then "we should really be able to learn something about how bears spend their time." We are led to believe that the two men, crawling stealthily on the ground or peeking through trees, are not far from the bears, even though the sequences featuring bears and men were surely filmed separately. We see the cute cubs playing a game of tag much as household pets would do, engaged in "amusing antics" accompanied by lighthearted music. Yet danger is ever present from coyotes and grizzlies, with Gros telling us at the outset that "nature can be harsh" as members of the animal kingdom engage in a Darwinian struggle in order "to create that delicate but natural balance" between predator and prey, with bears "successful in their fight for survival . . . in spite of man."

Just beyond the halfway mark, three scientists join Perkins and Fowler on an "exciting bear hunt," in which they use a tranquilizing dart to tag a grown bear. "No pain, just immobilized," we hear reassuringly before we learn that this hunt "will help scientists and conservationists learn more about" the species, "knowledge that will eventually help bears survive in the high country." Then at the very end Perkins tells another story of human-animal relations. In parks like Yellowstone, where the episode took place, bears that people hand-fed no longer feared humans and had become as dangerous as wild lions. "We should respect bears for what they are, magnificent wild creatures," we hear immediately before the credits roll, "and allow them to live unmolested in the parks and woods of the wild kingdom."

Another drug-and-tag story by Perkins, "To Rope a Grizzly" (1971), picks up where "Bears of High Country" left off but with the project having a different goal in mind and an unpredicted ending.[64] Ranchers had invited Perkins, now accompanied by Stan Brock, to track and capture "perhaps the most feared grizzly of all . . . the renegade, the killer of livestock," one that was "marauding ranch livestock." Because grizzlies were "becoming increasingly rare," Perkins noted, "we were determined to capture this fellow unharmed." Highlighting that in the Old West "many riders took part" in roping grizzlies, for this hunt "there were only two of us." In fact, their party consisted of Perkins, Brock, a "master tracker" Ollie, four tracking dogs, and the three men's horses. In many ways the episode follows the trope of old western films with cowboys on horseback chasing after a dangerous prey, one neither cute nor anthropomorphized like those in "Bears in High Country."

Their mission fails when the bear gets free from the lasso and chases one of the men up a tree. Now back in the studio, where Perkins and Brock untangle a chimpanzee from a rope they had used at the episode's beginning, Perkins can claim that there had been no attacks on livestock since their failed effort. "Even though he escaped our ropes," Perkins remarks at the end, as we see a grizzly in a photograph located on the wall behind the two men, "the grizzly is no match for a man with a gun. The grizzly has long been a coveted trophy because of its fierce reputation." There were only about five hundred left in the United States and that number will surely decrease, he notes, before concluding that man is the grizzly's "only natural enemy" but "also its only hope for survival in the wild kingdom." Perkins, like Disney Studios, had worked closely with conservation organizations such as the Audubon Society and the Wilderness Society, which endorsed films that pictured adventurers and scientists working in pristine nature to preserve wildlife. Yet it is possible that what we have here is less about preserving wild animals than protecting a rancher's private property.

Moreover, not unlike Disney's creations, the Perkins productions resemble what the Pulitzer Prize–winning television critic Howard Rosenberg in 2000 called part of "Show Biz." He noted that "*Wild Kingdom* deployed edgy music and edited footage to stress danger and drama." If "drug risk to animals was rarely mentioned, peril to taggers" drove many narratives—obviously not to Perkins but to his sidekicks, featured in "stagey sequences." We see Perkins, he continued, "as if he were witnessing this mayhem in the wild," but of course only in "his dreams," since filmmakers relied on stock footage "cut into the action to make Perkins seem in jeopardy and more of a participant than the creaky, anchored host that he mostly was."[65]

Next in line chronologically, and also shaped by commercial imperatives, is *The Man Who Loved Bears* (1979) by Marty Stouffer, independently coproduced with his cinematographer brother Mark and narrated by Will Geer.[66] If ever there was a movie that treated a wild animal like a human one, this was it. Films that traced an animal through its life cycle were common in these years, but Stouffer had a particular version of that narrative. In two thirty-minute segments of highly and unconvincingly staged scenes, we see the story of Marty, a nature writer living for a year in a cabin in the Colorado wilderness, where he adopts a newborn cub and raises it until it can live on its own. Inspired and initially frightened by seeing a large adult male grizzly, which Stouffer says must be the only grizzly living in the wild in Colorado, he stays up all night reading the tragic stories of how trappers, hunters, mountain men, and cowboys slaughtered "millions" of grizzlies in the Rockies in the nineteenth century. In the morning he goes to a zoo, where he is saddened to see grizzlies "reduced to begging for peanuts." Next, he heads to the zoo's nursery, where a nurse hands over to him a six-week-old female cub so he can feed her with a bottle. As he holds her, the cub licks his face, and as Marty confesses that he knows little about babies, he responds with "Hello there, Baby." The narrator notes, "Marty was the only mother the little grizzly ever knew," a statement that underscores the film's contrast between a nurturing man who acts as a mother to a baby cub and hunters determined "to satisfy some primitive feelings" by achieving "manhood through killing."[67]

So begins the story of Stouffer devoting "several years of his life to a crazy dream—to teach the little bear," whom he names Griz, "the ways of the wild and then give her freedom in the wilderness where grizzlies once thrived." Yet he worries that the "love for her human mother" will "make her prey for hunters," at which point we see a man shooting a rifle. Danger also lurked in a world where animals struggled to find enough to eat and avoid being eaten themselves. In addition, Stouffer wonders whether the cub could eventually "find a mate in the mountains where no grizzly had been seen for many generations" and whether "a zoo-born bear" can survive "in this harsh world." Back in his cabin, he takes care of the cuddly cub "with as much devotion as a human can bestow on an infant." As would be true with Timothy Treadwell, we often see Stouffer talking to his beloved bear as if she understands him. Wondering

Marty Stouffer playing on the floor with Griz from *Wild America*, season 5, episode 7 (1986). Screenshot.

whether the cub could "ever grow into anything as powerful" as the "beast" he had encountered in the wilderness, Marty set out to teach Griz "the ways of the wild" before eventually freeing her.

Stouffer worries that how he nurtured the young bear would mean that Griz would not fear the humans who might trap and kill her. So he devises a scheme, even though he is saddened by the thought of being separated from Griz. Finding an old bear trap in an abandoned cabin, he realizes he can use it to "make her fear, even hate humans, although it meant she'd also hate me." Trapped, Griz was "scared, she was betrayed, and she knew it was because of me." As a freed Griz walks away, Stouffer realized how conflicted he was, since he wanted her to be independent but also to return. A year later, determined to see her one last time, he finds her and says, "Hey, Griz, it's me, Marty." Griz, no longer a cub, rears up and supposedly recognizes Marty. She "seems to want to go to him but then she seems to remember the trap. . . . Marty understood, it was as he had planned." When Griz meets a large male bear, it is something Stouffer had long hoped for. Stouffer, a man living alone with no apparent family connections, found that "his dream was becoming a reality," as mating meant "the next step was baby grizzly." We watch the two adult bears walk off, presumably to mate. At the film's end Geer asks whether they will survive. The answer: "Of course they will. If man will let them," for people have "the power to destroy everything. Perhaps man cannot change," though he can realize that "true wilderness is the key to our own life. He may know that to love wildlife is to love all life including his own. He may comprehend that there is in each of us a little of, 'THE MAN WHO LOVED BEARS.'" This we hear at the very end as we see a flashback of Marty bottle-feeding Griz.

Two years after the showing of *The Man Who Loved Bears*, PBS acquired the rights to the Stouffer franchise, producing and then airing additional versions in 1982. These films, packaged as the *Wild America* series, already had more than a modicum of success but now became wildly popular, with some episodes attracting the highest Nielsen rating of any regularly scheduled series on public TV. Over time Stouffer films surpassed the reach Perkins had achieved: broadcast on hundreds of stations in the United States and others around the world, during some weeks reaching hundreds of millions of viewers. It was the robust development of cable TV and media deregulation beginning in the early 1980s that enabled wildlife films to move from the margins of television programming and to reach vast audiences at home and abroad, packaged by a series of shifting alliances on both commercial and public television channels. Stories on *Wild America*, the Nature series on PBS, various enterprises by National Geographic and Disney, and the Discovery Channel and its sister operation Animal Planet offered a vast array of animal shows, a small but important portion of which focused on bears. Production and distribution costs were lower than other genres because performing animals, unlike performing people, appeared gratis; films could rely on tested formulas and archival footage; one show was capable of being offered again and again; and audiences that appealed to advertisers and sponsors were reliable and affluent.[68]

Nine years after Stouffer's fable came a very different one, *The Bear* or *L'Ours* by the French director Jean-Jacques Annaud, produced as an independent film outside any TV series. Based on James Oliver Curwood's 1916 novel *The Grizzly King: A Romance of the Wild*, which in turn relied on an 1885 story from British Columbia, it offers a different take on the family romance among bears.[69] Though not able to avoid the sentimental, with extraordinary animal photography and stunning scenery, it opens on a grizzly mother comforting her male cub. Soon after, a rockslide kills the mother, and we then follow the surviving cub as he explores nature. Before long another kind of danger intrudes when two hunters stalk and then shoot, but only injure, a huge Kodiak bear, like grizzlies a subspecies of brown bears. The two bears soon meet one another. Initially the Kodiak rebuffs the cub's offer of comfort, but before long we see the cub affectionately licking the Kodiak's wounds, followed by affectionate nuzzling. Over time, just as the mothers in the versions by Disney and Stouffer taught cubs how to thrive, so now in good anthropomorphic fashion we see the Kodiak act as the educating parent. Of course, this is likely fiction, since male bears were more apt to threaten than protect an orphaned bear.[70]

Scenes then alternate between the threats the hunters pose to the bears' existence and the pleasures of life among bears—not only mating but also a performance in an anthropomorphically referenced scene of the cub's psychedelically induced dream. The potential conflict between men and bears ends when the Kodiak refrains from killing one of the hunters, who in turn prevents the Kodiak's death by firearm. Near the end we see the two bears hibernating in a den, where they fall asleep next to one another. Curwood's words on the screen tell us more joy comes from letting bears live than from killing them. As we have seen with the recent histories of zoos and circuses, *The Bear* represents, as a historian of wildlife films notes, one of history's "small pivot-points of change and progress, a quiet chapter in the story of humanity's advancement."[71]

Throughout the film we hear the voices of the hunters but never that of a narrator. Yet as the credits roll, we learn of the extent of human involvement in the film. First are the standard reassurances that "no animals have been maltreated or injured during the making of this film." Then comes a more positive note that in a world where "human behavior" threatens the lives of bears, "fiction, dreams, and emotions" encourage "their indispensable protection." At last, we find out just what that means cinematographically. "Credit to Steve Martin's Working Wildlife," which has in its stable over one hundred animal actors.[72] For *The Bear* the enterprise provided the Kodiak, Bart the Bear, who turned in an Oscar-worthy performance in this and other movies. In addition, what enabled us to see dramatic encounters, especially between hunters and bears, were the "animatronic bears created by Jim Henson's Creature Shop." So on-screen was relatively little anthropomorphism and, aside from the hunters, no human presence, but behind-the-scenes lay the power of human interventions and creativity.[73]

Then there is *Bears*, which appeared in 2019 on PBS as part of its long-running Nature series. Relying on technologies, it offered a stunning survey of the species worldwide within a pristine nature that is both dangerous and awe-inspiring. Like Disney's version two-thirds of a century earlier, it made humans invisible.[74] Yet imputing human traits to bears proved unavoidable, in this case especially when it comes to the subject of mating. We learn that a bear's back-scratching "is like leaving a calling card" in a "dating game."

Moreover, *Bears* is a peopled world. To begin with, there is the ever-present voice of the narrator, Olga Merediz. Then scattered throughout the hour-long special are references to famous fictional bears. When attention turns to the sloth bear, the connection is to the "real-life" one in Kipling's Baloo. More prominently featured are comments about "the endearing real-life Paddington, the spectacle bear," even though in the forest "marmalade sandwiches are not an option." The narrative also refers to the problematic relationships between bears and humans. Threaded throughout the film are scenes of bears playing in swimming pools and on porches and breaking into trucks, cars, campers, and dumpsters in search of food.

In the end, however, there is too little acknowledgment of the impacts of humans, let alone extended analysis of how politics and economics threaten wildlife. To be sure we hear brief mentions of how rising temperatures and shrinking hunting grounds put pressure on their habitats and food sources and threaten the well-being of bears. There are also vague images of what I think is an oil refinery and of people walking through a frontier town. We listen to unexplored statements of how "current trends" threaten their existence because "people are increasingly encroaching on the wilderness." Yet like almost every film featuring bears, this one has to have a happy ending—two cubs who achieve independence from a mother; a bear drugged and tagged so that science can help it; a grizzly that men and dogs are unable to capture; and a small cub and huge grizzly that hunters decide not to kill. So at the end of the film the audience learns that bears "need our help" and "willingness to share space. If we give them a chance, their brains, brawn, and ability to adapt will do the rest."[75]

Among the most recent important cinematic treatments of relationships between humans and bears is *Cocaine Bear* (2023), ostensibly focusing on the life of a bear but more accurately, as is true of so many other bear films, about human nature. Highlighting the drug-induced murder and mayhem a black bear exacts, it also has hints of kinder, gentler animals. Based on, but taking liberties with, a 1985 story that took place in Georgia's Chattahoochee-Oconee National Forest, it uses a warning about drug use by First Lady Nancy Reagan and other period evidence to reference how Americans in the 1980s grappled with the scourge of crack cocaine. For our purposes, the movie's complicated plot is less important than its explorations of interactions between humans and bears. Throughout, we witness the violent and often murderous actions of the bear, who has ingested or aspirated cocaine. This is true even though the actual 1985 drugged bear killed no one. Yet the 2023 version (tinged by zany incidents) relied on the magic of computer-generated images and the performance of actor/stuntman Allan Henry as the "Bear Performer" to offer a rampage-filled horror film. Referencing the work of Werner Herzog that explored the life and death of Timothy Treadwell earlier in the century, Mark Kermode, writing in *The Guardian*, noted, "It may not be *Grizzly Man* meets *Scarface*, but it leaves *Snakes on a Plane* standing on the runway."[76]

Despite the violence that dominates so much of the story, hints appear of more amicable relationships between human and nonhuman animals. Near the beginning, reassuring words appear on the screen: "Black bears are not motivated by territoriality. They will seldom attack bears in their vicinity." Soon we see the first of many images of Smokey Bear, who protects humans and forests. The wildlife activist Peter (Jesse Tyler Ferguson) makes clear that he prefers not to call animals "animals," followed by his remark that "bears are very peaceful" and attack only if people threaten them. The mother of a teenage girl, Sari (Keri Russell), refers to the advice Mama Bear and Papa Bear of the Goldilocks story had offered about being careful in the woods. At one point, we see a teddy bear lying on the floor of park headquarters and someone petting a pet lizard. A small lovable dog appears again and again to remind us of how we can adore pets who provide comfort. We see peaceful sheep in the back of a truck. When he encounters two cute cubs, teenager Henry (Christian Convery) says, "They look like polar bears," to which Sari responds reassuringly by insisting "they're harmless." She follows up by observing that Cocaine Bear is "protecting" her cubs, an impulse reinforced when we see mother and cubs gamboling. Yet despite how this cultural historian can find so many hints of friendly and comforting animals, the film focuses overwhelmingly on how dangerous black bears are. After all, Cocaine Bear kills the animal-loving Peter and near the film's end Cocaine Bear and her cubs disembowel the drug dealer Syd (Ray Liotta).[77]

"The wildlife film and the television genre," writes the media scholar Cynthia Chris as she draws on Michel Foucault, "comprises not only a body of knowledges but also an institution for their containment and display."[78] And that applies specifically to the bear films discussed above. They reveal how filmmakers skillfully worked to capture members of the species for viewers to enjoy and learn from. In the end of course, actual people, and the precedents and institutions they rely on, use staging that profoundly shapes what we see in nature films generally and those on bears specifically. As Nigel Rothfels has noted, we see the results of "the basic conceit of most nature films that no one (much less an extensive crew) stands behind the camera and that what we see before the camera is an unmediated, unedited experience of 'Nature.'" In addition to the labor of unseen crew members, making films involves sequences planned beforehand, "animals are enticed, coerced, or otherwise manipulated into becoming performers; and overall storylines are fashioned to meet specific, conventional narrative expectations."[79] To this Rothfels would surely add expectations governed not only by already established formulas but also by what corporate and NGO sponsors as well as network executives require in order to boost ratings.

Filmed stories of bears, which to varying extents deploy music and a narrator, often rely on familiar clichés such as that science will protect wildlife; various degrees of anthropomorphism; the vision of pristine and often spectacular nature; the tension between education and entertainment; the importance of the life cycle; and the relationships between parents and children. They also frequently involve a cycle of peril (often with a Darwinian emphasis) and safety as other animals, including humans, threaten bears; staged presentations of relations between people and bears suggesting an intimacy that relies more on fantasy than reality; and attention to politics that even if present is vague. Later versions, such as Annaud's *The Bear* in 1988 and *Bears* on PBS in 2019, struggled, or so it was claimed, to avoid projecting human characteristics onto bears and let bears represent themselves.[80] Although conservationists often collaborated with or supported the wildlife films, few of those involved acknowledge how filmmaking intruded on and interrupted the animals being shot by cameras but not guns, or how media may well have encouraged troublesome nature tourism.[81] Moreover, also problematic are the relationships between us as viewers and bears as performers, something that turns bears into familiar clichés and obliterates their distinctive characteristics. As Sherry Simpson notes, spectatorship involves "the risk of bears becoming just another commodity, not for businesses but for viewers. . . . Our trophies were close-up photographs and exciting stories. Once an animal becomes reduced to a collectible, it flattens into mere diversion."[82]

I could focus on any of these films to explore how they are made, and each case would be somewhat different, even though they all have much in common. However, I will concentrate on *The Man Who Loved Bears* because of the contrast between what we see on-screen and what Stouffer wrote about the filming, as well as controversies about his work more generally. In his 1988 book, *Marty Stouffer's Wild America*, he revealed what we do not see on the TV screen. To begin with he made clear that he understood bears in human terms. "Something about them reminds us strongly of ourselves," including how they epitomized "the old-fashioned term 'rugged individualism.'" Moreover, when Griz was "very young, she reminded me of a live teddy bear." Griz, he noted, "was every bit as devoted, crafty, playful, manipulative, and loving" as was his young daughter, who he was raising when he wrote the book. Ranchers had blocked his attempt to reintroduce grizzlies into Colorado, so he decided to raise a grizzly cub and introduce it into the wild of the San Juan Mountains, hoping it would find a mate and produce offspring. With the help of his brother and two friends, he'd make a documentary film so he could build public support and convince the state legislature to support his efforts to restore the state's bear population. He knew he could have purchased one from a circus so that he could rescue it from a miserable life in captivity, but he could not raise such a bear and then release it. He thought about purchasing a cub in a commercial market, which offered bears that would end up in zoos, circuses, and hunting preserves. Instead, he went to the Oklahoma City Zoo, which had a cub it would sell him if he could prove his more benevolent intensions.[83]

Though what appeared in the book and on the screen were similar, there are important exceptions. On-screen we never see his brother, their friends, or a camera. Stouffer noted that when he brought the cub to his cabin, he quickly learned that teaching her was relatively easy, but *"filming* her was pure chaos." Several scenes did not make it into the final cut, including the story of campers who let Griz into their VW bus, which she turned into shambles, and another story of her trying to break into a remote ranch house. More importantly, in the book he told of how he and his brother tailored the film so that CBS would fund and then show it. Not at all interested in the disappearance of grizzlies from the region, "they wanted a sentimental human-interest story about a man and his pet bear, along the lines of Walt Disney's films"—one "full of drama, comedy, suspenseful cliff-hangers, and happy endings." To a considerable extent Stouffer complied by including "fictional sequences": Among these were his discovery of an adult male grizzly, which in fact was a tame one supplied by an enterprise that did likewise for Disney films; one happy ending that showed an adult Griz with her cubs; and another where he said goodbye to Griz a year later. When Mark and Marty presented what they had produced, CBS rejected the film, but they did succeed in getting ABC to air it. And it turned out to be a great success, on TV, in theaters, and for Stouffer's career.[84]

His future assured but his heart broken—because in truth he never saw Griz again, and he regretted the compromises commercialism had forced him to make—Stouffer decided that he "never wanted to 'go Hollywood' again." Rather than doing "made-up human-interest stories that were shot from a script using tame animals," he would "tell the stories of real animals, free and wild within their wilderness domain, in a truthful and educational manner," so that audiences would understand the challenges wild animals faced.[85] To be sure, initially Stouffer enjoyed fame and fortune. His shows on *Wild America* are among the most successful ones PBS has offered. Aired on hundreds of its stations, at times they captivated more than 450 million viewers in a week, with sales of recorded versions reaching more than $60 million.

But this story did not have a happy ending. In three 1996 articles in the *Denver Post*, reporters Mike McPhee and Jim Carrier accused Stouffer "of staging scenes in his documentaries, mistreating animals, and defiling public lands."[86] Though PBS cleared him, a court case resulted in the Aspen Center for Environmental Studies being awarded $300,000 and revealed, in the words of the historian Gregg Mitman, "further disclosures from former animal handlers and staff of Stouffer's production company. Allegedly, caged, tethered, and tame animals and splices of footage shot in different locations were used to construct the dramatic chase, kill, and mating scenes" in *Wild America*.[87] In response, Stouffer insisted that what comprised staging was open to interpretation.[88] Of course the accusations did not refer to *The Man Who Loved Bears*, even though in this 1988 book he had revealed his reliance on staging.

With bears on film, staging appears in many different contexts. In 2015 the Smithsonian's National Zoo launched a series called #PandaStory "to give the public a behind-the-scenes look into the world of saving giant pandas" on loan from China. Part of panda diplomacy that reached back to the early 1940s but intensified in 1972, in August 2022 the zoo celebrated fifty years of its giant panda program. "No panda party is complete without a cake," the zoo announced.[89] Elsewhere on its website, viewers can find out about pandas, with much attention to their life cycle, including the processes of reproduction.[90] Inevitably, Disney followed suit. In early March 2022, a few weeks before the Smithsonian's birthday party, Pixar launched *Turning Red*. The film focused on a girl named Mei who at age thirteen "discovers a welter of new emotions—rage, acute embarrassment, lust—that cause her unexpected transformation into a big fluffy red panda."[91] Just as many films focused on the life cycle of bears and the National Zoo's website on sexual reproduction, so too, observers noted, *Turning Red* concentrated on menstruation in a girl's coming of age.[92] In November 2023 the group of pandas at the National Zoo returned to China. Even with relationships between the United States and China so strained over trade and territory, in late 2024, Bao Li and Qing Bao, two giant pandas, returned to Washington. "They're my favorite animal," Sofia Valle, an eighth grader, said of pandas—and anthropomorphically, "They're so fluffy! And they're lazy like me."[93]

The story of a polar bear named Gus even more extensively enabled Americans to fathom their emotional lives by learning about what a bear experienced. From the mid-1990s until his death in 2013, twenty million Americans tracked Gus's traumatic experiences. In 1994 his keepers at Manhattan's Central Park Zoo had noticed that for hours on end he compulsively swam in a figure eight pattern, the *New York Times* reported, "as if prepping for the Polar Bear Olympics." The zoo paid $25,000 to an animal behaviorist, who changed Gus's regimen and prescribed Prozac, treatments that eased the symptoms somewhat. When he died the writers of his obituary noted that there were "not a huge number of ways to become famous as a polar bear," but "Gus somehow man-

Cover of *What's Worrying Gus? The True Story of a Big-City Bear* (1995) by Henry Beard and John Boswell.

aged to do it by behaving like a perfectly ordinary New Yorker: he was neurotic."[94] In songs, children's books, and a play, observers pondered the meaning of this bear's life. "Gus was the model New Yorker," one observer noted, "screwed-up, acting out, groping to ease an unnameable pain," what another observer called "a symbol of the stress of living in New York."[95]

In *What's Worrying Gus? The True Story of a Big-City Bear* (1995), Henry Beard and John Boswell offered the most extensive, anthropomorphized riff. The cover suggested that like any neurotic New Yorker, Gus ended up on an analyst's couch. Inside was the story of how he got there. In the Arctic he "was fed up with the whole polar scene" and wanted to see stars "like Liza Minnelli and Jackie Mason . . . real lights—the lights of Broadway!" rather than "those dumb Northern Lights." So he headed for Manhattan, where he encountered all sorts of opportunities and problems: being refused entry into a restaurant because "this animal rights nut at the door won't let me in because I'm wearing real fur"; realizing "it was creepy how much the bear" at the American Museum of Natural History "looked like Uncle Norris"; and making and then losing a fortune working at Bear Stearns. As he hit rock bottom, he was arrested for hawking a peep show but struck a plea bargain with the judge, who agreed to let him "do community service entertaining kids at the Central Park Zoo," where "all the crazies in this screwy town are right where they belong—behind bullet-proof glass." If "you want my opinion," he mused, "this whole city is a zoo."[96]

Contemporary social media also offer abundant representations of bears in virtual captivity.[97] Instagram and X (formerly Twitter) feature seemingly unending images of bears: invading suburban backyards or trying to break into cars, living in the wild where they devour fish, and stuffed animal versions that comfort family members, as well as hefty and hairy gay men.[98] YouTube provides access to a wide variety of sites—on the NFL's Chicago Bears, of course, but also the full range of possibilities, from majestic creatures to "This bear killed 6 people in three days," which attracted well over a million viewers.[99] Facebook opens up especially rich and popular sources. Among them, "Cartoon Bears Are Still Bears (and More)" offers its 1.5 million followers a series of brief tales that turn iconic stories of friendly bears into vicious and terrifying ones.[100]

Among the bears most closely tracked on a social media site are the contestants in Fat Bear Week that appear on Explore.org's #BearCams. With the introduction of webcams at a site in Katmai National Park and Preserve, more than a million people annually from around the world have voted in a competition to identify the fattest bear. "Park rangers use their yearlong observations to create biographies for each animal," noted the *New York Times* reporter Remy Tumin in early October 2022. She described how we know more about the distinctive characteristics of these bear celebrities than we do about virtually any other ones, "noting their complex palates (freshly caught salmon versus scavenged leftover salmon), personality traits (playful or defensive) and, of course, heft."[101] Fans following Fat Bear Week weighed in on the competition. "Grandmaj" remarked that "the contest allows the bears protection and more folks will appreciate them for the critters they are and not a reputation placed on them way back when settlers were first coming into the country. The beauty found via these cams goes unmatched by nearly every other place in the world." On the other hand, at least one observer could not resist the temptation to turn from reality to representation. "When Otis was interviewed about today's bracket and his choice between Grazer and 151," wrote mwagner51, referring to the reigning champ, 480 Otis, "he merely answered 'Gentlemen prefer blondes.'"[102] As the *Wall Street Journal* noted in a front-page story, "Otis may be Alaska's biggest celebrity both in popularity and circumference."[103]

Facebook reveals how important gender is in the world of bears. The headline "Momma Bear Struggles with Cubs" shows her helping her offspring cross the highway as drivers of a long line of cars wait. And attracting even more viewers is "Orphaned Bear Cubs Saved After Man Becomes Surrogate Mother."[104] Gender plays important roles in the ursine world. We see the prominence of masculinity in the world of gay bears, with the likelihood that most celebrity bears are male, and, in chapter 9 of this book, with a male bear sexually satisfying a human woman. Yet even more present is maternalism. Sometimes it is a man who is the nurturer, something seen so prominently with Marty Stouffer. But more often women play that role, from Boas's report of a woman adopting a bear on Baffin Island to the mother bear in Disney's *Bear Country*.

Then there are bears of video game fame. "Some bears will always be bad news, of course," announces the author of "The Bear Essentials: Top 10 Best Video Game Bears of All Time!" The author notes, because some bears "are fierce and intimidating animals" but "untold millions of teddy bears have been gifted to kids around the globe . . . this list will include cuddly bear cubs, ruthless killing machines, and pretty much everything in between." We've already seen how Monokuma, a popular video game bear that is part of the Japanese video game Danganronpa series, captures the dichotomy of cute and terrifying. Its split image, we learn, "reflects the duality between good and evil." Sometimes Monokuma "acts like a cute and cuddly teddy bear not unlike Winnie the Pooh," but at others "he's a sinister bear who's defined by anger and cruelty" and "shows no compassion or pity for anyone," even those he executes. Moreover, his shape-shifting quality inculcates a sense of dangerous unpredictability.[105] Thus, this video game, like virtually all representations of bears in other media, emphasizes how compelling is the tension between two of the predominant emotions that bears evoke.

Captive bears appear in museums, zoos, circuses, homes, films, social media, and video games. Although I write of these as separate places, in fact both human and nonhuman figures, as well as cross-media influence, underscore the permeability of such borders. A few examples will suffice. Hagenbeck exhibited his animals at world's fairs, circuses, and zoos and in a variety of print media. How people previously saw animals on television or in a movie theater shapes their expectations and experiences when they go to a circus or a zoo—and of course this operates in the opposite direction. Taxidermists design exhibits at museums and then ply their trade for zoo designers. After more than a half century working at Washington's National Zoo, in 1944 William Blackburne retired as its head keeper; he arrived there with his animal training skills having been sharpened at the Barnum & Bailey Circus.[106] Mark Dumas moved fluidly between the worlds of pets, advertising, and films with his polar bear Agee. And as if to remind us of how bears travel across time, space, and media, there is the case of the bears associated with Grizzly Adams. As figments of media's imaginations, they reappeared in stories in magazines and books—and then in the 1974 film *The Life and Times of Grizzly Adams*. As actual bears they appeared in menageries in the Bay Area in the 1850s and in P. T. Barnum's shows in 1860. And oh, yes, they made at least one more appearance. After the death of Grizzly Adams himself, those in charge of his estate put the animals he had captured and trained up for sale. In 1863 Carl Hagenbeck and his father purchased five bears that had once belonged to Adams—listed as one black, two brown, and two grizzlies.[107]

Understanding bears in captivity involves acknowledging that in myriad situations bears work as performers, while almost all the time their captors—scientists, filmmakers, artists, and exhibit designers among them—provide the labor that enables us to appreciate, imagine, love, and control them. Some bears labor under painful conditions, including those that struggle to capture food bystanders throw their way or when trainers use negative and positive reinforcements to train them to perform for our pleasure. Others are in "retirement," having died naturally or been killed so that they can reappear in museums. Mixed motives drive captors, ranging from cruelty to loving protection, and shaped by the commitments to increase profits, the pleasure of entertainment, and the desire to educate. And then we find situations where bears work under relatively benign conditions for our benefit—as they roam in wild animal parks or are captured only by the camera lens. We witness bears in captivity, sometimes warned about the dangers to bears of life in the wilderness but less frequently about the dangers people pose to bears.

Despite some rare instances of resistance, representation, captivity, and domination suffuse the presentation of bears, famous and not-so-famous ones. In almost every venue, humans control how they perform. With bears' appearances contrived to varying extents, the agency of humans rather than of bears powerfully persists. For generations people have benefited from how humans controlled the behavior of bears being held in zoos and circuses. They have also derived pleasure from bears captured as pets, in print, on-screen, in social media, and in videos. Yet over time captivity has involved less violence and in many cases at least the appearance of less domination. After all, the difference between bear heads displayed in gentlemen's clubs and Oldenburg's proposed playful teddy bear statue is considerable. As outright violence decreased, projection of human traits onto bears intensified, a process that reached its apogee on-screen, with family romances in dramas such as *The Man Who Loved Bears* and *L'Ours*.

However, if with some exceptions depicted bears are no longer threatening, the stories of bears in captivity underestimate how people endanger them. Unfortunately, especially with zoos but also more generally, we focus on how captivity protects bears from threats they would face in the wild. All too rarely do we acknowledge that captivity endangers rather than protects them. Holding bears in zoos, circuses, and even in homes as pets is hard to justify. Whether representational captivity of bears endangers real ones living in the wild is an intriguing question but a difficult one to answer.

6

Teddy Bear

ANOTHER ONE QUICKLY DISAPPEARS

AND FREQUENTLY REAPPEARS

✳

One of American history's great bear legends centers on how President Theodore Roosevelt inspired the creation of the teddy bear. As the story is told, the bear involved made only the briefest of appearances before members of TR's party slaughtered it, with TR not directly involved. As with the tales of Hugh Glass (though in this case the bear in question is the victim rather than the perpetrator), the actual bear quickly disappears and then prolifically and almost immediately reappears. If the actual bear died, it lived on in so many versions that it is no exaggeration to say that the story of TR and teddy bears marks a major turning point in the history of bearmania. Shortly after bears were, well, everywhere, part of a melding of commerce and culture resulting in the appearance of bears in so many media, all of which quickly reached a national audience. And in the last third of the twentieth century, another explosion of bears took place, this one in more media. Like so many other stories about bears, this one is dramatically less about them and significantly more about us as people who rely on bears—more representational than real ones—to explore cultural meanings. This is centrally true about how understandings of childhood have changed from Roosevelt's time to ours, with teddy bears going from stuffed animals resting next to a child falling asleep, either naturally or under the influence of anesthesia, and then, beginning in the 1980s, to objects of critical assessments through their association with imperialism and the patriarchy.

Moreover, the story itself is full of ironies and odd twists and turns. In the 1880s, when he was in his mid-twenties, the future president was one of those elite Eastern Easterners (such as the artist Frederic Remington and the author Owen Wister) who went west to transform himself from an effete young man into a manly adult one. The great teddy bear incident emerged much later from TR's refusal in 1902 to kill a singular, relatively small bear in the American South— almost two decades after he killed many much larger ones in the American West. In the earlier period, Roosevelt's time in the Dakota Badlands afforded him an opportunity to be reborn, as he distanced himself from the debilitating childhood illness that afflicted him; the constricting expectations his parents had for him; the problems a gentleman faced in an America transformed by urbanization, immigration, and industrialization; and the deaths of his mother and first wife within hours of each other in February 1884. Against these challenges, the West offered opportunities. After all, some observers saw him not as manly but as effeminate. Indeed, on his way west, a reporter characterized TR as "a pale, slim young man with a thin piping voice and a general look of dyspepsia about him . . . boyish looking," appearing more like an Eastern tenderfoot uncomfortable in his own body than a virile Westerner.[1] His chance to test himself against wild animals came in early September of that year when he saw the "huge, half-human footprints" of a bear. The next day he proudly killed what he called a "monstrous" grizzly weighing about twelve hundred pounds and standing almost nine feet tall. "I found myself face to face with the great bear," he wrote when back east, and "doubtless my face was pretty white, . . . I could see the top of the bear fairly between his two sinister-looking eyes; as I pulled the trigger I jumped aside out of the smoke, to be ready if he charged, but it was needless. . . . As you will see when I bring home his skin, the bullet hole in his skull was as exactly between his eyes as if I had measured the distance with a carpenter's rule." In the following few days, he and a companion killed three more bears, including a cub TR shot, as he bragged, "clean through him from end to end." Years later he wrote, "There were all kinds of things of which I was afraid of at first, ranging from bears to 'mean' horses and gunfighters; but by acting as if I was not afraid I gradually ceased to be afraid." As the historian David McCullough has noted, TR's experience in the Badlands restored "him in body and spirit" and gave him a topic he could write about with passion—what life in the West meant to the nation's identity and to his own.[2] This was so even though at the time many animal protectionists, including George Angell, head of the Massachusetts Society for the Prevention of Cruelty to Animals, criticized Roosevelt as a big game hunter.

The association of Teddy Roosevelt with teddy bears had its origins years later, soon after he became president of the United States in September 1901 following the assassination of William McKinley. In June he had written of his desire "to kill a big grizzly of silver tip with our knives, which would be great sport."[3] In mid-November 1902 he had his chance on a hunting trip in Mississippi, alas, apparently with a black bear. His tracker was Holt Collier, an African American born enslaved around 1848 who during the Civil War had served as a scout in the Confederate army. Beginning with his first success at age ten, in his lifetime Collier killed more than six thousand bears. His lifelong connections with the prominent Hinds family of Mississippi and his reputation as a skilled tracker and organizer of hunting expeditions led to his being hired to help TR. During the outing in Mississippi, three reporters, leading figures in business and politics, and famous big game hunters accompanied the president. Aided by well-trained dogs, "with the instinct of an old bear hunter," as the reporter for the *Washington Post* wrote at the time, on November 14 Collier trapped a bear. Often referred to as a female, the bear weighed well over two hundred pounds and stood over six and a half feet tall. The hunt occurred on the banks of the Little Sunflower River near Smede's Station, seventy miles north and west of Jackson. When the bear "grabbed one of the hounds and crushed it through its spine," Collier "knocked the game over with a blow on the head" and then "roped the bear and tied him to a tree."

Summoned to the scene by a messenger, Roosevelt "would neither shoot nor permit it to be shot" but ordered, "'Put it out of its misery.'" One of his companions, or perhaps Holt himself, "ended its life with his knife." "The aggrieved Holt" remarked that "if the colonel had stayed whar I put him, he would 'er done got this yere one," as the reporter wrote, using dialect and describing African Americans as either Negroes or darkies. With what for the bear was a distinction without a difference, whoever composed the story's headline had a different take: The president "refused to make an unsportsmanlike shot." Although someone else killed the bear with a knife, the takeaway was that the compassionate president had saved the animal. After all, as another part of the headline called out, the bear "did not fall a trophy to president's Winchester."[4] The next day the author of a story in the *Washington Post* observed both that "the bear killed yesterday furnished meat for the camp last night and to-day" and that the "Bruin was in luck: Mr. Roosevelt again failed to get a shot."[5] The November 18 issue noted that bears were engaged in a "conspiracy to keep president from shooting them."[6] On the next day, when the president left Mississippi to hunt more explicitly political quarry, the *Washington Post* reported, "President Roosevelt's Bear Hunt in Mississippi ended and he has not had even a shot at a bear." Try as members of his party would, "they could not even get a bear within range of the President's rifle."[7]

Accompanying that article was a cartoon titled "After a Twentieth Century Bear Hunt" by the paper's cartoonist, Clifford Berryman. It showed the president leading his party away, overseen by a bear looking down from a hill and holding a newspaper whose headline read "HOW CAN YOU BEAR TO LEAVE ME." There is a canine ambulance to Roosevelt's left with a dead or dying dog on top and in front of him a bear cub being led away reluctantly on a leash, to which is attached a tag reading "Back to the Zoo." This was likely a reference to one of two zoos established in the 1880s—the national one in Washington or the New York Zoological Park, which a young Roosevelt had helped found. En route to the nation's capital, the train stopped in Tennessee, where "a rawboned mountaineer" suggested that "the bears in Mississippi had proved too wild for the President." No, he replied. "Perhaps they were Democratic bears and took to the woods on my arrival."[8] Yet despite Roosevelt's failure to kill a bear on this excursion, actual failure turned into symbolic success. Berryman's mocking self-portrait of 1904 is less well known than another one—issued in several versions beginning on November 16, 1902—that gained iconic status. Some claimed that the title, "Drawing the Line in Mississippi," referred to a disputed border line between Louisiana and Mississippi or to Roosevelt's efforts to resolve the problem of the racial color line. The more likely explanation and the one more favorable to Roosevelt's reputation is that the line he was drawing underscored his refusal to kill the cub with his rifle.[9] Berryman's cartoon of November 19 had mocked the president. This more famous one celebrated Roosevelt's sportsmanlike conduct by picturing a cute, innocent, and vulnerable bear cub held on a leash. Here Roosevelt stands taller than both the bear and the man controlling the bear. Moreover, TR now appears kindly, especially when his facial expression is compared favorably to the sterner one of the bear's captor. The cartoon pictured Roosevelt using his left hand to signal that he would not shoot the tethered animal by using the rifle he held in his right one. Like all versions, it inaccurately pictured the man holding the cub as white rather than African American.

The scholar Donna Varga suggests that the version picturing TR's refusal to shoot the bear emerged when Berryman responded to pressure to produce

THIS IS QUITE AS NEAR THE "REAL THING" AS I WISH TO GET

A 1904 self-portrait
by cartoonist Clifford
Berryman. National
Archives and Rec-
ords Administration,
National Archives
Identifier 2979338.

one more in line with a favorable interpretation of the president's actions. This one, she believes, "replaces Berryman's original challenge to Roosevelt's hunting practices with reverence."[10] It was, she remarks, "a not-so-nuanced sardonic pronouncement on Roosevelt's conservationist proclamations and his accusations of extravagant hunting practices of others, while himself engaging in excessive animal slaughter" as he and others had been doing for decades in the American West.[11]

Yet in late November other cartoonists quickly doubled down on mockery. One titled "A Happy Day in Bearville, Mississippi" pictured a group of bears celebrating around a sign that read "Teddy Has Gone but We Are All Here Yet." Another, under the title "No Hit, He Who Laughs Last Laughs Best," revealed a large, smiling bear who holds a "No Hit" target shaking hands with a grinning President Roosevelt. Nonetheless, the narrative favorable to Roosevelt endured. Among the hundreds or more of drawings that followed was one

Clifford Berryman,
"Drawing the Line
in Mississippi,"
Washington Post,
November 16, 1902.

that appeared when he ran for reelection in 1904. Berryman pictured Roosevelt with his running mate, Charles W. Fairbanks, and a bear cub holding a flag calling for "Four More Years of Theodore."[12]

However, the focus on how TR refused to kill the bear, which was eventually the main takeaway, was problematic. With the bear weakened by how long the dogs had chased it and then clubbed by Holt Collier, for Roosevelt to have put her out of her misery by shooting her would have been an act of unsportsmanlike cowardice that the reporters on-site would have broadcast to the nation. After all, disposing of her with his rifle would violate the "fair chase" rules of the Boone and Crockett Club, an organization of big game hunters that TR played a key role in founding in 1887.[13] Thus, what concerned Roosevelt was adverse publicity about the hunt. As he wrote in a letter soon after, since he never actually shot a bear this time, "naturally the comic press jumped at the failure and have done a good deal of laughing over it." He worried that if the press covered future hunts there would be "so much silly and brutal newspaper talk as to leave an unpleasant impression upon the immense number of our people who know nothing whatever of hunting and who accept as true what they see in the press." Consequently, in planning future hunts he avoided mentioning bears.[14]

The longer story of Teddy Roosevelt and teddy bears highlights several transformations. One underscores the almost immediate disappearance of the actual bear. Another reveals that soon after 1902 was when, not without precedents, bear stories exploded out of print and into an enormous range of expressions in popular culture. The third involves Roosevelt understood not as an avid hunter killing wild animals but as one who saved and protected them. As Varga writes, the dead bear Roosevelt's hunting party ate for dinner was "to be reified as a human-like cub who was released by a mythical presidential aficionado" well before the formation of the advocacy group PETA.[15] A fourth concerns the shift, already seen in some quarters, such as with Goldilocks and the Three Bears, in how people understood bears, changing them from ferocious, threatening beasts into comforting, childlike animals that enabled children to imagine they could love. The bear cub tied to a tree morphed into the legendary teddy bear in comforting captivity in children's bedrooms. Ironically, if by actually hunting bears TR became a man, then by being hunted and symbolically pardoned, the real bear became a stuffed teddy bear. This underscores the familiar contradiction between how Americans kill real bears but love inanimate ones.

As would later happen with Smokey Bear, so with teddy bears: seemingly endless versions emerged over time in every possible medium as new types of popular culture proliferated. From stuffed animals that appeared soon after the Mississippi misadventure to links to Black Lives Matter in 2020, teddy bears represent not danger but the comfort of childhood innocence. First on the scene, and then over time by the millions, were toy teddy bears.[16] Well before 1902, toy bears had found their way into children's bedrooms, arms, and dreams. However, their emergence as specifically teddy bears happened soon after Teddy Roosevelt returned to the White House from Mississippi. And they did so from two sources, so the frequently told stories go—in Brooklyn from the candy store run by Russian Jewish immigrants Rose and Morris Michtom and in Germany from Margarete Steiff and her nephew of the already well-established manufacturer of stuffed toys that bore their last name.

The Michtoms ran their mom-and-pop store in Bedford-Stuyvesant, selling candy during the day and sewing stuffed animals upstairs in the evening. Inspired by Berryman's drawings, by Christmas 1902 they reportedly developed a toy bear they called Teddy, which they placed in the store window for sale with other toys accompanied by a sign calling it "Teddy's bear." Seeking permission to use his nickname, Morris supposedly wrote the president, sending him a bear dressed as Roosevelt might be outfitted, complete with gold chain and leather vest. Although the letter to Roosevelt has never been located, we may have his handwritten response. "I don't think my name is likely to be worth much in the toy bear business," he allegedly wrote, "but you are welcome to use it."[17] With the toy extensively available for sale by Christmas 1903, in 1907 the Michtoms founded Ideal Novelty Company, which as Ideal Toy Company would sell millions and millions of teddy bears.

At some point after TR's adventure, at the Leipzig fair, Hermann Berg, on the lookout for new products for the American doll company George Borgfeldt and Co., espied a bear on offer from Steiff. He authorized the production of three thousand that would be shipped off to New York for sale at the legendary F.A.O. Schwarz toy store in Manhattan and that some reports claimed were lost at sea. In short order, surely by 1907 if not earlier, sales of teddy bears soared—if not as high as Ursa Major in the sky, nonetheless into the sales stratosphere. It was not long before teddy bears looked less and less like real bears and increasingly like the cute, childlike, soft, and vulnerable tens if not hundreds of millions of toy versions that so many of us have fallen asleep next to.[18] Teddy bears are so beloved, writes the Finnish scholar Anu Valtonen, because it's "their cuteness, bearness and softness as well as their unique role as intimate bedmates that makes them so special." Moreover, because they evoke a sense of helplessness, "they manifest and embody human vulnerability."[19]

I drafted these teddy bear origin stories about Roosevelt's 1902 Mississippi expeditions before finding out how problematic if not outright apocryphal they were. A Google Scholar search led me to find the exacting scholarship of Donna Varga, and in our ensuing correspondence she set me on the road to understanding how Teddy Roosevelt's adventure led to the creation and then popularization of teddy bears in ways that challenge the oft-told tales. As if to confirm the importance of interspecies relationships, she led me to an article by Charles Moose in an October 2002 issue of *Teddy Bear Review*. There and elsewhere, I learned that the tales of how the Michtoms developed their teddy bear enterprise are good folklore but bad history, with the story of the exchange of letters between Roosevelt and the Michtoms as one example. To be sure, at some point Ideal Novelty Company did produce teddy bears in great numbers, though exactly when this began is not entirely clear. Surely it was not within days or months, or perhaps even years, of Roosevelt's fall 1902 expedition. Similarly, in 1902 Steiff introduced its first jointed bear covered in mohair, but it was a while before the connection with Teddy Roosevelt was made. But particulars of that story are also apocryphal, including the loss of so many of them at sea. Before long, perhaps as early as 1908, Steiff labeled its toys "Teddy" bears. Though in many quarters they were still known as Roosevelt bears, by the fall of 1906 the shift from Roosevelt bears to teddy bears seems to have begun.[20]

It turns out that the story of TR inspiring teddy bears most likely occurred not because of clever entrepreneurship in Brooklyn and Germany but as the result of the work of Seymour Eaton, the prolific Canadian-born American publisher, writer, and editor. As the author of doggerel poems about two teddy bears, notes a knowledgeable observer, he "helped fix the bear in the public mind as a symbol for Roosevelt." Some credit him with being the first to attach the name "Teddy" to the plush toys that were already gaining in popularity.[21] Perhaps in late 1905 but certainly by early 1906, Eaton began publishing in newspapers poetry for children about Roosevelt bears. He briefly wrote under the name Paul Piper to avoid ruining his reputation as a more serious author known for practical education books. Initially serialized in a score of newspapers for twenty-nine weeks, the poems appeared later that year in a book featuring Teddy-B (for black or brown) and Teddy-G (for gray), two realistically sized, anthropomorphized, and friendly bears. They had left the Colorado wilderness where TR had been hunting that spring to explore the worlds humans inhabited. Eaton wrote that the two bears gave themselves those names based on materials that members of the president's hunting party had left behind. In the fall of 1906 *The Roosevelt Bears: Their Travels and Adventures* brought together some of the already published stories, and the next year the rest of them found their way into *More About Teddy-B and Teddy-G, the Roosevelt Bears*. Other volumes appeared before long.

Although Eaton used the term *Roosevelt bears*, not *teddy bears*, his books played an important role in making the connection between Teddy Roosevelt and teddy bears. One stanza widely circulated in 1906 captures the quality of his poems and how he linked the two Teddies:

> The "Teddy" part is a name they found
> On hat and tree and leggings round,
> On belt and boot, and plates of tin,
> And scraps of paper and biscuits thin,
> And other things that hunters drop
> When they chase a bear to a mountain top.[22]

A typical story followed Teddy-B and Teddy-G as they explored America and eventually ventured abroad. The chapter on their visit to Boston carries the weight of high-minded stereotypes that ascribed culture-seeking intelligence to bears. When they arrive at the Boston Public Library, they asked, "'Is Boston culture made of beans? / And does it take but a single week / For Boston

Illustration from
Seymour Eaton's *The
Roosevelt Bears: Their
Travels and Adventures*
(1906).

No. 1. The Roosevelt Bears at Home
" Two Roosevelt Bears had a home out West
In a big ravine near a mountain crest."

children to learn their Greek.'" Then they sat down and read books "To study
Emerson and the Autocrat." Realizing how hungry they were for Culture, they
returned books to the library's stacks "And told the man they'd come again /
And study Holmes and Emerson."[23]

What the Boston poems revealed was specific culturally and geographically.
The bears stayed with Priscilla Alden and her brother Will on Beacon Hill.
They traveled there from the city's South Station, "with flowers strewn along
the street" and merchants having closed their doors and giving "their clerks
each double pay." Perhaps children reading the book would connect this Priscilla Alden with the woman of the same name from the seventeenth-century
Plymouth Colony, whose life Henry Wadsworth Longfellow had chronicled
in his 1858 poem *The Courtship of Miles Standish*. It would take a similarly cul-

tured child to realize the Autocrat was Oliver Wendell Holmes Sr. In Eaton's Boston, there are no Irish citizens competing with African Americans to climb up from the lower rungs of the city's social and economic ladder. "No literary merit is claimed for it," Eaton wrote of his work. He was offering "simply a good, wholesome yarn, arranged in merry jingle and fitted to the love of incident and adventure which is evident in every healthy child."[24] Though children were apparently his target audience, as children's literature his books had yet to convey what teddy bears would eventually become. After all, while acting like humans, Teddy-B and Teddy-G were not plush toys but realistically sized bears, not comforting, cuddly, and cute stuffed animals but large adult animals who could introduce sophisticated children to the sights and sounds of America. Tour guides, not toys.

Soon Anna Held, a Ziegfeld Follies star at the time married to Florenz Ziegfeld, evoked the teddy bear in a different way and medium. To publicize the Broadway show *A Parisian Model*, in early 1907 Held sang "Will You Be My Teddy Bear," its poetry equal in quality if not in reach to what appeared in Eaton's books.

Come away with me, be my Teddy B
I'm so blue,
Come to me, do
Teddy it's true
I'm longing for you

Elsewhere, male performers dressed in bear suits appeared with women on their backs and holding large toy bears. Such a scene appeared on the vitally important Broadway stage during pre-radio days and when movies were only beginning to circulate. While on tour in the nation's capital, timed to coincide with Roosevelt's delivery of the State of the Union Address, a member of the cast went to the White House and met with the president. All these cultural expressions undergirded why the August 1907 issue of *Playthings*, the magazine of the toy industry, confirmed that teddy bears were here to stay. "We stand on the Teddy bear question," one article's author wrote, "where we have stood for the past year, and that is firmly in the belief that bears have come to stay and that sales this year, at all seasons and any particular season, will be better than last year."[25]

The commercialization of teddy bears was now rampant. The craze had fully emerged from hibernation, and when it did, teddy bears changed from Eaton's full-sized, intelligent ones into small, silent toy ones. In mid-October 1906, the *New York Times* announced that toy bears named Teddy-B and Teddy-G were selling like proverbial hotcakes. "Everybody is buying a Roosevelt Bear," the paper reported, having noted that earlier their "frolics on an Eastern trip so amused young readers" of the paper. Now they had "become a fad. Automobilists carry bears as mascots. Children cry for 'em, and even 'society' is taking up the toy as a novelty."[26] On Christmas Eve, the paper printed a poem by Mary Means Naughton that began "A sorry little Teddy Bear / Crept sadly through the snow," thinking there would be no present for him under the tree. On Christmas morning, his mother took her child to a tree, inside of which "hung a honey-comb / For that good little bear."[27] The New York Zoo named two bears recently arrived from Colorado Teddy-B and Teddy-G. Entrepreneurs rushed to produce clothes for teddy bears. Postcards and magazine covers featured the lovable bears, and Uncle Remus acquired a teddy companion. There was even a 1907 "Teddy Bear Two-Step" song.

After Roosevelt's hunting trip in 1902 and the ensuing proliferation of teddy bears from 1906 to the present, teddy bears have made their appearances in virtually every medium and almost always as innocent and comforting. "The public endowed teddy bears with a bundle of positive traits," writes the historian Robert E. Bieder as he ascribes ample powers to inanimate bears, "including trustworthiness, loyalty, friendliness, warmth and dependability."[28] In the new century's first decade, parents gave their children teddy bears and told them stories based on that figure. The music for "The Teddy Bears' Picnic" appeared in 1907, with the lyrics following a quarter of a century later in 1932. Though for children it was "safer to stay at home," if they did venture forth, they'd "see them gaily gadabout," for "they love to play and shout" since they "never have any cares."[29] From then until the present, teddy bears appeared virtually everywhere. Topping the list of bear-related children's literature, and in a way that emphasized Atlantic crossings originating with Steiff's creations, were two British-born anthropomorphic bears connected to Teddy discussed in a previous chapter—A. A. Milne's 1926 Winnie-the-Pooh and Michael Bond's 1958 Paddington Bear.

Indeed, in the years after World War II teddy bears seemed to be everywhere. They appeared in movies, including *Alfie* in 1966, and in characters such as Care Bears, Teddy Ruxpin, and SuperTed beginning in the 1980s. A teddy bear had a starring role in the 1981 version of *Brideshead Revisited*. Teddy bear fandom found its source in the magazine *Teddy Bear Times & Friends*, first issued in 1983. The Great American Teddy Bear Rally initially took place in 1981. Dozens of teddy bear festivals occur every year. Teddy bear museums appeared and proliferated around the world. The first one in the United States opened in Naples, Florida, in 1990 but closed fifteen years later.[30] September 9 is National Teddy Bear Day, "a perfect time to celebrate your childhood friend," that "special cuddy teddy," or so I learned from the website that lists over fifteen hundred national days.[31]

One of the reasons the final third of the twentieth century figures so prominently in the expansion of teddy bear culture is that this is when they crawled from the world of children to that of adults.[32] As the triumph of the therapeutic took hold, adults saw teddy bears as offering solace and comfort—what Varga describes as providing a "transcendence of time and space, a material means for bringing back as lived adult reality the supposed simple and innocent times of an undefined era of a bygone childhood."[33] Adult teddy bear culture developed its own language—*arctophiles* to describe teddy bear lovers; *hug*, a gathering of them; *artists' bears*, specially designed ones handmade in limited numbers; and *bearapy*, denoting an approach to mental health care assisted by a loving animal.

Moreover, therapeutic teddy bears worked their magic not only in the offices of therapists but also in the wider public world. The 1995 terrorist attack on the Alfred P. Murrah Federal Building in Oklahoma City produced abundant expressions of sympathy, via teddy bears prominently, despite officials asking for no more.[34] I have not seen the memorial in Oklahoma City, but fresh in my mind is a visit to the New Museum in Manhattan in 2016, where I saw *The Keeper*. The curators called this exhibit "a multi-floor presentation dedicated to the act of preserving objects, artworks, and images"—and not just any objects but thousands of teddy bears gathered from homes and family albums.[35] Originally curated by Ydessa Hendeles, previously shown in Germany, Canada, and South Korea, and based on the Teddy Bear Project, this exhibit featured, according to those who developed the original show, teddy bears with "semi-human attributes, which invite the projections of people's imaginations. It falls somewhere between a pet and a person—a silent comrade, and, like the photographs, the bearer," so to speak, "of confidences."[36] Or in the words of the material on offer for the New York version, "the exhibition also emphasizes images and objects that testify to historical trauma or dramatic events, representing the act of preserving as a resolution to bear witness and to remember. Clandestine efforts to save or protect, often taken at great risk, attest to an indefatigable faith in the power of images to heal and comfort, and a desire to honor what survives in spite of the effects of violence or time."[37]

As I began working on this chapter, what surprised me more than anything else (though perhaps it should not have) was the use of teddy bears in the world of medicine, from offices of mental health professionals to pediatric surgical units in hospitals. Therapists had long used teddy bears, along with other stuffed animals, dolls, and toys, to engage with young patients in one version or another of play therapy. Yet as a definable field, Teddy Bear Therapy, as the practice is known, emerged in the late twentieth century. It relied on and extended long-standing approaches that deployed play as a way therapists could help young children communicate what was bothering them as they dealt with trauma, sadness, and anxiety. Unable to articulate their concerns and reluctant to confide in anyone, children, under the right circumstances, would be able and willing to make an exception with teddy bears. After all, more than any other animal, bears had developed a reputation of being huggable, comforting, and childlike. Indeed, as an example of capitalism's inventiveness, there is some evidence that over time the design of teddy bears changed because adults who purchased them preferred toy bears that appeared to be nurturant, their faces more human and their bodily proportions more like that of a young child.[38]

The roots of Teddy Bear Therapy were many, including multiple strands of psychoanalysis that originated in early twentieth-century Vienna, around and expanding the work of Sigmund Freud; the mutual storytelling technique of Richard Gardner; Donald Winnicott's focus on the importance of play; and the humanistic, self-actualizing, and person-centered approach of Carl Rogers, especially as applied to children by Virginia Axline. The approach to Teddy Bear Therapy, wrote three prominent practitioners (including Charl Vorster, who is credited as its founder), relied on exchanges between the therapist and a child that center on stories about troubles a teddy bear had encountered, as similar as possible to the ones the child had experienced.

In the first session, a child selects a teddy bear to take home and bring back to later sessions. Then, relying on the power of play and storytelling, the child, usually between four and twelve years old, identifies with and communicates through the teddy bear. Gradually, the therapist guides the child in helping the bear deal with and understand the problems the bear has faced, with the therapist gently helping the patient learn from the parallel situations. "The inclusion of the teddy as the one with the problem, and not the child," three authors note, "thereby changes the child's position from a disempowered position to an empowered position." This means that "by assisting the teddy with resolving his problem, the child is in actual fact dealing with his or her own problem." As a result, "the child is empowered by the teddy bear who now needs his or her help to solve problems." If it turns out that the bear is pursuing unproductive solutions, the therapist suggests other options, in the process helping the child explore alternatives. The child, guided by the unconditional acceptance and empathetic responses of the therapist, can "explore how changes to the teddy and the teddy's relationships in the family, or broader system, ultimately bring about resolution of the teddy's problem" and thus the child's as well.[39] Over time, family members or caregivers are brought into the therapeutic circle since they are key players in the process of healing that draws on the insights and approaches of family systems. Left implicit in professional presentations such as this one is why a teddy bear is the obvious selection among many possible toys and stuffed animals. There was no need to make clear the reason behind such a decision because this was long after teddy bears had become the comfort animal of choice.

"Doctor, Is My Teddy Bear Okay? The 'Teddy Bear Hospital' as a Method to Reduce Children's Fear of Hospitalization" is the title of a 2008 study carried out in Israel. The results revealed lower levels of anxiety among preschool children who had visited a pretend hospital where they acted as parents to their beloved teddy bears.[40] Teddy bear hospitals and teddy bear clinics, available in the developed world at least since the 1990s, replicate many of the techniques used in psychotherapy, using teddy bears to empower children in anxiety-provoking situations. After all, if Milne's Winnie-the-Pooh said, "I am a bear of very little brain and long words bother me," then a child might come to the rescue. This approach to health care teaches children about wellness and familiarizes them with what must be for them strange settings and procedures, thus helping them overcome, or at least lessen, their anxieties.

In some cases, the goal is educational for a future that might not happen. For example, the UMass Memorial Children's Medical Center Teddy Bear Clinic recently called on children to "pack up your teddy bears and your parents and join us for a fun-filled day" for an "interactive health and safety fair." After having "your face painted" and entering "a raffle for a free bicycle," you could learn "about your bodies, what to expect at a hospital visit and tips for staying safe at home."[41] At a typical clinic, scores of children are given teddy bears, which they take from station to station. They learn how to use a stethoscope to listen to a heartbeat (first on their bear and then on themselves), eat healthily, stay physically fit, perform a pretend surgical operation, administer an inoculation to their bear, and repair a broken bone. "I still remember what it was like as a child to visit the doctors," remarked Stephanie Lee, a recent graduate of Brown University's medical school. She recalled an earlier time when she had encountered "these big people in white coats" who invaded her personal space and performed procedures she did not understand. Having become one of those "'scary'" physicians herself, she now wanted "to help kids become more comfortable during a doctor's visit by taking the time to show and explain things in a more friendly environment at the Teddy Bear Clinic." However, she and her peers also learned something valuable from the clinic—how to communicate with children in terms they could understand instead of in the language doctors had learned in medical school.[42]

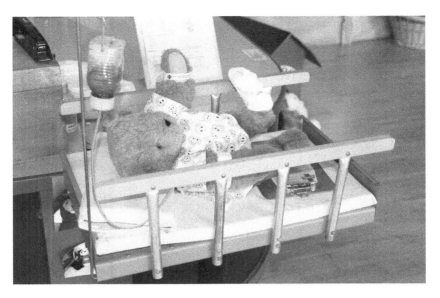

Bear recovering in Vermont Bear Hospital. Photo by Ryan Taylor, LRPS.

In other cases, play gets more immediate when a child faces a hospital stay and serious medical interventions—far removed from a teddy bear picnic but closer to the peril a real bear faced before Teddy Roosevelt came to the rescue. As in a therapist's office or a pretend hospital, so in a real one: A teddy bear can comfort a child or enable young patients to articulate their fears. In addition, there is evidence of the benefits of administering an anesthetic, nebulizer, or intravenous fluid with the help of a teddy bear. "Most kids will respond to the shape of a teddy bear because they probably have one at home," remarked the Southern California physician Conrad Salinas, because it was "much less threatening than if you use a scary piece of medical equipment that looks like a big hose spewing vapor at them. . . . Instead of being apprehensive, they can hug the bear and not even realize they are getting medication."[43]

But wait! To shift once again from the real to the pretend, we turn to surgery at a teddy bear hospital. You can go to your local or regional one, but if you want the best care, send yours off to the Mayo Clinic or Cleveland Clinic equivalent, the Bear Hospital, which is part of the Vermont Teddy Bear operation, so to speak. "If anything ever happens to your Bear," the entry on their website reads, even as it makes clear that their hospital only takes care of Vermont Teddy Bears, "we will nurse him or her back to health. . . . Every once in a while a tragedy will strike—a dog attack, a chance meeting with a lawn mower.

When this happens it is very easy to become upset, lose your cool, maybe even freak out! But NEVER FEAR, health care is here, and we are not just talkin' any old health care, we are talkin' FREE, full coverage health care for your Bear's entire lifetime." What follows is a form to fill out and instructions for how to ship your bear to Vermont, accompanied by the warning that you must provide the return address, since "Bears aren't good with directions and will be unable to find their way home without help." Then the tone shifts back to serious matters, assuring you how well your bear will be taken care of, what with "premium accommodations including the finest health care staff, exceptional dining facilities and use of the day spa." Yet it ends with a promise no real hospital would offer: "If by chance your Bear was too badly injured with no hope of recovery, we will replace your Bear with a new one for FREE!"[44] We see the teddy bear recovering, with all the appropriately reassuring symbols present—a bandaged leg, a shirt decorated with smiley faces, and nourishment coming from an intravenous tube apparently filled with honey.

As would be true with coverage of Smokey Bear, so with teddy—over time highly critical attention emerged. Even around the time of his Mississippi hunt, critics of TR's imperialism, including W. E. B. Du Bois, offered judgments that would resonate with those offered more recently. In the mid-1980s Donna Haraway published her influential critique in the pages of the progressive, postmodernist journal *Social Text*. The title of her essay, "Teddy Bear Patriarchy," may have suggested that she would focus centrally on the connection between the two Teddies. She did not mention the hunt in Mississippi, the president's sportsmanlike gesture, or the rapid emergence of teddy bears. Yet her discussion of Manhattan's American Museum of Natural History, including TR's role in its history, made clear the critical implications for understanding the relationship between the two Teddies. She focused on eugenics, race, gender, class, nature, and power represented by the 1939 statue of TR at the time placed prominently outside the museum. At its Central Park West entrance, she noted, stood the "statue of Teddy majestically mounted as a father and protector between two 'primitive' men, an American Indian and an African, both standing and dressed as 'savages.'" This involved, Haraway continued, the story "of the commerce of power and knowledge in white and male supremacist monopoly capitalism, fondly named Teddy Bear Patriarchy." Theodore Roosevelt's life underscored the importance of the process of regeneration by violence. The slaughtering of animals justified by shout-outs to education or conservation saved not only TR but also America from threats to virility caused by the excesses of turn-of-the-century runaway immigration and wanton luxury. Roosevelt's adventures, she insisted, were grist for "the tales of a pure man whose danger in pursuit of a noble cause brings him into communion with the beasts he kills, with nature. This nature is a worthy brother of man, a worthy foil for his manhood." For millions of Americans, children especially, teddy bears that originated in a failed hunting expedition in 1902 brought plush comfort. Yet for Haraway, Teddy Bear Patriarchy represented something familiar to TR and many men of his generation and background: "preserving a threatened manhood" grounded in stopping decay and supporting racial purity by bolstering activities central to preventing "decadence, the dread disease of imperialist, capitalist, and white culture."[45]

Decades later, and unlikely in response to Haraway's essay, the American Museum of Natural History announced that it was taking steps to remove the equestrian statue from its prominent place at its entrance. "Over the last few weeks," remarked the museum's president, Ellen V. Futter, on June 21, 2020, "our museum community has been profoundly moved by the ever-widening movement for racial justice that has emerged after the killing of George Floyd. We have watched as the attention of the world and the country has increasingly turned to statues as powerful and hurtful symbols of systemic racism." The city's mayor, Bill DeBlasio, supported the recommendation because, he remarked, the statue "explicitly depicts Black and Indigenous people as subjugated and racially inferior." Prominent descendants of TR supported the decision, and Futter carefully made clear that the objection was to what she called the statue's "hierarchical composition" and not to TR himself, whom Futter called "a pioneering conservationist."[46] Not to worry, however. Teddy bears, like Teddy Roosevelt, could be called on to represent laudable causes. Indeed, exactly one week after Futter's announcement came the story that in Los Angeles, the Bear the Truth organization used teddy bears in support of Black Lives Matter by placing well over a thousand teddy bears in front of City Hall.[47]

If Haraway focused on Teddy Roosevelt but not teddy bears, in four scholarly articles published between 2009 and 2013 Donna Varga successfully connected the two Teddies in ways that parallel the post-1970 critical analysis of Smokey.[48] She charted the transformation of wild animals, including bears, in children's toys and stories beginning in the 1890s. She emphasized how they had changed from dangerous threats that had to be killed to comforting animals that had to be cuddled. In the process came the blurring of the distinctions between humans and animals—with innocence connecting them. Imaginary bears, she showed, offered comfort to children at the same time real kids returned the favor. Commodifying teddy bears turned them into products of consumer culture that might, she argued, offer comfort but also blocked people from more genuine human relationships with bears and even distanced them from the challenges of engaging in transformative battles for social change.

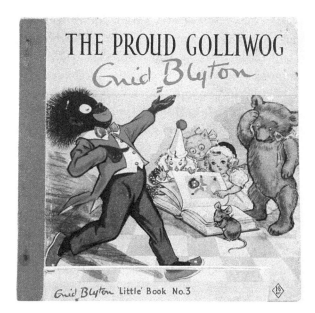

Cover of Enid Blyton's *The Proud Golliwog* (1951).

In the United States the depictions of children cuddling bears featured white youngsters. In Britain racism was rampant in teddy bear culture, seen especially in the intertwined lives of teddy bears and golliwogs, renderings that circulated in North America as well, often contrasting the innocence of white childhood with caricatured references to minstrelsy. This can be seen in the cover illustration from Enid Blyton's Little Book series, which combines images of a friendly bear overlooking innocent children reading a book—in which there is a racist picture of a golliwog who also appears, in even more horribly stereotypical ways, on the cover. More generally, offering a teddy bear as a present was one thing, but giving food, clothing, and shelter to people in need was another, a more worthy endeavor, meaningfully important to both giver and recipient. "The basis of teddy gifting culture in the commercialization of emotions, with its emphasis on the individual's personal feelings and inner needs," Varga has noted, "causes it to replace political action and reinforce the very conditions of subjective and social alienation."[49]

Conceived in the first decade of the twentieth century and over the ensuing decades born and reborn in many ways and many media, teddy bears remain one of the most iconic and beloved of the imaginary species, providing culturally significant opportunities to enable us to think about what representational bears mean. They underscore the importance of several major shifts. They reveal the intensifying anthropomorphism of representational bears and of their importance as celebrities. In both the Dakotas and Mississippi, TR and his associates violently asserted their power over bears. Yet through time, beginning with Seymour Eaton and later with therapeutic applications, fictional teddy bears emerged as stuffed animals—intelligent and empathetic, capable of providing comfort not just passively but actively too. As they did so, they remind us that as early as the first decade of the twentieth century, despite the varied species of North American bears alone, the category "bear" had often denoted a generalized and undifferentiated animal, far more imaginary than real. Moreover, despite relatively recent critiques of how they represent racist and violent imperialism, they continue to comfort children and even adults in the United States and around the world.[50] Teddy bears that help children overcome their fears of hospitals and adults and children alike their traumatic experiences show that sometimes anthropomorphism promoted border-crossing and reciprocal relationships between people and bears even at a time when violence elsewhere characterized the relationships between people and bears. Seeing teddy bears as huggable should remind us of the tension between cuteness, vulnerability, and the potential for violence. We see this in the display of innocent teddy bears in Oklahoma City, in connection with Black Lives Matter, on an operating table, or in a museum exhibition that explores traumatic events.[51]

And in the end, here's the irony. The real, living bear that Teddy Roosevelt refused to kill makes only the briefest of appearances before being cooked and eaten by members of TR's party. The teddy bear that emerged with extraordinary rapidity as a famous celebrity is something else, embodied in many representational and ideologically significant versions.

Off the Poster and Out of the Zoo

SMOKEY BEAR GOES EVERYWHERE

Unlike Teddy's bear, Smokey Bear had an extended life as an actual bear even though, like the one TR refused to kill, most of us know little of what he was actually like. Smokey first emerged as an imagined creature in the early 1940s as part of an effort to protect the wilderness from fires after both images from Disney's *Bambi* and those of squirrels were deemed problematic. Then the rescue of a black bear cub injured in a New Mexico forest fire offered a real live symbol, eventually relocated to the National Zoo and adding material for a robust and long-lasting public relations campaign. Before long, Smokey appeared everywhere—on posters, as stuffed and cuddly animals, on membership cards for clubs that children could join, in the words of the prominent Beat poet Gary Snyder, on-screen, and in song.[1] Smokey stands tall in the ranks of anthropomorphized bears as an American black bear (*Ursus americanus*), which are strong and swift, can weigh over five hundred pounds, and can reach almost seven feet in height. Although black bears rarely attack humans,

Americans encounter them as much as any other species because they exist in greater numbers in places into where we are increasingly intruding. Yet most representations of Smokey make him kind and gentle.

With the start of World War II, those in charge of preventing forest fires, the vast majority of which were caused by human carelessness, grew concerned. With so many workers involved in the war effort, it was becoming increasingly difficult to staff firefighting efforts. Lumber harvested from forests was crucial to the war effort—with over 300,000 board feet going into the making of one Liberty ship. Interested in developing a public relations program to limit the number of forest fires, in 1942 representatives of the US Forest Service joined officials at the newly established Wartime Advertising Council, a prime example of cooperative efforts between the federal government and private corporations so common in American history in times of crisis. Thus was born the Co-Operative Forest Fire Prevention Program and its Wildfire Prevention Campaign, which in the postwar period operated under the sponsorship of the Advertising Council. During the war and after, these organizations relied on a prominent advertising agency, Foote, Cone, and Belding, drawing on "the same true and tested methods of advertising used to sell oranges, toothpaste, and other commercial products," according to a Forest Service representative in 1956. Under the slogan "Smokey Says—Care Will Prevent 9 out of 10 Forest Fires," the campaign helped reduce such fires.[2] Public service announcements linked protecting wildlife from fires with the war effort, deploying racist and threatening images of a Japanese man holding a match with slogans such as "Our Carelessness, Their Secret Weapon."[3]

By 1944, eager to counter the attacks on advertising during the 1930s, those involved in preventing forest fires realized that what was needed was a national campaign, a reassuring message rather than a threatening one, and an attractive image of an animal to sustain the campaign's appeal. Initially, they relied on images from the 1942 animated Disney film *Bambi*, in which a white-tailed deer faced a terrifying forest fire caused by hunters who carelessly let a campfire get out of control. On the poster, Bambi appeared along with Thumper the Rabbit and Flower the Skunk, all of them (like Smokey) appealing to children. Disney loaned the use of Bambi and his friends for only a year, and the Forest Service declined to agree to what the studio insisted on for an extension, especially costly royalties. Attention then turned to an alternative. The initial design featured squirrels, but as the author of an internal memo remarked, "The squirrel is a nuisance and just a damn rodent to farmers and rural people."[4] Moreover, it was hard to imagine how either Bambi or a squirrel could successfully fight forest fires. Discussions in the Forest Service shifted again, this time to a search for an anthropomorphized and nonthreatening depiction of an animal larger than a squirrel that "could stand upright and demonstrate forest safety practices."[5] As someone said at the time, the squirrel didn't have "the human interest" of "the Bear, whose human-antics appeal to, amuse and instruct all ages in all localities urban and rural."[6]

In early August 1944, officials met at the Department of Agriculture. Richard Hammatt, the head of the Forest Fire Prevention Program, wrote his colleagues that he was considering a "characterization (Disney manner?) of a (cub?) bear in a green (unburned) pine forest setting." It would have specified features, such as "nose short (Panda type); color black or brown; expression appealing, knowledgeable, quizzical; perhaps wearing a campaign (or Boy Scout) hat that typifies the outdoors and the woods. A bear that walks on his hind legs; that can be shown putting out a warming fire with a bucket of water"; who like G. I. Joe was carrying a rifle.[7] A teddy bear provided no model, since it was understood as cuddly rather than strong and protective. The Forest Service hired *Saturday Evening Post* artist Albert Staehle, who in 1936 had provided the image of Elsie the Cow for the Borden Dairy Company, to create the first bear poster, one that depicted a humanized, nonthreatening animal. When Staehle submitted an illustration of a naked bear, those in charge balked, so he was clothed. As the writer for Smokey's own website later remarked, there was a "need to find an animal symbol . . . and nothing seemed more fitting than the majestic, powerful (and also cute) bear."[8] Thus, in 1944, was born Smokey, named after "Smokey" Joe Martin, a New York City firefighter who in 1922 suffered blindness and burns in a dramatic rescue effort. Dressed up as a forest ranger in jeans, wearing a distinctive hat, and pouring water on a smoldering campfire, Smokey had an official birth date of August 9, 1944, with the first poster delivered two months later.

If World War II was one doula helping to birth Smokey, another more specifically in play was the effort by Japanese military leadership to use wildfires as offensive weapons. In the spring of 1942, their navy had fired explosives from submarines off the coast near Santa Barbara, California, hitting an oil field close to the two-million-acre Los Padres National Forest. Then, in November 1944, Japanese authorities deployed an additional tactic when they began to launch nine thousand unmanned balloon bombs, carried across the Pacific Ocean from Japan by high-altitude winds. Before the war ended, 350 successfully made it to America, landing in Hawaii, in Alaska, and on the mainland as far east as Michigan. Yet they failed in their mission to hamper America's war effort by igniting major fires. Had the public known what the Japanese were doing, it would surely have fanned the anti-Japanese flames that had led to the incarceration of Japanese Americans in internment camps. However, to deprive government officials in Japan of strategically useful information, a generally successful gag order remained in effect.[9] Nonetheless, the connections remained between the Japanese as enemies, sabotage, fires, and national defense. The Japanese "could illuminate the whole West Coast by setting our forests on fire," remarked a Forest Service official as he called for the public-private partnership to work together in "a war atmosphere—a patriotic fever."[10]

The Smokey Bear campaign was one of those the Advertising Council sponsored over many years, including some that focused on automobile safety and cancer prevention. But this particular one grew by whatever is the bear equivalent of leaps and bounds. In 1947 Smokey gained a deep voice when Jackson Weaver, a radio personality in the nation's capital, projected calm and benevolence by recording his voice with his head placed in a barrel. At the same time the slogan morphed into "Remember . . . Only YOU Can Prevent Forest Fires" and more than half a century later into "Only You Can Prevent Wildfires." By the early 1950s, corporations, led by the Advertising Council and Foote, Cone, and Belding, annually contributed $8 million worth of free advertising that relied on a wide range of media to spread the word.[11]

In response to the proliferation of commercial products featuring Smokey that had begun to appear during World War II, in 1952 Congress passed the Smokey Bear Act. The law criminalized the unauthorized use of the name and image of Smokey Bear and allowed the licensing of commercial items, with the resulting income to support fire prevention efforts.[12] Products featuring Smokey generated royalties and spread like wildfire, with one list in the mid-1950s including items such as a "Smokey teddy bear, wallets, belts, T-shirts, scarves, ash trays, blue jeans, hats, books, comic books, automobile cigarette snuffers, songs, records." Prominent among other efforts to spread the word and prevent forest fires was the launching in 1952 of the Smokey Bear Junior Forest Ranger program, with each member pledging to help Smokey; in return they would receive a "personal" letter from him along with a membership card, a bookmark, and a copy of the "Smokey the Bear" song. Every week thousands of letters reached Smokey, in some years the numbers surpassing those the nation's presidents received. In the mid-1950s, a young girl informed him that she was "helping you prevent forest fires by watching my daddy when we are out riding in my car. If my daddy throws a cigarette out the window, I fine him 10c, but if we are near a woods, I fine him 25c."[13]

If a New York City firefighter provided Smokey's name, the "real" Smokey was born in 1950. In the spring the Capitan Gap Fire, caused by human carelessness in New Mexico 150 miles southeast of Albuquerque, raged through 17,000 acres. An orphaned cub three months old and weighing five pounds had sought safety by climbing up a tree. Hearing "a faint sound like the whimpering of a sick child," the Forest Service ranger in charge recalled decades later, soldiers on a rescue mission "discovered a tiny cub bear clinging to the charred bark of a pine tree," with his feet's soles bleeding and "his seat . . . blistered." Rescued with the help of some Taos Pueblo Indians and initially named Hotfoot Teddy, he was taken to Santa Fe, where he was cared for by a veterinarian and by Ranger Ray Bell and his family. But when the frightened cub became difficult to care for, he had to be moved.[14]

Flown to the nation's capital, he was greeted by a large crowd that included members of Congress, forestry officials, the Secretary of Agriculture, a representative of President Harry S. Truman, and ordinary citizens. Smokey was moved to Washington's National Zoo, where he lived for a quarter of a century. Now famous and promoted by celebrities ranging from Jack Benny to Louis Armstrong, Smokey attracted millions of inquiring visitors. Because he received thirteen thousand letters a week or more, responded to by his personal secretary, the US Postal Service in 1964 designated 20252 as his very own zip code. Later, well after he died, he learned to speak Spanish and acquired his own Instagram, Twitter, and Facebook accounts.

In 1962, zookeepers introduced him to a female, Goldie Bear, in the hopes they might produce an heir. That effort having failed, they instead had Smokey and Goldie adopt a young bear, Little Smokey. In the spring of 1975, the zoo let Smokey retire and renamed the younger bear Smokey Bear II. After Smokey I died on November 9, 1976, he was buried in Smokey Bear Historical Park in Capitan, New Mexico, where the graveside plaque reads "This is the resting place of the first living Smokey Bear . . . the living symbol of wildfire prevention and wildlife conservation." Over time Smokey joined Santa Claus, Mickey Mouse, and the American president as the most recognizable figures in America. Yet the irony is notable. As Alice Wondrak Biel, a historian with years of experience working for the National Park Service, put it, the long story of Smokey Bear "had a scenario that mimicked a classic dime novel, but in reverse—a real bear whose real story could add to the aura of the already fictional Smokey Bear. Accordingly, they turned the story of the real Smokey into the biography of the cartoon Smokey, hybridizing the real with the fictional to powerful effect."[15]

Few if any other animals received so many prominent obituaries. The *Wall Street Journal* memorialized his passing on the front page of its November 11, 1976, issue, while the *New York Times* relegated its story of how "Smokey Bear Dies in Retirement" to page 16.[16] Yet the *Washington Post* topped all others. On the front page of an inside section under the headline "S. Bear, Fire Fighter," B. D. Colen wrote of the passing of Smokey Bear, "an employee of the National Park

Service . . . at his home in the National Zoo." Continuing the tongue-in-cheek emphasis on how human he was, Colen remarked, "Mr. Bear was perhaps better known to Americans than any personality other than the president." The obituary noted the marriage of Mr. Bear "in 1962 to the former Goldie," before hastening to add that he "was not a blood relation, despite the similarity" of their last names. Nine years later, "the still childless couple adopted a youngster," who had recently taken "over for his father following Mr. Bear's retirement." The conclusion persisted in following the conceit by saying that "his wife, of the home in Washington," survived him, as did their son.[17] In his maturity he had a cumulative income of more than a million dollars, derived from authorized use of his name and image.[18] This meant that, adjusted for inflation, his earned income sustained him, his wife, and his son well into the ranks of middle-class American families. Though Smokey in captivity had a nasty temper, the Advertising Council, an astute observer noted, portrayed "him as a cross between a teddy bear and a benevolent forest ranger, hidden under the fur of an authentic bear."[19]

Together the authorized and unauthorized products that amplified his fame were so extensive that a robust but incomplete sampling occupies 115 linear feet on the shelves of the National Agricultural Library.[20] There and elsewhere one can find posters, postage stamps, movies, costumes, songs, radio and television programs, and dolls, most of which project cuddly, friendly representations of Smokey Bear rather than suggestions of how dangerous a black bear might be.

Were there world enough and time, let alone potential interest of readers, this historian might devote an entire scholarly book to the study of representations of Smokey. Suffice it to say that the overwhelmingly familiar depictions of him as warm and fuzzy started with posters and soon emerged on postage stamps and with children's toys, stuffed animals especially. As Sean Munger astutely wrote in 2020, "Smokey worked because he seemed so wholesome and innocent," and "anthropomorphic bears are hard to resist as lovable characters." Adding to that, he noted the connections between Teddy Roosevelt, teddy bears, and environmentalism, as well as "a participatory message" connecting people, young ones especially, that emphasized "civic responsibility and democracy."[21]

The first advertisement, featured on a poster drawn by Staehle, appeared in August 1944.[22] With the seemingly unending images in advertising campaigns that followed, some aspects persisted while others changed. A shovel was often added but the jeans and hat were ever present, however much their size and shape changed. Typically, Smokey was half-man as forest ranger and half-bear as forest protector. Alone in 1944, he was eventually joined by others—Forest Service rangers, children, cubs, and even a Bambi-like fawn. In 1944, Smokey

OUR MOST SHAMEFUL **WASTE!**

⊗ *Remember*– **Only you can**
PREVENT FOREST FIRES!

Fire prevention poster with Smokey holding a fawn reminiscent of the one in Disney's *Bambi*. The name and character of Smokey Bear are the property of the United States, as provided by 16 U.S.C. 580p-1, and are used with the permission of the Forest Service, U.S. Department of Agriculture.

seemed to be having no difficulty dousing a small fire. In some later renditions, forest fires in the background rage out of control. Throughout the long histories of Smokey, with his brawn, shovel, and overalls he often appeared dressed as a working-class male, whose target audiences included children and those having the inclination and resources to hunt, camp, and go on vacations. Often images of Smokey Bear picture him as reassuringly gentle, working like he does to protect our world from the ravages of fires. In one example, Smokey, dressed in his familiar hat and blue jeans, gets back at Disney by holding a fawn with a forest fire burning in back. Similarly, a poster features Smokey with his familiar hat and jeans, along with two cute, smaller bears that are also fashionably dressed.

The use of postage stamps in the campaign to prevent forest fires began in 1945 with the image of a squirrel and a blaze behind it, even though the broader public relations campaign had already replaced the rodent with a bear. By 1947, the US Post Office offered the first of scores of stamps that deployed a bear—including an unnamed, portly one accompanied by two highly humanized cubs,

Fire prevention poster depicting Smokey with two young, domesticated bear helpers. The name and character of Smokey Bear are the property of the United States, as provided by 16 U.S.C. 580p-1, and are used with the permission of the Forest Service, U.S. Department of Agriculture.

albeit relying on not very compelling artistry. On a regular basis the post office has issued stamps that used much-improved artistry to get the message across persuasively.[23]

Then there is a whole series of toy bears, beginning in 1944 when Knickerbocker Bears added to its long-established offerings by acquiring the license to produce Smokey Bear dolls. Ideal Toy Company, which earlier had created and marketed the teddy bear, produced one of the first licensed versions of a toy Smokey. Since then, a torrent of products has flooded the market.[24] Embroidered patches, camp blankets, "Snuffit" ashtrays, hats, shoelaces, comic books, faux matchsticks, pins, bookmarks, pencils, figurines, handkerchiefs, and every kind of book imaginable. Smokey even made appearances in two iconic parades—Macy's Thanksgiving Day Parade in Manhattan and the Tournament of Roses one on New Year's Day in Pasadena, California. Some of these came to market with government-issued licenses and some of them not. Surely with some exceptions, such kitsch may have done more to support commercial

Smokey Bear celebrates his eightieth birthday in the Rose Parade, Pasadena, California, in 2024. Photo by author.

enterprises than to prevent forest fires. Perhaps the high point of expressive loyalty produced by the Smokey Industrial Complex came in 2004 with the celebration of his sixtieth birthday. Bambi reappeared at an elaborate party held in Southern California's Universal Studios Theme Park. The sons and daughters of wilderness firefighters blew out the candles on his birthday cake while Smokey Bear received a huge Hallmark birthday card.[25]

In addition to these representations of Smokey Bear, there are some one-offs connected to the moment of their creation. Among the first was the 1952 song "Smokey the Bear," originally performed by famous country music singer Eddy Arnold and written by Steve Nelson and Jack Rollins, who earlier were responsible for the much chillier "Frosty the Snowman." Over the years, the artist Rudy Wendelin recalled, as he emphasized how he had anthropomorphized Smokey, "The part I had was the humanizing conversion. Over time we replaced Smokey's claws and paws with more human-type hands; the paws became rough fingers. . . . We softened his sharp pointed teeth" so that "Smokey didn't look so much like a wild animal. We had created a more human, friendly and acceptable appearance."[26] The lyrics by Nelson and Rollins included "Prowling and growling and sniffing the air. He can find a fire before it starts to flame. That's why they call him Smokey, that's how he got his name." To make the song work, the song writers inserted the word "the" between the bear's first and last names.[27]

In the late 1960s the multimedia campaigns may have reached their peak, or at least one of many. The year 1966 witnessed the appearance of the General Electric–sponsored animated television movie *The Ballad of Smokey the Bear*, featuring the voice of James Cagney. More than almost any other cultural production, this one presented the anthropomorphized combination of a domestic mother, a family man father, and cute children so typical of the 1950s. Countering the story of an orphaned Smokey of 1942, which might have frightened children, it pictured highly gendered domestic scenes: a young Smokey seeing his girlfriend, of whom his parents disapproved; a Mrs. Smokey sending her husband off to play with his two nephews; and the cub Smokey being rescued by his father, who in the rest of the movie teaches his son not to be afraid of forest fire.[28] From 1969 to 1971, Jackson Weaver performed as the official voice of Smokey on seventeen episodes of "The Smokey Bear Show." An ABC Saturday morning television presentation, it drew on earlier Dell Comic Books published from 1955 to 1961. Recognizing that times had changed and making sure fear did not undercut cuddly anthropomorphism, the producers no longer offered up the earlier story of two bears that were Communist spies.[29]

Depictions changed in 1969 with the words of the Beat poet Gary Snyder, one of several examples inspired by cultural and social movements of the last third of the twentieth century. His poem, he remarked retrospectively, appeared "at a time when the nascent environmental movement was trying to stop the spread of nuclear power. We needed some strong, vital imagery to help us." Born out of a belief in Buddhism, Snyder's Smokey represented a commitment to "protect life down to the smallest little creature, protect our community, maintain our own practice, and honor impermanence, all at the same time." Reaching back in history and across cultures, Snyder connected Smokey with traditions the Forest Service knew nothing of, but, he insisted, "that was part of the fun of it all, turning the establishment's imagery on its head."

"A handsome smokey-colored brown bear standing on his hind legs," the poem read, "showing that he is aroused and watchful. Bearing in his right paw the Shovel that digs to the truth beneath appearances, cuts the roots of useless attachments, and flings damp sand on the fires of greed and war." His jeans, Snyder continued, symbolized the "slaves and laborers, the countless men oppressed by a civilization that claims to save but often destroys." Using language neither the Advertising Council nor the Forest Service would have deployed, he wrote of Smokey "trampling underfoot wasteful freeways and needless sub-

⊙ 7.14.05   *Smokey Bear Thanka*   ⊛ Capparell

Illustration highlighting Beat poet Gary Snyder's "Smokey the Bear Sutra" (1979). Lorraine Capparell, watercolor, 2005.

urbs, smashing the worms of capitalism and totalitarianism," and taking on the task of helping those who followed him to become "free of cars, houses, canned foods, universities and shoes, [and to] master the Three Mysteries of their own Body, Speech and Mind." He "fearlessly" worked to chop "down the rotten trees and prune out the sick limbs of this country America and then burn the leftover trash." As a conclusion, Snyder wrote, "If anyone is threatened by advertising, air pollution, television, or the police, they should chant SMOKEY THE BEAR'S WAR SPELL: DROWN THEIR BUTTS, CRUSH THEIR BUTTS." In 1969, turning familiar representations inside out, the environmental and antinuclear movements thus inspired a Beat poet to offer one statement in opposition to the hegemonic presentations of Smokey Bear.[30]

Around the same time, American soldiers offered another adversarial response to the iconic Smokey. During the war in Vietnam, the Pentagon, the CIA, and USAID launched Operation Ranch Hand, which used Agent Orange to defoliate dense forests in Southeast Asia so pilots could detect enemy movements below. By the late 1960s, they named their planes "Smokey Bears" and used the slogan "Smokey the Bear" to describe a maneuver when a flight mechanic, instead of throwing a grenade out of the plane, left it inside so that the smoke, exiting the cockpit window, thwarted the mission. At some point, most likely close to when that specific operation ended in 1971, someone at an American Air Force base created a poster that changed the words on the traditional Smokey poster to read "Only you can prevent a forest."[31]

If Donna Haraway's influential text of the mid-1980s, "Teddy Bear Patriarchy," represented a powerfully critical response to the circulation of teddy bears, the same was true for Smokey in the 1970s during battles over land rights in northern New Mexico. In *The Milagro Beanfield War* (1974), the novelist John Nichols offered a vivid, fictionalized version of long-simmering conflicts over land and water. In his telling, on the one hand were government officials, including those with the Forest Service, who controlled vast stretches of land. They were enabling a developer to build a vacation resort for the wealthy. In opposition was a town resident who threatened to derail the project by illegally irrigating his bean field as he rallied residents, most of them Hispanos, known also as Nuevomexicanos, scraping a living together as descendants of Spanish-speaking settlers who had inhabited the land for centuries. They often joined with Indigenous peoples to create mestizo communities. Because Forest Service policies benefited the developer, "big timber and mining companies, and out-of-state hunters and tourists" rather than the poor locals, Nichols wrote, they tended to look upon Smokey "as a kind of ursine Daddy Warbucks, Adolph Hitler, colonialist Uncle Sam," and the developer Ladd Devine III "all rolled into one."[32]

So the locals responded how marginalized rebels often do, and not only by supporting the illegal takeover of land and water rights. They also transformed small wooden statues of Smokey produced under the auspices of the Forest Service and intended for sale to tourists. These were a sacrilegious version of santos, small statues of the Roman Catholic saints or the Virgin Mary cherished and displayed in people's home. Townspeople, Nichols said, bought or stole the Smokey Bear knockoffs by the dozens. Once home, "they poured kerosene on the little Smokeys and lit them," Nichols wrote provocatively. "They hammered nails into the little Smokeys; and in a great many other imaginative and bestial ways they desecrated" the carved icons "in hopes of either destroying the United States Forest Service or at least driving" it off their land. When a Forest

El Gran Robo
de Nuestra Tierra

Poster protesting "El Gran Robo," translated into English as "The Great Theft," from Jake Kosek, *Understories: The Political Life of Forests in Northern New Mexico* (2006).

Service official attempted to save the Smokey statues from further desecration by bringing them to district headquarters, in the middle of the night locals responded. Relying on novelistic imagination, Nichols writes of them killing several Forest Service horses and then shoving "a little Smokey statuette . . . halfway up the ass of each dead horse." They painted "Chinga Smokey!" (Fuck Smokey) on a government truck; "whittled down" another santo "so it could be jammed up the truck's tailpipe"; and set fire to the district headquarters and as a result destroyed the hundred or so remaining statues.[33]

If Nichols offers a fictional account of opposition to the Smokey/Forest Service alliance, the UC Berkeley professor of geography Jake Kosek expands on this theme by mobilizing oral histories, folklore, and anthropology as he focuses on hill towns in northern New Mexico. There locals view Smokey with adversarial disdain. Subject to the symbolic violence that Nichols described, Hispanos see Smokey "as a vicious and despotic land thief."[34] Inspired by the battles over land rights of the 1970s, they understand him not as the beloved and benevolent icon millions of Americans envisioned but as a powerful symbol of theft, driven by racism and nationalism, of land stolen from them and then controlled by federal authorities who utilize it in ways that undermine their well-being.

In the 1940s, when the Forest Service introduced Smokey, federal officials had recognized local resistance rooted in historic antagonisms. That was now intensified by a sense that warnings about the danger of forest fires in effect accused locals of being unpatriotic folks when they actually used fires carefully to manage land and animals, locals whose outsider status and conflicts with the government authorities compelled their resistance. As an advertising executive involved in the campaign to promote Smokey remarked in 1947, "Sabotage of the forest is still a serious threat today and we still have an enemy of the forest to conquer. . . . It is not from overseas but from both a deviant and uneducated group and from the insidiousness of Americans' own carelessness."[35]

Many citizens of northern New Mexico envisioned an unholy alliance among missionaries, federal officials, and absentee landowners, many of whom lived in the nation's financial centers. As a result, Kosek asserts, in the postwar period Smokey became "an important site of struggle not as an abstract symbol but as a site through which the complex mixture of land struggles, racial exclusions, and nation building are mediated and made manifest in the lived daily experiences of Northern New Mexicans." At various points, in government policies and cultural representations, they came up against a racialized nationalism that threatened to marginalize them. As Kosek shows, in northern New Mexico Smokey remains "the consummate representative of white colonial paternalism, unjust land dispossession, and state authority."[36]

For decades, different ways of understanding land use policy centered on balancing the claims between preservationists and those wishing to use forests for hunting, logging, and residential developments. Although correlation is not causation, the campaigns that relied so heavily on Smokey Bear, and that dovetailed with and legitimized the Forest Service's fire-suppression strategies, may have dramatically decreased the number of wildfires the nation experienced. In 2011 the average annual acreage burned in wildfires had decreased to 6.5 million from a figure of 22 million in 1944. Yet in the 1970s, like their nineteenth-century predecessors, scientists emphasized the importance of ecological balance and, along with environmentalists, increasingly identified the Smokey Bear Effect as the process by which the prevention of forest fires actually provided dead trees and the growth of underbrush as fuel for fires. Thus, the official policy of suppressing fires, supported by the Smokey campaign, may have sometimes done more harm than good. After all, scientists pointed out that though people's carelessness caused some blazes, forest fires were part of the natural order of things. Add to that the way climate change created drier conditions and you have situations in which any number of factors, including lightning, could cause a rapidly developing and difficult-to-control conflagration, something increasingly witnessed in Western states in the early twenty-first century. In response, the federal government developed new approaches designed to prevent or limit the spread of dangerous fires. This change in policy also involved a shift in Smokey slogans when in 2001 his official motto became "Only you can prevent *wildfires*."[37]

Indeed, some well-informed observers believe that over the long term Smokey and the policies he has represented were highly problematic, even as government practices persisted in emphasizing the importance of fire suppression. Early in the new century, skeptical opposition grew. In 2007, in a paper titled "Be Careful What You Wish For: The Legacy of Smokey Bear," two Forest Service researchers stated, "The long-standing policy of aggressive wildfire suppression has contributed to a decline in forest health, an increase in fuel loads in some forests, and wildfires that are more difficult and expensive to control."[38] Though the Forest Service and the merchandisers it supported saw no reason to end reliance on Smokey, Stephen Pyne, the nation's leading historian of fire, called on him to "retire with dignity."[39] In 2018, around the same time Pyne issued his call, a *Washington Post* reporter pointed to over a hundred wildfires "blazing through Western states, charring" millions of acres. All this highlighted an ongoing debate about whether Smokey was responsible for the fires destroying forests, given his role as "the pitchman for the federal government's aggressive wildfire suppression policy." After all, commented Richard Minnich, a professor of earth and planetary sciences, we don't say, "Only You Can Prevent Earthquakes."[40] Then, in 2020, Sean Munger asserted that the policies promoted in the name of Smokey Bear, by relying on the blunt instrument of suppression, were highly problematic. "I'm not going so far as to denounce Smokey," he declared, "who is, after all, as American as apple pie; but let us acknowledge at least that his legacy is not as squeaky-clean as the character we wish he was."[41]

In the annals of famous bears, the chronology of Smokey is unusual—the story begins with a representational bear invented in the nation's capital during World War II; emerges as a real one who travels from New Mexico to the National Zoo and back to New Mexico; and then morphs into everything from a family man to a symbol of capitalist exploitation. The Disney empire, which plays an outsize role in so many other bear stories, inadvertently gave birth to representational Smokey and later underwrote only a minor appearance in the short animated production *In the Bag* (1956). Absent Disney's power, what created and sustained Smokey was the full force of the culture industry's powerful combination of government and corporate entities that involved federal and advertising agencies, songwriters, copywriters, newspapers, toy manufacturers, and even a Beat poet. Smokey's history underscores the importance of two critical moments in American history: the years during and around World War II as incubators of the intensification of bears as celebrities and then the late 1960s/early 1970s as pivotal years when Smokey morphed from an innocent animal to a dangerous one.

Although those involved in the campaigns that created Smokey Bear used the word "humanize" to describe what they were doing to bears, real and imagined, we might more properly describe what happened as domesticating or anthropomorphizing.[42] What emerged were images and understandings that marginalized the real Smokey and blurred the differences between people and bears, part of a familiar process of projecting contemporary values onto the continually changing image of bears. This shape-shifting or distinction diminishing was similar to what often happened when postmodernists entered the arena of interspecies relationships well after the birth of Smokey on a poster in 1944 or in a New Mexico forest six years later. To be sure, in the worlds of Smokey Bear, there is an *Ursus americanus* in nature we see, with a cub found escaping a forest fire by climbing up a tree as well as black bears—father, mother, and son—on display in the National Zoo as an artificial but necessary family. And then there is an unending number of representational black bears modeled on Smokey in almost every possible commercial form. In the imagined world, the blurring of relationships between humans and animals is complicated.

Yet it is notable that from 1944 on, the danger depicted was usually not any violence a person might carry out against a bear, or a bear against a person, but the way humans threatened forests. Of course, there are many other hybrids—anthropomorphized figures in the worlds created by Disney and Dr. Seuss, for example. But none of these imagined animals is so involved in highly organized public relations efforts involving government organizations and corporations committed to shaping public policy and the natural world. That is what makes the stories of Smokey Bear so complicated, compelling, and problematic. Moreover, in the final three decades of the twentieth century and into the twenty-first, government officials, scientists, conservationists, environmentalists, and Indigenous citizens fought over what Smokey represented. These struggles underscore the troubled ways in which conflicts about how people used or abused nature revealed tensions that settler colonialism provoked among opposing classes and ethnic groups.

Smokey Bear bears comparison, so to speak, with other well-known bears. Paul Shepard explores how earlier examples represent different stages of human development. Teddy bears with very young children. Winnie-the-Pooh as the "animated teddy" for somewhat older ones. Paddington, "who strives to join the modern human world" as "the city cousin" of Pooh who lives in "a literal rather than symbolic world . . . the civilized little bear of latency, . . . the consumer and conformist in us, whose bearishness will gradually recede beneath a civil interior." Smokey graduates "from the freedom-loving pubescence" that Yogi Bear represents, "into the bureaucracy itself." It is possible to imagine Smokey as "a man in a false face," for at least Pooh and Paddington are "helpful fictions as we grow into our human condition. But the Smokey mask conceals a deeper, authoritarian mischief, corporate demagoguery, the cunning of expropriation and the politics of deception by appeals to our sense of security in the guise of a bear." As a result, "the tender, surrogate bears of our youth vanish into the figure of a man who has assumed the lineaments of a bear, whose real interest is cutting down trees, whose exhortations, cautionary admonitions, rules, and objectives are the euphemisms of 'forestry' and progress."[43]

Smokey eventually emerged as an animal capable of intelligence and empathy. Both he and teddy bears were protective—Smokey early on of the forests and teddy throughout of children. Teddy and Smokey both feature abundant blurring and crossing of the line between human and animal identities—teddy more so than Smokey, with adults as well as children. With Smokey there is at least one actual bear, discovered clinging to a tree in New Mexico, residing in the National Zoo, and then buried near where he was originally found. However, with Teddy, unlike with Smokey, the real bear makes the briefest of appearances in the story and then a cub simulacrum emerges before appearing again and again in cartoons, stuffed animals, and every other form. Minor Ferris Buchanan, the biographer of Holt Collier, opened his book with an appropriately revealing story that highlights the unreal reality. When Buchanan and his wife took their children on a visit to the Memphis Zoo, a young daughter "protested our leaving without seeing a real Teddy bear," and it was immediately "obvious that she thought a Teddy bear was real, much as I suppose she would have believed in the Easter Bunny or Santa Claus." When he responded that "there was no real Teddy bear," his daughter "cried inconsolably" and then asked, "'If it is not real, where did it come from?'"[44] Had she visited the National Zoo and seen Smokey Bear, she might have felt differently.

8

Out of the Closet

BEARS IN THE GAY WORLD

✕

Hairy, hefty, and aging, members of the gay bear subculture celebrate and erot-icize what they see as their resemblance to bears as they attempt to counter the images of male homosexuals as younger (cubs) and slimmer (otters). Role-playing as animals accentuates their masculinity. As part of the broader story of the development of gay liberation, they compare themselves to bears in an ef-fort to foster a sense of individual and group identity in powerfully imaginative yet at times problematic ways. Since the 1980s in the United States and then spreading around the world, this subculture has largely existed in media worlds outside the mainstream one that features so many other bears.[1]

If in American culture more broadly stories of bears circulate with no appar-ent narrative boundaries to contain them, in this case tales remain in a largely self-contained media world. Moreover, rather than projecting human traits onto bears, gay bears do the opposite—impute ursine qualities to human beings. More so than elsewhere, bears are abundantly representational and without human-like agency that might highlight their emotional and cognitive powers.[2] Gay bears celebrate their own masculinity in ways that involve free-floating references, rarely connected to actual or even imagined animals. Elsewhere are stories about sexual relations between nonhuman male bears and human women.[3] In the cases of the gay bear subculture that I know of, rare are discussions of sexual or romantic cross-species congress with bears, real or imagined.

Although the gay bears came into prominence in the 1980s, there is a significant prehistory that reaches back at least to the mid-1960s. Among the important precursors were the Girth-and-Mirth and Radical Faerie movements that first appeared in the mid-1970s. And in scattered urban areas by 1980, some gay men, as noted by the chronicler of the world of gay bears Les Wright, connected gays with representational bears. Gay bears placed "a small teddy bear in a shirt or hip pocket," he notes, in order "to emphasize being into 'cuddling,' that is resisting being objectified and reduced to preferred sex acts."[4]

The movement to link gay men with bears gathered strength, with 1986 as the time when organizational expressions began to take hold. This happened especially in San Francisco and initially through computer bulletin boards, at private "Bear Hugs" parties, and in what was then the underground magazine *BEAR*.[5] "The rise of a bear community," notes Wright, "is inseparable from the AIDS epidemic."[6] The emergence of gay beardom came soon after the discovery of HIV/AIDS, which the CDC first announced in early June 1981, news that quickly spread in the gay community and elsewhere.[7]

Many in the emerging gay bear community developed commitments to "cohesion, nurturance, and mutual aid as a response to the acute sense of isolation and alienation they had experienced," according to Wright. He also cites a commitment to sex-positive and more careful ways of life. In the wake of horrific deaths, gay bears were asserting the importance of life and a robust masculinity. Significantly, given the image of AIDS-stricken gay men as emaciated, the emphasis on the hefty male body suggested a commitment to life, what Wright calls "the spirit of survivorship and . . . a way to transcend the hell of AIDS by joyfully seizing the day."[8]

By the early 1990s, the subculture found expression in increasing numbers of organized activities and organizations across the nation and around the world. Among them were an International Bear Expo that included the crowning of an International Mr. Bear; hot tub parties, bear clubs, and bear bars; more varied and extensive means of electronic communication, especially with the development of the World Wide Web; the proliferation of bearaphernalia; and publications that followed *BEAR Magazine*, not only in mainstream gay newspapers but also in the magazines *American Bear*, *Bear Fax*, and *American Grizzly*.[9]

"We are not dealing with a well-organized, members-only, card-carrying association," writes Tim Martin, the editor and publisher of *American Bear*. Instead, what emerged was "the advent of a pervading spirit that is often more a shared personal experience," one that involves something "deeper than skin and body hair."[10] Even though the world he is referring to was more organized than he avers, his point is nonetheless accurate: who gay bears are and what characterizes them is very much up in the air. This subculture is an integral part of the broader gay and lesbian revolution, despite tensions between this particular group and the worlds of both lesbians and other types of gay men. Especially notable is an effort to position gay bears in contrast to identification of gays as effeminate men.[11] As Wright has noted, gay bears were distinguishing themselves "from 'twinks'—the gay mainstream image of the young, blond, smooth-skinned, gym-buffed, presumably shallow and air-headed Southern California 'surfer' or *GQ* model type."[12]

It is convenient to define a member as someone with "a large or husky body, heavy body hair, a lumbering gait, an epicurean appetite, an attitude of imperturbability, a contented self-acceptance of his own masculinity," remarks Wright. Yet many observers opt for more capacious definitions that embrace variety and depend less on physical attributes than on personal and psychological ones.[13] Perhaps Scott Hill's statement, "We are a community woven together by an appreciation of masculinity and genuineness in a man," best summarizes a broader view.[14]

The world of gay bears involves considerable variety and frequent attempts at inclusivity. Although bicoastal urban communities gather most of the attention, groups exist in rural, small-town, and fly-over America.[15] Moreover, there are complicated and robust discussions of the racial and class composition of this world. As one knowledgeable participant/observer notes, as he points especially to those who live in cities, "it is clear that the majority of Bears are white, upper-middle class, white-collar professionals." In opposition to this demographic are those with sartorial connections to blue-collar culture.[16] Another contested issue emerges in debates over sexual practices. Members of the gay bear community insist on the importance of nurturing relationships while also "accommodating the realities of casual sex" and a wide variety of other practices.[17] Finally, it is hard to avoid issues surrounding the relationships to mainstream culture, especially the role of capitalism and commercialism. As is true with any cultural movement, even adversarial or outsider ones, commodification and gentrification always loom as threats.[18]

In a wide range of media, though most of it rarely accessed by people outside the community, there is an extensive world involving gay bears.[19] The most important periodical is *BEAR Magazine*, which first appeared in 1987 in a few dozen xeroxed copies and now circulates as a glossy publication widely available in the United States and abroad. Another publication, *RFD: A Country Journal for Gay Men Everywhere*, reminds us of the importance of gay bears outside major urban areas. Among others are *American Bear, Bear World Magazine,* and *A Bear's Life Magazine.* The photographers John Rand and Chris Nelson offer visual images of community members.[20] Social media, including multiple Facebook, X, and TikTok sites, helps connect gay bears with each other. A series of films explores relationships and communities of gay bears.[21]

The movie (and a rare one at that) that most fully references an animal bear, although only at several removes from a real live one, is the twenty-two-minute 2011 *I F*CK*D P*DD*NGTON B**R*, once available online but now no longer so. It features Jimmy Justice as narrator and actor, who in terms of hair and heft bore little resemblance to most gay bears. He offered a narrative of a sexual and romantic relationship to a man he named Paddington Bear, a story the London media hyped. Aside from costuming in a bearskin, mentions of a paw, and frequent references to Paddington, there were no suggestions to actual bears or fictional ones. Much of the film features Justice narrating the story, a version of Paddington sitting on a table next to him. At one point he tells the story of his mounting Paddington in order to have sexual relations with him.[22]

Similarly referencing animal bears, principally in their titles and at moments metaphorically, are innumerable festivals that bring gay bears together, with the annual July one in Provincetown, Massachusetts, the most legendary example. Among those in attendance are men who don bear-referencing clothing, typically far removed from any connection to actual animals.[23]

This is, the town's tourism website announces, "the largest gathering of bears in the world. Tens of thousands come to Provincetown" and go to "parties, bars, and clubs throughout the town. You know what you're getting into when you attend. And no, we're not talking about *actual* bears."[24]

The statement about the absence of real bears in Provincetown underscores an important point. When I began to work on this chapter, I thought I'd be able to explore how those involved in this subculture depicted or wrote about actual bears. Before long, however, I discovered that most visual and even rhetorical evidence offers images or references not of bears as animals but of gay men as bears. Most of what I write about elsewhere in this book involves stories of real bears or representational ones. However, in this instance the references to bears strike me as overwhelmingly metaphorical, with men projecting ursine characteristics onto themselves. Or as Bernd Brunner notes in his 2007 *Bears: A Brief*

Four gay men celebrating Bear Week on Cape Cod. Provincetown Office of Tourism.

History (without referencing the world of gay bears), admirers of nonhuman bears "must usually content themselves with a variety of fetishistic substitutes—or settle for a so-called bear in the form of a bearded, powerful man."[25]

Although there are many images of gay bears, relatively rare are examples that feature real or imagined ones. Early images appeared in George Mazzei's 1979 "Who's Who at the Zoo: A Glossary of Gay Animals."[26] The cover of the Les Wright book *The Bear Book* highlights his credentials, including that as the nation's most important coordinator of writings about gay bears. Moreover, the cover offers what are relatively rare pictures of animal bears from within this community, in this case friendly and playful ones.

Wright's *Bear Book II* contained an insert with twenty-six photographs of gay bears, four of which referenced nonhuman bears: one a picture of a gay bear wearing a bear outfit, whether fake or a real pelt is not clear; a second, of two gay bears cuddling, one of them holding a small statue of a bear, perhaps an unidentified Native American object; a third of a gay bear standing, with a picture of the head of a grizzly placed over his shoulder; and a final one revealing bear paw tattoos, one on each of a man's buttocks. Similarly, the flag of the International Bear Brotherhood features a representation of a bear paw in the upper left-hand corner. And finally but importantly in terms of visual representations

Cover of Les Wright's *The Bear Book: Readings in the History and Evolution of a Gay Male Subculture* (1997).

is this rare reference in a picture and words to parallel sexual practices. "Brown Bears Caught Performing Oral Sex," reported Megan Gannon on livescience .com. "The club of fellatio-loving animals just gained new members" when scientists "observed a pair of male brown bears in captivity in Croatia that regularly engaged in oral sex over several years."[27]

If we turn our attention to the bearotica stories, we find scattered references to nonhuman bears. In over two hundred pages of Jonathan Cohen's novel *Bear Like Me* (2003), I could locate only one relevant passage. When talk turns to going to the Global Bear Gathering in Sweden, one gay bear says, "I think there must be some sort of biological imperative that kicks in.... Isn't that when salmon swim upstream to spawn?"[28] And in Ron Suresha's edited 2004 book titled *Bear Lust: Hot, Hairy, Heavy Fiction*, a few passing, metaphorical references appear to "a bear hug" and "heartfelt hairy hugs to bear cubs and grrr-pals."[29]

Several references to bears as animals appear in a chapter in the sociologist Peter Hennen's *Faeries, Bears, and Leathermen: Men in Community Queering the Masculine* (2008). They strike me as exceptionally rare examples of references to an actual live creature in the extensive literature of the world of gay bears that I have read. Drawing on his experience at several gatherings, especially during summer camping trips, Hennen talked of how two campers "had seen *real* bears." But when they returned to tell what they had witnessed, their fellow gay bears offered "not a word about the danger the hikers had so obviously placed themselves in." Maybe, he remarked, "the testosterone-laden air made it possible to forget about mama" bear, who would attack to protect her offspring.[30]

Elsewhere Hennen offered more symbolic but scattered references to bears and their habitats. Mentioning how gay bears invoke their love of life in the wilderness even though the subculture was a largely urban phenomenon, he discusses how centuries-old manly return-to-nature movements had involved an escape from "the perceived feminizing forces of civilization" while also linking "Bear masculinity with heteronormative masculinity." In a parallel historical contextualization, he wrote of how, by using teddy bears as symbols of tenderness, members of the gay bear subculture followed the example of Teddy Roosevelt by "unintentionally" suggesting that "manliness was intimately linked with whiteness." He also explored typologies in the subculture, including the identification of grizzlies as "more mature and demanding Bears" and polar bears as "older Bears with white or grey hair." He pointed out that in 1997 Wright had mentioned how "the gay mass media" sold "to the Bears consumable, standardized images of 'real' bears." And he noted that some gay bears collected bearaphernalia, including one who had a stuffed and mounted head of a real bear and a Baccarat bear.[31]

However important to me as a historian are references to actual bears and to a handful of collectible, imagined, or metaphorical ones, to Hennen other issues mattered more, gendered power especially. His chapter on gay bears was one of three that explored what the subtitle of his book called "Queering the Masculine." "Bear masculinity," he insisted, "must be developed and sustained intersubjectively, within the community itself, an interactive process that is greatly facilitated by the symbol of the bear." Drawing on the work of Pierre Bourdieu, especially his *Masculine Domination* (1998), Hennen explored issues of body image, sexuality, and gender. Interested in whether this subculture was oppositional or accommodating, he concluded that its members embraced a "hegemonic masculinity" and "heteronormativity." "Perhaps one day the Bears featured here," like those in "the wild," he remarked at the very end of this

Cover of Ray Kampf's
*The Bear Handbook:
A Comprehensive
Guide for Those Who
Are Husky, Hairy, and
Homosexual and Those
Who Love 'Em* (2000).

chapter, will "emerge from hibernation with a ferocious hunger" and "demonstrate the same ferocious hunger for change in the gender politics governing resistant masculinities."[32]

In other sources, some examples refer to cross-species phenomena, albeit ones that, given their rarity and brevity, underscore the limited attention gay bears pay to actual bears. Metaphorical references dominate Ray Kampf, *The Bear Handbook: A Comprehensive Guide for Those Who Are Husky, Hairy, and Homosexual and Those Who Love 'Em* (2000). One example is his brief discussion, "A True 'Fairy' tale—*The Three Bears*: a look at a three-way relationship," that is, a ménage à trois where, unlike in the Goldilocks story, "there are not three beds but one California King." And on the front cover of the book appear contrasting drawings of a "Real Bear" from the world of gay men and a "really good at faking it" picture of an animal bear.[33]

In "Bearaphernalia: An Exercise in Social Definition," the librarian and scholar Robert B. Marks Ridinger mentions bears in astronomy, religion, and myths but, leaving parallels or connections implicit, does not connect such representations to those in the gay bear world.[34] Jack Fritscher, a historian and activist, mentions but does not explore the importance of teddy bears and heavenly bears to the communities of gay bears.[35]

Then there is Pierre De Mey, a French bear who discovered gay bears while on postdoc study at Harvard. He lists the teddy bear as one type of gay bear, albeit an "unsexed type"—with its image "that of a sweet companion, always ready for a cuddle."[36] And Scott Hill used "Aroused from Hibernation" as the title for his essay on how he developed a sense of his identity.[37] Pointing to bears mentioned in the Bible, in a Hindu epic, and among Native Americans, Suresha, a prominent author in the gay bear community, remarked that "despite many positive archetypal images of the bear mammal . . . contemporary American culture views the creature as negative and fearsome." This was, he continued, not like how "most self-identified urban bears see themselves, or would care to see themselves represented" but as "a surly, uncouth, or shambling person."[38] And then we find a clever reference, a rare example of one to a popular story about bears. *Bear Book II* included "In Goldilocks's Footsteps," an essay by Elizabeth A. Kelly and Kate Kane that positioned its authors, like Goldilocks, as intruders. The essay starts with the female authors remarking, "Maybe it begins like the fairy tale in which once upon a time Goldilocks finds herself an uninvited guest at the home of three bears."[39] And as discussed above, there is the reference to Paddington, this one hardly cuddly, in the film *I F*CK*D P*DD*NGTON B**R*, described as taking "us behind the closed doors of the nation's favourite stuffed bear to reveal a sordid world of adultery, debauchery and ultimately tragedy."[40]

In addition to all these scattered, largely metaphorical references to bears in multiple media, I could find only one serious essay that explores the meaning of how this subculture deploys images of bears—in this case of the relevance of bears in Native American cultures. The geologist Michael S. Ramsey contributed an essay titled "The Bear Clan: North American Totemic Mythology, Belief, and Legend" to Wright's first *Bear Book*.[41] He drew on his command of Native American cultures that he developed while a graduate student at Arizona State University, often specifying distinct traditions of different groups. He mentioned the familiar transition in representations of bears from the wild and frightening to the cute and fascinating. He focused on how to some groups of Native Americans the grizzly bear "was one of the most powerful totemic spirits in all of nature," which found its expression in legends and myths, as "sacred and possessing of individual spiritual powers," so much so that they became "one of the most powerful religious symbols in many indigenous cultures." Conjuring the animal "as a brother, a kindred spirit, and a teacher," he wrote that some Native Americans saw in the bear an animal that had wonderfully similar traits to themselves. He discussed at length what bears mean to Native Americans and how those meanings found expression in myth and ritual practices, focusing on the bear as Healer, Creator, Warrior, and Renewer. More generally, he mentioned both how humans anthropomorphized bears and "projected ursine qualities onto themselves and others."

He then turned to the roles of bears in the gay subculture. What he wrote implicitly contrasted the robust role of bears there with what was evidenced elsewhere. "No longer seen strictly as a wild and fearsome animal," he noted, "it has become the fuzzy childhood toy, the oafish cartoon character, and the leading symbol of fire prevention." With "loveable names" such as Yogi and Winnie, "this bear character is stripped of those qualities that made it so important among Native Americans." In contrast, he wrote of how "the bearish man is perhaps most evident and well-organized within the bear community that exists in gay America," whose attributes he discussed. "In the bear we see a mirror of our animalistic side, the epitome all that is wildness." If to Indigenous people "this represented power, spirituality, and nature," then "to modern man," he insisted, without making clear if he was talking generally or specifically of gay bear men, "freedom, strength, and playfulness are its virtues." Though they shared a nomenclature, he noted, actual bears and gay ones differed in what that meant. He acknowledged that many of those involved in the world of gay bears "use both abstract and realistic representations of the bear, its paw print, and vocalizations as symbols for the group," as well as in clothing, jewelry, and tattoos that spanned "a wide range from Native American emblems and icons to modern representations of the bear to more specifically homoerotic forms." He insisted on "the basic and continued realization of the similarities between humans and bears" as "the strongest premise that binds the ancient bear cults with those of today." Grasping at straws in a way that confirms my judgment about the rarity of interspecies comparisons, he remarked that "perhaps the most direct connection that can be drawn between the two is the use of symbology to express one's love of, and membership within the given group." Yet in the end, he acknowledged that any "linkage" between the two communities "seems tenuous at best."[42]

Another gay bear offered remarks that went beyond stating a "tenuous" connection between gay bears and bear species. "Bears, as we think of them, don't actually exist," remarked the musician Ned Wilkinson. "Men with qualities we consider 'ursine' do exist. The only thing that makes any man a 'bear' is his own self-image or the image that others see in him" and not the "result of any objective reality," since how an individual gay bear presented himself was "guided purely by his own subjectivity."[43] Wilkinson, unlike Ramsey, offered a brief discussion of the relationships between actual bears and gay bears and as a result produced essentialized Native American culture; rather than identifying specific practices of specific groups, he offered sweeping analyses that categorized "Native Americans" in overly unspecified, archaic, simplistic, and static ways.

Then there is some evidence of an interest in exploring connections between human and nonhuman bears in Suresha's *Bears on Bears*, 340-page collection of interviews of those involved in the gay male subculture. As in other sources, scattered mentions of cubs, bear paws, the wilderness, hibernation, legendary bears, and even "ursomasculinity" occur.[44] Beyond that, three authors emphasized how otherwise rare and superficial are cross-species references or understandings. Jack Fritscher, having noted that real bears hibernate but gay male ones do not, remarked, "There's a point where anthropomorphism fails." More extensively, Suresha mentions that "the number of points of commonality between four-legged creatures and humans is amazing. We could be taking from this identification a wealth of meaning to serve our own personal transformation. Yet if you ask most men who identify as Bears what they feel they have in common with the four-legged creature . . . all they can think of is the hair, maybe the girth. Not a word about strength, endurance, speed, courage, fierceness, appetite. In fact, most Bears think bears are slow, dumb, fat animals." Driving the point home, Chris Wittke, who writes frequently for BEAR *Magazine*, suggests how superficial the parallels are. "I think *bear* is a nice metaphor, as in 'he's a bear of a man,'" he noted before going on to insist that until recently he believed the bear metaphor "had been stretched to the breaking point—probably around the ten-thousandth time somebody made a 'husbear' reference." Now, however, he "would recommend that people not pin hopes on a Bear movement, because it's just a metaphor! Fun is good, fur is good; expanding our sexual vocabularies is great. I guess that's all."[45]

Unlike the simultaneous appearance of other examples in so many widely available media, representations of bears in gay culture were mainly available to insiders. Context is important here. The year 1986 was a major turning point when the subculture took hold organizationally. This occurred amid the AIDS crisis, when gay men were being culturally demonized as spreaders of a lethal virus—to which the celebration of gay bears offered a powerful alternative. Gay bears emerged in the 1980s into a world populated by other admirable representatives. Among them were Garfield's companion Pooky, a teddy bear with a starring role in the 1981 version of *Brideshead Revisited*, the publication of

The Tao of Pooh in 1982, the first issues of the magazine *Teddy Bear Times & Friends* in 1983, the appearance of Donna Haraway's "Teddy Bear Patriarchy" soon after, and in 1987 both the opening of the exhibit of Winnie-the-Pooh and Friends in Manhattan and the publication of Julius Lester's first book that recast the story of Brother Bear. This was a crowded world, but the attention of gay male bears turned not outward to real bears or to these varied cultural representations but inward to focus on the role of their bodies, masculinities, personalities, and commitments as they struggled to gain a more secure and honored place in the world of gay men. The emergence of gay bear culture in the late 1980s was consequential in another way. The invention of the World Wide Web in 1989, of Google as a search engine almost ten years later, and then subsequent social media such as Facebook set in motion forces that enabled both the spread of the gay bear subculture and my ability to research it. A number of consequences followed. It enabled me to explore a world that, unlike so many other examples of representational bears, exists in a largely self-contained media world. To be sure, printed books enabled me to explore this world, but so too did new media. The official birthday of the internet is January 1, 1983, which means it was available a few years later when the culture of gay bears arose. This reminds us that today the internet gives not only this researcher but also gay bears living outside major metropolitan centers access to this intriguing world. It reveals both the fragmentation and the hyper-proliferation of how Americans encounter representational bears.

Gay bears present rare perspectives in the annals of how we explore bears representationally. To be sure, gay bears participate fully in the trajectory seen elsewhere over time—the increasing embrace of the anthropomorphic assumption that bears are cuddly and lovable. However, as the Jimmy Justice film's referencing of Paddington reminds us, overwrought desire often erases the border between cute cuddling and violence.[46]

In almost all other cases—notably with teddy, Smokey, Brer Bear, and Winnie-the-Pooh—what is involved is people imputing human characteristics to real or representational bears. As part of a process of cultural appropriation, gay bears do the reverse of what we see elsewhere—impute characteristics of bears as animals to human beings and often in a non-self-reflexive way.[47] Gay bears focus not on bears as like people but on people as like bears. Even so, as we have seen so often with representational bears, because bears remind us that they are like us, they provide fertile opportunities for representational adoption. This is so even though gay bears focus on secondary physical characteristics of bears, especially heft and fur, have little interest in exploring other aspects of interspecies commonalities, and offer few examples of cross-species relationships. The history of gay bears underscores the ways gender and sexuality have profoundly shaped how humans have related to bears. Significantly, despite references to hibernation, this world reveals almost nothing about the lives of actual bears. Moreover, in their intense but often vague identification with bears, gay men provided yet one more example of how by the late twentieth century the ways humans understood bears eliminated any sense of the distinctive specificity of individual bears or species among them.

9

Timothy Treadwell and Marian Engel

BEARS, HUMANS,
AND DANGEROUS EROTICISM

✕

Timothy Treadwell's life and death with bears is the third of the legendary stories that, like Marian Engel's 1976 *Bear: A Novel*, mixes danger, attraction, eroticism, violence, and anthropomorphism, albeit in ways that complicate narratives of change over time. Ostensibly a story about a young man trying to connect with bears, it is actually one that reveals how Treadwell relied on bears to solve his own problems and that predictably ended tragically, unlike the trajectory Engel's novel offers. The historian Jon T. Coleman identifies Treadwell as "the most direct of Hugh Glass's descendants."[1] And on a *Dateline NBC* program, the anchor Stone Phillips introduced Treadwell as "part Dr. Doolittle, part Grizzly Adams."[2] With the help of Jewel Palovak, in *Among Grizzlies: Living with Wild Bears in Alaska* (1997), Treadwell told the dramatic, often fabricated story of his life with bears for thirteen summers in remote areas of Alaska. Six years after the book's publication, these ventures ended in death for him, his companion at the time Amie Huguenard, and two bears. Along with a film by Werner Herzog, the book and what Treadwell said of his aspirations reveal how he tried to offer a moving story of redemptive salvation, marked by its subject's shape-shifting—how Treadwell's life among bears, in which he seemed to become one with them, temporarily saved him, even as he knowingly courted death. As a perceptive observer understood his situation, Treadwell was among "those who wanted not just protection and greater tolerance, but the establishment of diplomatic relations between the species, a breakdown of the adversarial wall that separates them from us."[3] Yet though this seemed possible in Engel's fiction, it was impossible in Treadwell's life.

"The path that led me to the land of the grizzly," Treadwell naively claimed at the outset of the book (mostly written by Palovak, his business partner and onetime lover), "was far more dangerous than the bears themselves." He grew up in suburban Long Island in a solidly middle-class household headed by a father who was a foreman for a construction firm. Treadwell insisted he was "just a bit mischievous, with the heart of a wild animal." Early on, he dreamed of being an animal because they "possessed the innocence and freedom that I could only wish for." So, in addition to sleeping with a teddy bear beside him, he "donned imaginary wings, claws, and fangs" and "was haunted by fantasies of riding away on a wild horse, or running far and fast with a pack of timber wolves." He also imagined becoming "a grizzly, roaming the great north." Then one day, "an incident occurred that would change my life," he said. He and a friend encountered "some older kids who were throwing frogs high into the air and splattering them on the muddy water's surface," killing them one at a time. Initially rebuffed by the older and tougher boys as he tried to rescue the innocent animals, he triumphed over his adversaries and succeeded in liberating the frogs. Thus, "an eco-warrior was born."[4]

However, the road ahead was perilous. In high school, already his drinking alcohol, driving recklessly, and getting arrested convinced him that in his "chaotic state, abandoning" his family "was the best gift I could give them." So he headed west, if not to the land of the grizzlies, then to Southern California. Living in a series of communities from Long Beach to Malibu, he remembered himself as "an overactive street punk without any skills, prospects, or hopes."[5] Addictions, he reported, quickly took over his life—initially to alcohol and then to cocaine, meth, quaaludes, and heroin. His life of violence and paranoia placed him on a self-destructive course. There were several alternative paths forward that did not work out. Hoping to get roles on television shows, he hired a Hollywood talent agent but failed to get a job he coveted as the bartender on the NBC sitcom *Cheers*, which went instead to Woody Harrelson. A doctor prescribed antidepressants to control what may have been bipolar disorder.

However, he took himself off his meds because he preferred the highs and lows to the more placid middle ground.[6]

What started him on the path to salvation was the intervention by a friend, a Vietnam vet who convinced Treadwell to turn his life around precisely as it was spiraling out of control. After a near-death experience, he knew that "somewhere, someplace, beyond the honk of horns and burning glare of city lights, was sanctuary." When his friend asked him where that might be, Treadwell supposedly replied that it would be a place with few people and "lots of wild animals.... This might seem crazy," he continued, "but when I was young I used to pretend I was a grizzly bear." That meant Alaska, his friend replied.[7]

A year later he rode a motorcycle to Alaska to spend his first summer there, this time in Wrangell–St. Elias Park, west of the border between Alaska and the southwest corner of the Yukon Territory. Coincidentally, 1990, the year of his first trip north, was when Doug Peacock published *Grizzly Years: In Search of the American Wilderness*, in which he recorded how, having returned from a stint as a Green Beret medic in Vietnam, he sought redemption living among the grizzlies in Wyoming and Montana. However, if both Peacock and Treadwell lived among grizzlies as part of intense personal quests, Peacock's book and experiences differed dramatically from Treadwell's. Peacock evidenced more respect for grizzlies on their own terms; carefully informed readers about how they hunted, mated, and communicated with one another; rarely if ever relied on anthropomorphism, even as he acknowledged their "grace and dignity," as well as their "enormous power and mystery"; remained acutely aware of how dangerously lethal bears could be; and never forgot that he was a human and they were grizzlies.[8]

After his initial foray Treadwell shifted to places in Katmai National Park and Preserve, located at the northeastern end of the long peninsula that stretches out from southwestern Alaska. Early on, he camped in an area he called Grizzly Sanctuary in Halo Bay along the Katmai coast. In 1994 he moved thirty-five miles away to Kaflia Bay, to an area he named the Grizzly Maze. Unlike the relatively open area of the Sanctuary, what characterized the Maze was dense brush created by alders, labyrinthine trails, and tunnels through which humans had to travel on all fours. Here great numbers of bears tromped, eventually ending up at coastal waters filled with salmon. Treadwell could not reach the remote areas along the Katmai coast by motorcycle. Rather, he took a nonstop flight from Los Angeles to Anchorage and then flew for an hour by jet to Kodiak Island. There he gathered provisions before flying about eighty miles on a small floatplane, whose pilot would drop him off near the shores in Shelikof Strait.

In September 2003, three weeks before his long idyll ended tragically, Treadwell wrote to Roland Dixon, a Colorado rancher, conservationist, and financial supporter. "My transformation is complete," he insisted, "a fully accepted wild animal—brother to these bears. I run free among them—with absolute love and respect for all the animals. I am kind and viciously tough."[9] That quote captures the drama of the narrative Palovak and Treadwell tell in *Among Grizzlies* about his first eight summers in Alaska, one characterized by dramatic and moving incidents, as well as by naive anthropomorphism. His first encounter with a bear typified his future responses. "A grizzly! My mouth dropped open in astonishment as the animal and I locked gazes," Treadwell wrote, and "in that moment of mutual recognition, . . . I gazed into the face of a kindred soul, a being that was potentially lethal, but in reality was just as frightened as I was" because of "decades of adversity caused by man."[10]

Over the years a series of encounters intensified Treadwell's transformation, even as he remained fully aware of the dangers involved. He refused to protect himself by using a pepper-based bear spray or a portable electric fence. He conveyed much of what he learned about actual bears, including that they had genuine needs and wills of their own. After all, he reported on incidents where grizzlies killed people, and more ominously, he knew they were "half-ton beasts with swords for claws. . . . All of them were capable of ending my life in an instant." Back in Southern California between Alaskan summers, he learned all he could about grizzlies, especially, he claimed, the threats to their existence by poachers looking to extract gallbladders for Asian medicine, developers taking over the wilderness bears needed to survive, and hunters seeking trophies. When he recalled seeing hunters, he remarked that they saw him as "just another eco-faggot Yankee from the lower forty-eight trying to take away their god-given right to shoot wildlife for fun and profit." Reflecting his complicated and problematic engagement with masculinity, he referred to the possibility that others saw him as gay, despite that he had a series of affairs with young, physically attractive women who pursued him. In discussing his annual trips to Alaska, he tracked the ways bears had rescued him from addictions. Though he acknowledged his mixed feelings about the extensive ecotourism he witnessed, he usually pictured himself as alone with bears and without either "quaint lodges with cheerful innkeepers and cable TV" or the anger and temptations he felt in Southern California.[11] Others saw him differently, one astute observer remarked, as someone with "good looks and goofy, surfer-dude demeanor."[12]

However much Treadwell learned about how dangerous bears could be, his discussion of his life among the grizzlies was romantic. Although people vilified and feared grizzlies, they "had let me in and had taught me the truth. Bears live in perfect harmony with their environment," he asserted, even though elsewhere he told how they preyed upon salmon and in this case their diet would be humans, "while we imperfect humans hold the fate of all living things on earth. We must save them." He prided himself on developing the knowledge and skills he assumed were likely to keep him safe, even though he was aware of dangers he faced. Again and again, he talked of the intimacy of his relationships with grizzlies, at one point dreaming of their "paw steps echoing in the inner depths of my soul" and at other moments falling asleep in their beds. Contradicting the reality of what they were like, he gave the bears he encountered cutely clever names such as Booble, Mr. Chocolate, Molly, and Mr. Goodbear (named after a teddy bear from his childhood). He spoke to them reassuringly and naively with words such as "'Good day, beautiful bear! . . . I would never harm you. You look like an angel.'" He sang them "a good-night song" and "told them I loved them."[13] And once he admitted on television that, one writer noted, he engaged "in a bit of intense impersonal research with one of his girlfriends, surrounded by bears doing more or less the same thing."[14]

Even though he acknowledged that "it would be quite interesting to know what the bears think I am," he nonetheless relied on projections, misinterpretations, and fabrications as he put his own feelings onto bears.[15] One critic insisted that Treadwell "misinterpreted the smallest action by a bear as a human-like act of either trust or affection."[16] The face of a bear he called Hulk, Treadwell wrote, "became animated, and I felt a warm feeling toward me. He was sad now, but one day he would love again." At another point he concluded, "Whatever their evaluation, it is abundantly clear that most of the bears I live among either tolerate me, or enjoy my company." Before long there developed what he insisted were feelings of mutual respect. Claiming he was one with them as he captured what it meant to become increasingly feral, he announced, "'I am Grizzly. I am *Grizzly*.'" So he "decided to behave like the bears, and dropped down to all fours. I was transforming, going through a metamorphosis. I felt wild and free." Once, as he left the Grizzly Maze, he communicated with the bears by whispering to them, "I'll fight for your freedom. Then I'll return to watch over you, I promise!"[17]

Threaded throughout his stories were references to his spiritual journey marked by revelation, resurrection, rebirth, and salvation. At one point he enacted a baptism ritual. "The rush of the face-to-face encounter" with a grizzly "lifted me into a euphoric state" and emboldened him to cross a river after having overcome his fear of doing so. No longer afraid, he summoned "the power of the grizzly within me" and "dove in and vigorously paddled across, snarling and growling the whole way. I was wild and free." Soon comes another of the many transformative moments. "I begged for forgiveness from a higher power," and then he made his pledge as he spoke to himself and to the bears surrounding him. "'I will stop drinking for you and all bears. I will stop and devote my life to you.' ... Now, on a faraway beach, my battle for preservation truly began."[18] Loyal supporters and postmodernist theorists alike might agree, as one perceptive observer notes, that Treadwell "feels he's knocking on the door of interspecies kinship."[19]

It turns out that what Palovak and Treadwell wrote combined fact and fiction. To begin with, Timothy William Dexter was his given name, which at some point he changed to Treadwell, as in "tread well" and also a name from his mother's side of the family. The claim that he was born in Australia, where he grew up as an orphan, was an exotic fabrication, as was the Cockney accent that fooled so many. Left out of the brief narrative of his life are the two years Dexter spent at Bradley University on an athletic scholarship until he lost that support because of a diving injury. Some skepticism is also in order about the stories of his descent into drug addiction that ended with violent confrontations with drug dealers. Missing from the book's narrative was the time he spent in Malibu, bartending and waiting on tables—and developing connections with the rich and famous that were critical to his career. In addition, Treadwell named his bear companions grizzlies, a more evocative title that hardly captures some of the bears he encountered—brown bears (*Ursus arctos*), which lived along the coast, rather than the smaller but more aggressive *Ursus arctos horribilis*, commonly called grizzlies, found inland.[20]

Also inaccurate was his claim that he was protecting bears from poachers or that Alaskan grizzlies, tens of thousands in number, were endangered.[21] Treadwell's insistence on how dangerous poachers were confirmed his sense that he was an eco-warrior and sustained him as he garnered sympathy, celebrity status, and support for what he did. Indeed, it was Treadwell and not poachers who violated rules and laws designed to protect bears in the region, such as not hiking in the dark, keeping a safe distance from bears, storing food carefully, and not using portable generators. Again and again, he came into conflict with officials from the Alaska Department of Fish and Game, the US Geological Survey, and the National Park Service, as well as scientists, photographers, knowledgeable amateurs, operators of ecotourism companies, and ecological activists. Officials at the Katmai National Park and Preserve, along with their higher-ups, debated whether to rein in his activities or impose serious sanctions.[22] Treadwell also harassed guides who took tourists to see bears. Moreover, reading *Among Grizzlies*, one would hardly know that, what with a robust tourist trade, Treadwell was hardly alone with "his" bears because the area was thick with scientists, photographers, and especially tourists brought there by scores of commercial operations.[23]

Also absent from the book was any sense of the people and institutions supporting his work. Despite the picture of Treadwell as a lone eco-warrior in Alaska during summers, in Southern California the rest of the year his celebrity status and eco-activism fed his egotistical fantasies and enabled him to garner emotional and financial support. As a bartender in Malibu, he captivated the attention of animal rights supporters among the region's Hollywood stars, executives, and publicity agents when he told stories of his adventures and displayed photos or videos to support his dramatic and heartwarming tales. All this led to producers interested in capturing what he did on film and to financial backers who helped fund his activities, including his summer excursions. "Hugh Glass represents an odd case," writes Coleman, highlighting how different was Treadwell's narrative from earlier ones. The central figure in the story of Hugh Glass "seemed uninterested in turning his injuries into a marketable narrative . . . and his reticence stands out conspicuously amid the flood of words and images generated by shark girls, bear men, and do-it-yourself amputees." Unlike Grizzly Adams, with the help of others Treadwell relied on experts who helped launch a multimedia campaign that developed a marketable narrative capturing images of grizzlies. With the help of Palovak instead of P. T. Barnum, Treadwell paraded grizzlies not down the streets of San Francisco and Manhattan but in a book, photographs, and videos to modern-day audiences.[24]

Donors sponsored his presentations at schools, initially impromptu and eventually highly organized. Combining childlike antics, dramatic visuals, and performative power, over the years Treadwell charmed and educated ten thousand children or more. "Watching him perform in a classroom," a sympathetic observer noted, "you saw a magician who explained the mysteries of bears and their lives in such a way that children emerged glowing, as if they too were the discoverers of wild America. Hearing him talk about his bears, by name, with their bonds of affection, quirky behavior and playful antics, you felt that you were let in on great secrets that few receive today or have forgotten as wilderness has been paved over and subdivided."[25]

In so many of these activities, the animal rights activist Jewel Palovak was crucial. The nature of their relationship shifted over time—long-term friend, lover for three years, coworker—yet above all Palovak was someone who skillfully amplified Treadwell's reach. She knew how to connect him and his work with producers, editors, journalists, schoolteachers, and sponsors. And as an author more skilled and disciplined than Treadwell, she was central in the writing of *Among Grizzlies*. More focused and steady compared to the moody and shape-shifting Treadwell, she was instrumental in creating Grizzly People, a grassroots organization "made up of exactly two people: Timothy and Jewel," a knowledgeable observer quipped with some exaggeration. They garnered support from Hollywood heavy-hitters such as Leonardo DiCaprio (a star of *The Revenant* a dozen years after Treadwell's death) and Pierce Brosnan, as well from major corporations such as Konica and Patagonia—all eager to burnish their reputations as environmentally concerned citizens or enterprises. Palovak created the website www.grizzlypeople.com, where people could help finance Treadwell's expeditions by purchasing his photographs or making donations. His work also attracted the attention of at least one major donor, Roland Dixon.[26] Treadwell never used his celebrity status to enrich himself. Instead, he lived very modestly but used the money he and Palovak raised to fund his activities, especially his presentations at schools and his summer expeditions in Alaska.

Slowly and then rapidly, Treadwell's story garnered media attention.[27] The first big break came in 1994, when *People* magazine featured a brief article, "Bears Fan." Lyndon Stambler sympathetically repeated Treadwell's fabricated stories. He mentioned experts who warned that what he was doing was dangerous but remarked, "Treadwell, blissfully singing to the great bears, doesn't worry about that."[28] Media attention and the fame that followed intensified with the publication of *Among Grizzlies* in 1997. A year later on the *Tom Snyder Show*, Treadwell got his message across. As "one of them," he was "always safe, always kind." When the host asked his guest if bears ever mated while he was near them, Treadwell replied, "Well, there was a time two years ago when I had a girlfriend up there and we, well, uh, her family might be watching so I shouldn't say any more."[29] An especially poignant moment came on the *Late Show with David Letterman*. As we see Treadwell walking onto the stage, a narrator introduces him by saying, "It was as if he had become a star by his own invention." After Treadwell, visibly awkward on the set, explained how he carefully interacted with bears, Letterman responded with a question. "Is it going to happen," he asked, "that one day we read a news article about you being eaten by one of these bears?" To this people in the audience responded with laugher, and Treadwell in turn said no as audience members interrupted him with guffaws.[30] He also made careless remarks that may have charmed his followers but subjected him to criticism from experts and officials. "They're party animals," he insisted colorfully but problematically about bears.[31] Yet in the end, one claim that Palovak and Treadwell made was true: bears did on rare occasions use their mighty powers to attack and kill people. This despite the fact that in the eighty-five years of Katmai National Park and Preserve not one person has ever been seriously mauled, let alone killed.[32]

That soon changed, dramatically and tragically. In late September and early October 2003, Treadwell and Huguenard were living at a campsite on the Katmai coast, across from Kodiak Island and close to a stream near where bears fed. In fact, bears aggressively fought each other to capture salmon, upon which they feasted so they could store fat and calories before winter arrived. Because Treadwell and Huguenard were there later this year than usual, the bears encountered were ones he was not used to interacting with. And given the area's unique climate and weather conditions, they were more ravenous and aggressive than usual, subject as they were to hyperphagia, a condition that impelled them to eat more than usual to prepare for hibernation. The couple had remained in the area longer than expected because of what turned out to be a fateful argument at the Kodiak airport with an airline employee over the price of flights back to Los Angeles. This caused them to return to Katmai National Park rather than find a way to proceed to Southern California. Treadwell knew full well the danger he was courting. In journals he kept, recovered after his death, he noted the increasing number of bears fighting one another and what he called "killer bears," three in number.[33] "I'm into the historically toughest and most exciting month," he wrote California friends in early September. "Tremendous storms, and huge gatherings of extremely hungry bears, more and more darkness—intense isolation. I'm going to make it, unless one of the killer bears gets me."[34]

On October 5, when she heard Treadwell being attacked by a bear, Huguenard rushed out of their tent. A video camera, its lens capped but its microphone on, captured a horrifying six minutes and twenty-one seconds of audio until the battery ran out. "Come out here, I'm being killed out here!" he shouted. "Play dead," she advised him when she saw his bloodied body. He rose but the bear attacked again, violently shaking him. Huguenard screamed once more, "Fight back!" "Hit it with a frying pan," he cried out as the bear continued to ravage him. "Go away, leave me, run! Get out of here," he shouted to Huguenard. He must have known that his life was about to end but hoped that what he said might save his companion. She did hit the bear with a walking stick, to no avail. And then that bear and another at the site took turns gorging themselves on the bodies of Treadwell and Huguenard.

The next day, Willy Fulton, a pilot who had often airlifted Treadwell back and forth between the Kodiak airport and the water near his campsites, flew in to pick up the couple. After he landed, he walked through the alders and, sensing something was amiss, returned to the plane. Before he arrived there, he saw a "pretty nasty-looking bear that I'd seen before," he later reported. Back on the plane, he flew over the site where Treadwell and Huguenard had camped. As he looked down, he saw a bear eating "a human rib cage" and knew either Treadwell or Huguenard was the victim.[35]

What he espied set in motion the activity of park and state officials, who came to the site and discovered the horrific evidence. They located the mutilated remains of both Treadwell and Huguenard close to where they had camped, some parts of their bodies hidden in a cache that one of the bears had created to prevent other animals from feasting on their remains. Officials shot a large adult bear that Fulton insisted had killed Treadwell and that had remained near the campsite, and then they killed a second, much younger one. A necropsy of the larger bear, a male weighing a thousand pounds, revealed some bodily remains, almost certainly Treadwell's, not Huguenard's.[36]

Innocent and/or complicit? A martyr and/or a fool? Knowledgeable and/or naive? Spiritually healthy and/or mentally ill? Scientifically sophisticated and/or amateurishly wrongheaded? Protecting grizzlies and/or endangering them as he chased after celebrity fame?[37] On the one hand were skeptics and detractors. Gary Porter, a guide who took tourists to see grizzlies, commented that Treadwell "made a fundamental anthropomorphic error. Naming them and hanging around with them as long as he did, he probably forgot they were bears," just as they may have forgotten that "some of the time, he was human."[38] Equally unsparing were the assessments of professionals who saw Treadwell as engaging in reckless, illegal, hypocritical, and unscientific behavior. G. Ray Bane, who had been the superintendent of Katmai National Park and Preserve in the 1980s, remarked that Treadwell "habituates the bears to reducing their normal tendency to avoid close human contact." Though he "may well have convinced himself and others that he was a modern version of 'Grizzly Adams,'" in the end he "caused the deaths of his friend and two park bears, plus probably endangering other people and bears by his actions."[39]

On the other hand, supporters, especially some animal rights activists, saw Treadwell as a saintly visionary, a tragic figure, a bear whisperer committed to protecting wild animals, grizzlies especially. One was Joel Bennett, Treadwell's friend and a naturalist, skilled filmmaker, and longtime member of Alaska's state Board of Game. Comparing him with Jane Goodall and Dian Fossey, Bennett believed that Treadwell had a unique capacity to establish genuine relationships with the animals he studied, loved, and sought to protect. He said all this even though he also acknowledged that Treadwell was "a showman, and clearly enjoyed his notoriety."[40] Louisa Willcox, Wild Bears Director for the National Resources Defense Council and someone after whom Treadwell had named a bear, praised him as a person whose work caused people "to reflect upon wild nature afresh, deeply, personally, and with a renewed energy. . . . Hearing him talk about his bears, by name, with their bonds of affection, quirky behavior, and playful antics," she continued, "you felt that you were let in on great secrets that few receive today—or have forgotten as wilderness has been paved over and subdivided."[41]

In 2005, two years after Treadwell's death, the esteemed German director Werner Herzog—whom the film critic Peter Bradshaw called "that connoisseur of extreme figures in far-off places," someone drawn to stories of people with distinctive personalities who pursued difficult if not impossible-to-achieve dreams—offered another assessment in the documentary film *Grizzly Man*.[42] Herzog did the voiceover but appeared on-screen very rarely. "Treadwell's over-the-top persona," Bradshaw observed, "is in contrast to the cool, deadpan drone of Herzog himself, who pays tribute to his intuitive skills as a film-maker, but repudiates Treadwell's Disneyfied view of nature, seeing in it only colossal coldness and indifference."[43] Herzog relied significantly on one hundred hours of videos that Treadwell shot in the last five years of his life, sometimes from a handheld camera and at other times one placed on a tripod. This provided dramatically more extensive material on bears than did the stories of Hugh Glass or Grizzly Adams in a film that offered a vision of nature unlike Disney's.

In contrast to some of his performances on late-night television shows, here Treadwell often seemed comfortable with himself—sometimes deadly serious and at others speaking boyishly in a high-pitched voice. At several moments, Herzog made it clear how carefully Treadwell worked as a filmmaker, sometimes redoing a scene as many as fifteen times. Even when Treadwell seemed most natural and spontaneous, it is important to remember that not only did Herzog's skillful editing create an artful documentary but also, when his subject was on-screen, he was always performing as he carefully crafted the narrative of his life. More often than not, Herzog mixed fascination and skepticism as he worked to picture Treadwell accurately as someone less interested in bears than in what they meant for his complicated and tortured soul. In the footage Treadwell shot and the documentary that Herzog produced, bears had abundant agency, seeming to exhibit savvy understandings of this human. Scenes that featured Treadwell revealed a man constantly aware of the dangers he was courting, something he tried to avoid through a combination of knowledge of how bears behaved, masculine toughness expressed verbally and through firm body language, sweet-talking, and courtly expressions of affection. Again and again, we see Treadwell on camera, acknowledging that bears could kill him. Yet though he was a "kind warrior . . . a Samurai, so formidable, so fearless of death," he acknowledged, "I will not die at their claws and paws."

Several scenes capture this range of responses. As a bear he named the Grinch approaches him, Treadwell says, "Don't you do that," and then repeats it again, this time more menacingly. For whatever reason, but Treadwell assumes as a result of what he said, the Grinch saunters off, and he responds by

Timothy Treadwell with a bear in the distance, from *Grizzly Man* (2005), directed by Werner Herzog. © 2005 Lions Gate Films. Screenshot.

quietly uttering, "It's okay. I love you." In another case, he comments that if you do not meet the challenge a bear poses, "you're dead. They can bite. They can kill. They can decapitate." Not long after, he walks right up to a bear, stands inches away, and says, "It's okay. It's okay. I didn't mean to get in your way." And as it walks away, he tells the bear, "Wow. It's okay. You're the boss." "I have no idea if there's a God," Treadwell announces at one point. "But if there's a God, God would be very, very pleased with me" because God would know how much he loves and respects animals and that "I am one of them." Then, in a sequence filmed a few days before his death, Treadwell acknowledges the omnipresence of danger when he insists that though he had "found a way to survive with them," he knows he "was on the precipice of great bodily harm or even death." In the last scene he shot, he faces the camera and insists, "I live for them. I die for them."

Even as Treadwell claimed he was not "a religious guy," in one extended sequence on-screen he "invoked higher powers" to save the bears he loved and lived for. Lying in his tent as he cuddled with his teddy bear, he worried that the lack of rain imperiled the ability of bears to capture fish in streams where water was running low. So he both prayed and angrily shouted to heaven. "If there's a god," he muttered as he mentioned deities of many faiths. Then the rain poured down so heavily that his tent all but collapsed, held up only by the camera's tripod. He had wrought a "miracle," he claimed, especially since he learned that the showers only came near where he and the bears were.

What the scenes of Treadwell on film reveal was his passionate conviction that animals, bears especially, saved him from death and gave him life. He talked of a time when even though he enrolled in programs to cure his alcoholism, his behavior continued to imperil his life. When he "discovered this land of bears," he recalled, "I realized that they were in such great danger that they needed a caretaker, they needed someone to look after them." And since if he were to take on that role, he could not be drunk, he "promised the bears that if I would look over them, would they please help me be a better person." They had "become so inspirational" that he gave up drinking. Thus, because of the miraculous gift animals had given him, he could "run so wild, so free, like a child."

Although Treadwell liked to picture himself alone with animals, in fact women played crucial roles in his life—in Southern California and in Katmai. Yet the footage revealed just how troubled and complicated were his relationships with people of the opposite sex, even as he expressed a preference for same-sex relationships. In a sustained soliloquy he spoke to the camera about these issues. "I always cannot understand why girls don't wanna be with me for a long time," even as he insisted, "I'm very, very good in the—you're not supposed to say that when you're a guy." On avoiding fights with girlfriends, he wondered whether being "a patsy" was "a turnoff to girls," using a noun appropriate for females younger than the women with whom he was involved. So instead, he "always wished I was gay. Would've been a lot easier, you know? You can just 'bing, bing, bing.'" After all—he persisted in relying on highly problematic images of gay sexual practices—"gay guys have no problem. I mean, they just go to restroom and truck stops, and they perform sex. It's like so easy for 'em." Unfortunately, he continued, "Timothy Treadwell is not gay: he adored girls," even though they "need a lot more, you know, finesse and care, and I like that a bit. But when it goes bad and you're alone, it's like, you know well, you know, you can't rebound like you can if you were gay. I'm sure gay people have problems too, but not as much as one goofy straight guy named Timothy Treadwell."[44]

Throughout *Grizzly Man*, Herzog offered attempts to explain and judge Treadwell, something that revealed the contrast between what Roger Ebert called "Treadwell's loony idealism" and "Herzog's bleak worldview."[45] On-screen, the pilot Willy Fulton commented that Treadwell "saw himself as Prince Valiant, fighting the bad guys with their scheme to do harm to the bears." Sam Egli, a helicopter pilot who assisted in the postmortem cleanup, observed that while Treadwell was trying "to do well," he was nonetheless "acting like he was working with people wearing bear costumes out there instead of wild animals." He only lasted as long as he did, Egli continued, because "the bears probably thought there was something wrong with him. Like he was mentally retarded or something." Dr. Larry Van Daele, a bear biologist at Alaska's Department of Fish and Game, saw Treadwell as someone who "tended to want to become a bear" and acted like one, although, Van Daele insisted, only Treadwell understood why he did this.

Along somewhat similar lines were the comments on-screen by Sven Haakanson Jr., who spoke with the authority that came from the combination of being an Alutiiq, having a PhD in anthropology from Harvard, and serving as the director of the Alutiiq Museum in Kodiak. Trying to be a bear (as Treadwell did), he noted, was not something that Indigenous people attempted. Not only was invading their world "the ultimate of disrespecting the bear and what the bear represents," it damaged them, for "when you habituate all bears to humans, they think all humans are safe." He said avaricious tourists stole bear parts from the Alutiiq Museum's exhibit, something he deemed parallel to Treadwell's exploitative boundary crossing. So when Haakanson looked at the situation from the perspective of his own culture, he knew "Treadwell crossed a boundary that we have lived with for 7,000 years. It's an unspoken boundary, an unknown boundary." And as we watch Herzog show footage of Treadwell crossing that boundary, we listen as Haakanson observes that "when we know we've crossed it, we pay the price."[46]

It was Herzog who offered the most probing and extensive exploration of what drove Treadwell, ultimately, to his cruel fate. As he shows the viewer bears running, simultaneously graceful and ferocious, Herzog helps us realize that Treadwell's footage reveals not so much about wild nature as it does "an insight into ourselves, our nature. And that, for me, beyond his mission, gives meaning to his life and to his death." In an extensive section, three-quarters of the way through the documentary, Herzog explored how Treadwell "became increasingly paranoid" about his enemies—not only the poachers (about whom there was so little evidence) but also those targets of his anger that were more present. In the filmmaker's words, Treadwell saw intruders as "an encroaching threat on what he considered his Eden." For example, Herzog showed footage of a time when what stoked Treadwell's ire was a guide who had brought tourists to the park's shore and then threw rocks at Freckles and Quincy in an attempt to dramatize danger and scare them off. The film also reveals that the major objects of Treadwell's fury were federal and state officials. Angrier and angrier at restrictions, Treadwell insisted it was he, and not representatives of officialdom, who truly protected bears. In extensive footage, Treadwell used vituperative swearing to dramatize his oppositional stance. "As far as this fucking government is concerned," he said, as he looked into the camera and at times stepped aside to make clear he was performing for an audience, "Fuck you, motherfucking park service."

Although Herzog admired his subject's filmmaking skills for producing footage the "studios, with their union crews, can never dream of," he deployed his own skills as a documentarian to convey how he understood his subject. Herzog's was an evaluation that implicitly stood in opposition to those who might view Treadwell sympathetically, as someone who heroically but tragically blurred the distinction between humans and animals. Herzog assumed "there must have been an urge to escape the safety of his protected environment," with Treadwell often writing in his diaries "of the human world as something foreign. He made a clear distinction," Herzog noted, "between the bears and the people's world which moved further and further into the distance. Wild, primordial nature was where he felt truly at home." What Treadwell filmed revealed both "human ecstasy" and "darkest inner turmoil, as if there was a desire in him to leave the confinements of his humanness and bond with the bears[.] Treadwell reached out, seeking a primordial encounter. But in doing so, he crossed an invisible borderline."

While Treadwell sought this encounter with bears, Herzog said, he courted danger. "Treadwell had a natural tendency toward chaos," with Amie Huguenard's own writing revealing how she saw her partner as "hell bent on disaster." As viewers see wild glacial formations, Herzog commented that "this landscape of turmoil is a metaphor of his soul." His subject offered a "sentimentalized view that everything out there was good," with the universe in "balance and harmony." In contrast, the documentarian made it clear how he differed from Treadwell, who "seemed to ignore the fact that in nature there are predators." For Herzog "the common denominator of the universe is not harmony, but chaos, hostility and murder." Unlike Treadwell, Herzog discovered "no kinship, no understanding, no mercy. I see only the overwhelming indifference of nature. To me, there is no such thing as a secret world of the bears," even though to Treadwell a bear could be "a friend, a savior." To drive home his point about how Treadwell's naivete caused him to overlook or minimize evidence that contradicted his worldview, Herzog showed footage of Treadwell looking at the body of a baby wolf that other wolves had killed and mentioning that adult male bears murdered their pups so they could have "fornication" with females. In the end, Herzog concluded, what Treadwell really opposed was "the people's world and civilization. . . . His rage is almost incandescent, artistic. . . . He's fighting civilization itself. It is the same civilization that cast Thoreau out of Walden and John Muir into the wild." In his diary Treadwell had written, "How much I hate the people's world."

Herzog's film ends with a shot of Willy Fulton, formerly a rodeo rider, flying his plane over Katmai National Park and Preserve as he sings a version of Bob McDill's "Coyotes." The lyrics emphasize how much of the West has disappeared—longhorns, Comanches, Geronimo, and outlaws including the nineteenth century's Sam Bass. "Treadwell is gone," Fulton adds. "He cursed the automobile" because he knew "this new world of asphalt and steel" was no place for a man like himself. Then, as the credits begin to roll, we see Treadwell walking off into distance with two bears as Fulton remarks, "He'd look off into the distance at something that only he could see. He'd say all's that left now are the old days. Damned old coyotes and me."[47] Implicit in this final sequence is that Treadwell loved this wild world because he was rebelling against "civilization," much more, it should be noted, than Grizzly Adams ever pretended to be doing.

I end these stories of emotionally charged, often violent and erotic encounters between Treadwell and grizzlies with Marian Engel's *Bear: A Novel* (1976). Her narrative insists on the power of a cross-species relationship that lacked the tragic ending of Treadwell's tale and gives a bear tremendous emotional power and autonomy. This tale is unusual because while men have authored most of the best-known narratives, a woman wrote this one—and she did so in an erotic story and one driven not, as was true for Treadwell, by troubled masculinity but by feminist commitments. Engel tells the story of a librarian from Toronto. *Mousy* is the word that comes to my mind at the description of this shy and quiet woman, who Engel says "lived like a mole."[48] During a summer, feeling as "if life in general had a grudge against her," she travels to an estate on a remote island in northern Ontario to inventory the book collection of the late Colonel Jocelyn Cary for the Historical Institute where she works.[49] And there she encounters a bear who wanders freely around the late colonel's property. The book jacket highlights key features of this short novel, featuring a bear calmly caressing a bare-breasted, enraptured woman with a blurb underscoring this as a "shocking, provocative novel with evocation of 'the forbidden, the unthinkable, the hardly imaginable.'"

Bear earned Engel the prestigious Governor General's Award for English-language fiction in 1976, an honor bestowed on Mordecai Richler five years before and Margaret Atwood three years after. Engel's novel revealed her interest in Canadian First Nations. She drew on the Indigenous story of *The Bear Princess*, and early on within the novel Lucy Leroy, a Cree woman, helps the main character understand how to approach the bear. Over time, *Bear* achieved cult status in North America, perhaps in line with what a blurb promised on the cover of one paperback edition: "The shocking, erotic novel of a woman in love."[50] Scholars, Canadian literary ones especially, have lavished praise on

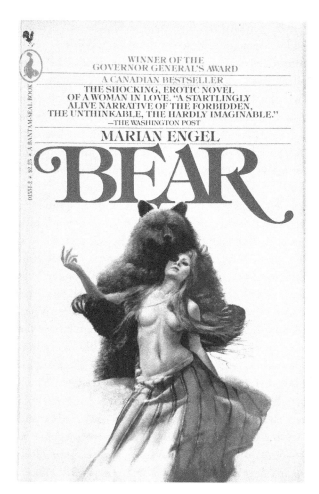

Cover of Marian Engel's *Bear: A Novel* (1976).

Bear. They have located it as a text in a range of traditions, including feminism, Canadian pastoralism and nationalism, fantasy, Gothic romance, soft-core pornography, and romantic quests in the natural wilderness seeking rebirths.[51] They might also have noted how common across cultures and time are stories of romantic and even sexual relationships between bears and women.

Engel offers the dramatic story of a woman in her late twenties named Lou who develops an erotic, sexual, and spiritual relationship with a bear, a relationship also marked by violence against her. "Not a toy bear, not a Pooh bear, not an airlines koala bear. A real bear," Lou remarks to herself when she first sees him, staring at her while he stands upright in a doorway—even as we remain unsure what species of bear he is. Throughout there are hints of feminism, what with references to Aphra Behn, Jane Austen, and Mary Shelley, as well as mention of a "letter from a feminist friend inquiring why she was not doing research on a female pioneer for International Women's Year." Only once does she mention the name she gives the bear—Trelawny, after Edward John Trelawny, who had written Shelley's biography. Going through the colonel's collection, Lou discovers studies of bears, with Engel skillfully weaving together snippets from what he left behind with Lou's encounters with nature, not only the bear but also around on the island. "In the lore of *Irelande*, she read later (safe inside and the bear chained up, the windows closed against insects, insulated)," Lou knew that a bear could be a god.[52]

She soon realizes that the bear is part of the household, and before long she has many friendly, even affectionate encounters with him. Two-thirds into the novel, such reports intensify. We read that "he licked her nipples stiff and scoured her navel. With little nickerings she moved him south," Engel continues. "She swung her hips and made it easy for him." The bear's tongue "was capable of lengthening itself like an eel" and found all her secret places. "And like no human being she had ever known it persevered in her pleasure. When she came, she whimpered, and the bear licked away her tears." Sometimes the bear is expressive yet at other times inattentive to Lou's needs. Although at moments the bear satisfies her sexually, Engel notes that what Lou "disliked in men was not their eroticism, but their assumption that women had none. Which left women with nothing to be but housemaids." The narrative continues, with scenes of erotic encounters alternating with descriptions of Lou's reading and cataloging. The bear comes to visit her and put his tongue "up into her cunt. A note fell out of the book: *The offspring of a woman,*" Engel reports, "*and a bear is a hero with the strength of a bear and the cleverness of a man.—Old Finnish legend*. She cried with joy."[53]

Near the novel's end, the encounters turn violent, with the erotic becoming spiritual as well. "'Tear my skin with your clattering claws,'" Lou implores the bear at one point. "'I am frail. It is simple for you. Claw out my heart, a grub under a stump. Tear off my head, my bear.'" Soon we read that after swimming with the bear, "she mounted him. Nothing happened. He could not penetrate her and she could not get him in," and he was quite unmoved. At the end of the summer and of the book, as Lou prepared to leave the island, there appears a violently erotic culmination. She looks down and sees that "slowly, magestically his great cock was rising," unlike a man's she notes, "it was red, pointed, and impressive." So Lou disrobed "and went down on all fours in front of him, in the animal posture." The bear, perhaps reminding Lou of the limits of the permissible and of his own nature, "reached out one great paw and ripped off the skin of her back" while he lost his erection. She shoos the bear away and falls "shaking into bed."[54]

The next morning, Lou thinks about what happened the night before, as Engel makes clear that however the bear acted, Lou was free to understand what he did and their relationship as she pleases. "He ripped me, she thought. That's what I was after, wasn't it, decadent city tart?" She looks in the mirror and "seemed to have the body of a much younger woman," noticing on her back that "one long, red, congealing wound marked her from shoulder to buttock. I shall keep that, she thought. And it is not the mark of Cain." Sitting beside the bear, she muses that "last night she had been afraid that the smell of blood on her would cause him to wound her further, but today he was something else: lover, God or friend. Dog too for when she put her hand out, he licked and nuzzled it." That night, as they lay together, "she felt pain, but it was a dear, sweet pain that belonged not to mental suffering, but to the earth." After Lou leaves the island and begins the drive home, in the book's final sentence, Engel notes, "It was a brilliant night, all star-shine, and overhead the Great Bear and his thirty-seven thousand virgins kept her company." The novel's last words bring us back to what Engel uses as its epigraph. "Facts become art through love," Kenneth Clark had written in *Landscape Into Art* (1949), "which unifies them, and lifts them to a higher plane of reality; in landscape, this all-embracing love is expressed by light."[55]

In contrast with texts that chart how vicious bears can be, including a story of a man who seeks recovery in the Alaskan wilderness, here is a feminist tale. Set in a more domestic place, a bear's violence, as well as his sexual encounter with a woman, is spiritually transformative. *Bear: A Novel* is an early example of what would become prominent in the ensuing decades—probing reconsiderations of emotionally positive relationships between humans and animals. More centrally, if the novel points forward, Engel drew inspiration from feminism that began to take hold in the 1960s. This is a tale about how women (clearly Engel and perhaps Lou fictionally) draw inspiration from female authors who have come before them. Closer to the surface is Lou's sexual awakening, not at the hands of a man but at the body parts of a male bear. Above all, understood in the context of the stories of Hugh Glass, Grizzly Adams, and Timothy Treadwell, *Bear* combines the violence of bears with a woman's rebirth. Treadwell did not survive such an encounter, but a fictional Lou did. A flight of fictional fantasy, but hardly more so than most of the others that focus on how people experienced bears. With Engel's novel, we encounter a counter to the stories of Glass, Adams, and Treadwell. Engel both offers erotically reciprocal relationships and allows the bear to speak, so to speak, as we see when the narrative reveals that it has a personality and will of its own. Both Treadwell's story and Engel's highlight the relationships between violence and eroticism—in the former case violence a bear inflicts on a man who had earlier relied on bears for his own salvation and projected onto them a range of emotions, including erotic ones. With Engel's story, a bear's violence gives a woman intensely erotic pleasures as well as physical pain.

Written over almost two centuries, these stories of celebrity bears—of or by Hugh Glass, Grizzly Adams, Timothy Treadwell, and Marian Engel—offer varied takes on bears themselves and on relationships between them and humans. Bears make appearances as violent and loving, carnal and spiritual. People anthropomorphize, terrorize, tame, and love them. They project onto them a wide variety of human feelings, in some cases ascribing agency, intelligence, and rich emotional lives to them. With Hugh Glass a bear makes few appearances in the original story, even though it sets in motion complicated narratives, the interpretations of which vary greatly over time, mixing dangerous attacks and transcendent inspiration. In the original story, commercial exploitation appears at the hands of trappers but only much later by media in search of revenues, most notably in Hollywood's *The Revenant*. Grizzly Adams not only befriends and sleeps with bears but more prominently hunted, captured, violently tamed, and extensively displayed them for profit out west and back east.

The story of Timothy Treadwell has no clear line between affection, danger, and commerce. Treadwell goes further than Adams in developing close relationships, in exploring what reciprocity means, and in giving them voice, personalities, and characteristics not unlike those of humans. In this case, cross-species relationships exist mostly through Treadwell's imagination. Treadwell and Herzog capture bears on film, while near the story's conclusion bears violently dominate humans. But in the end, far more dramatically and lethally than was true with Grizzly Adams, the results are tragic as Treadwell fails to recognize the limits of his understanding of bears and of his power to court them. From Glass to Adams to Treadwell to Engel, there is clear progression toward anthropomorphism and cross-species relationships. Yet there is also more violence in these two stories than with Glass or Adams, deadly in one case and sexualized in the other. Engel's narrative, which conveys the most intense and complicated relationships between a human and a bear, also grants the bear tremendous agency.

All of this is to say that these stories offer no simple linear historical arc. Moreover, although they emphasize how dangerous and even lethal attacks by bears can be, in some versions they also present visions of affection and transcendence. Ironically, true in all cases but especially so with Treadwell, bears can be both deadly and inspiring. Hugh Glass, and not the bear who attacked him, was the celebrity. With stories connected to Grizzly Adams, Timothy Treadwell, and Marian Engel, there is more balance between the level of fame human and animal subjects achieved. To be sure, Treadwell's Booble, Mr. Chocolate, Molly, and Mr. Goodbear are imaginatively fictious. Engel's Trelawny is known only to literary cognoscente. Lady Washington, Ben Franklin, and Frémont are better known as historical figures than as bears that Adams named. Only his Samson, who appears on the California flag, achieved appreciable notoriety. We do not know the names of the bears who killed Treadwell and Huguenard. Maybe some bears are too dangerous to be celebrities.

Coda

Few social movements have deployed symbolic animals to promote their causes. To be sure, there is the one representing the Black Panther Party. Yet more generally in the 1960s and 1970s, most protesting groups did not rely on the evocative power of an animal to advance their causes. In contrast, environmentalists deploy images of polar bears in ways that turned them into evocatively useful celebrities to mobilize the support of *Homo sapiens* for *Ursus maritimus*. The German sociologist Dorothea Born has charted how this iconography developed. Drawing on depictions of polar bears in *National Geographic*, she explored the processes by which "a polar bear, adrift on a melting ice floe, a polar bear desperately clutching to some blocks of ice, or a polar bear expressing emotions of sadness or distress" came to be linked with the dangers of climate change. She revealed how the image of polar bears began to shift from dangerously threatening to helplessly threatened, a change that intensified beginning in the 1980s. Then, for a dozen years beginning in 1992, anthropomorphized polar bears became "increasingly linked to climate change although the issue itself" was yet to be "foregrounded." Starting in 2004, polar bears' connection to climate change was "presented as an uncontested fact," with increasing attention given "to the consequences that warmer temperatures and the earlier breakup of ice have for polar bears." Now, it was not just those bears that were endangered but the ecosystem they inhabited as well. "Their

Polar bear holding bagged chunks of ice available from a commercial ice machine but not from nature. Illustration by John Cuneo.

misery and sorrow," Born noted, "function as a stand-in for humanity's problems and the drifting ice floe becomes a metaphor for earth's vulnerability."[1]

Many Inuit who live in the Arctic region see the threats to polar bears very differently, in ways that underscore the problematic cultural biases of environmentalists. Nowhere is this clearer than in the 2010 documentary *Qapirangajuq: Inuit Knowledge and Climate Change* produced by Ian Mauro and an Inuit named Zacharias Kunuk. Relying on interviews of Inuit people, the footage reveals that Native Americans, unlike environmentalists, worry about polar bears proliferating. Focusing on local conditions, they view bears' increasing numbers and their movement from ice to Native villages as adversely impacting inhabitants' lives. To them, threats to their way of life come from outsiders, especially wildlife biologists they identify as "Southerners," who patronizingly look down on Native peoples. As Ursula K. Heise of UCLA's Institute of Environment and Sustainability notes in her probing discussion of the film, what is involved in the contrasting meanings of the lives of polar bears is a "struggle over cultural and political sovereignty." For Inuit peoples, "the real species that is everywhere, out of place, and dangerously invasive is conservationists rather than polar bears." She juxtaposes this view with that of Euro-Americans, who see danger not from a local perspective but from a "transcendently planetary" one.[2]

In striking contrast, for most environmentalists endangered polar bears are symbolically resonant as symbols of how global warming is affecting the Arctic as much as any region on the planet. Sea ice is crucial to the lives of actual polar bears because it provides the surfaces on which they travel as they hunt for seals, the main component of their diet. It is possible that eventually there will be relatively little sea ice in the region. In mid-2020, Henry Fountain, a reporter for the *New York Times* who specializes in the science of climate change, noted that unless reversed, such changes would "force the animals onto land and away from their food supplies for longer periods, . . . Prolonged fasting, and reduced nursing of cubs by mothers, would lead to rapid declines in reproduction and survival." In February 2024, a *New York Times* headline warned that "Videos Show Polar Bears Struggling Not to Starve."[3] Pictures of polar bears as endangered remain a powerful force in raising money, consciousness, and support for action.

The examples of their deployment are abundant. The first English-language edition of *Little Polar Bear* by the Dutch author Hans de Beer (not da Bear) appeared in 1987 and before long became the basis for a series of multimedia expressions. In 1993 Coca-Cola launched its Northern Lights campaign, widely circulated in many media and featuring an animated version of the animals drinking Cokes as they watch the aurora borealis. Nineteen years later, in response to activists who cast skeptical eyes on the corporation's commitment to protecting the environment, Coca-Cola promised to donate $2,000,000 a year for the next five years to the World Wildlife Fund, a small portion of either its profits or its advertising budget.[4] Al Gore's film *An Inconvenient Truth*, released on May 24, 2006, pictured two polar bears, not unlike what this illustration conveys, struggling to survive as carbon-burning-induced global warming melted the Arctic ice. A few weeks earlier *Time* magazine's special report on global warming featured another example of a lonely representative of the species struggling to survive as sea ice disappeared. The issue's cover revealed a polar bear along with the caption "Be Worried, Be **Very** Worried." A year later the cover of *Vanity Fair* tripled down by displaying three celebrities in a way that underscored the vulnerability of polar bears: a photograph by Annie Leibovitz of Leonardo DiCaprio, who worried about the Berlin Zoo's polar bear, Knut. In 2010 Nissan playfully deployed a famous polar bear in an ad for its all-electric car Leaf.[5] In late 2013 Greenpeace launched a campaign using "a giant polar bear—Aurora," leading "a procession to the doors of Shell's London HQ to protest about plans to drill for oil in the Arctic."[6]

Two polar bears on melting ice, a diminishing resource so vital to their survival. FloridaStock/Shutterstock.

A 2013 Greenpeace protest highlighting how corporations drilling for oil imperil the environment. Chris Harvey/Shutterstock.

More recently, warning that "as their ice habitat shrinks, skinnier and hungrier bears face a grave challenge to their survival," the World Wildlife Fund offers "Symbolic Adoptions" of polar bears for $60, including a "formal adoption certificate" and a letter addressed to the donor.[7] Polar Bears International, founded in 1994, relies on familiar imagery of one polar bear affectionately nuzzling another to support International Polar Bear Day. Launched in 2011, the holiday now takes place every year in late February at a time when cubs are sleeping safely with their mothers.

"Why do we have the polar bears in our masthead?" asks the website of the environmental organization A Warmer Planet. "Of course they are fuzzy and cute," its copywriter explains while doubling down on the power of representations, "but they are also one of the most illustrative symbols of the effects of climate change on wildlife as they require an environment that is being rapidly changed by a warming climate." What followed was a defense of the use of the image. "With their dependence upon the vanishing sea ice, and seals, the only hope for survival of polar bears as a species is a sudden reversal of Arctic warming, which is highly improbable, or zoos." Acknowledging that "literally thousands of other species also have specialized habitat and nutritional requirements and are also threatened with extinction due to climate change," it nonetheless insisted "the polar bear is indeed an appropriate symbol of the effect of climate change upon the wildlife of our planet."[8] In so many ways such images support campaigns to slow or reverse the impact of global warming, hunting, poaching, toxic waste, suburban development, tourism, and extraction of natural resources.[9]

Advocacy groups and governmental organizations have mounted campaigns to combat the adverse effects of climate change, including those that endanger polar bears. The year 1948 saw the establishment of the International Union for Conservation of Nature (IUCN). In 1965, within it there developed the Polar Bear Specialist Group (PBSG) that brought together scientists committed to carrying out the research in support of the protection of polar bears. This in turn led in 1973 to the Agreement on Conservation of Polar Bears, by which all nations where the species lived—Norway, Denmark, Canada, the United States, and what was then the Soviet Union—committed themselves to intensify and coordinate research and protection. In the United States, a key moment came in 2008 when the Department of the Interior listed polar bears as threatened under the terms of the 1973 Endangered Species Act. This resulted from the efforts of the Center for Biological Diversity, Greenpeace International, and the National Resources Defense Council. Together they had won a victory in court by successfully challenging the efforts of the administration of President George W. Bush to stop dragging its feet.[10] *Scientific American*'s headline announcing the Department of the Interior's decision claimed, "U.S. Protects Polar Bears Under Endangered Species Act."

Yet in fact the practical consequences of the victory hardly matched the headline's promise. The 1973 act, as the author of the story underneath made clear, "will not be used as a tool for trying to regulate the greenhouse gas emissions blamed for creating climate change." Powerful were the forces arrayed against scientific evidence of the diminution of sea ice in the Arctic region, the intensifying activities of advocacy groups, and the recent deployment of polar bear iconography. After all, the article noted the lack of protection the government's decision offered against hunters (whom it identified as Natives but not outsiders) and the reluctance to interfere with the activity of industry in the region, especially by energy corporations. In addition, a representative of the free-market Cato Institute, along with politically powerful climate deniers, expressed skepticism about the scientific data on climate change. "What has become clear through this heavily litigated process," insisted the Republican senator from Oklahoma, James Inhofe, "is that listing the polar bear as a threatened species is not about protecting the polar bear but rather advancing a particular political agenda." As he had claimed earlier, global warming was "the greatest hoax ever perpetrated on the American people."[11]

In the 1880s Franz Boas viewed the relationships between humans and polar bears in two opposing ways—we were either slaughtering them or developing mutual cross-species, emotionally positive, and powerful relationships. The deployment of polar bears in the fight against global warming presents a third, as evocative and iconic political weapons in the fight to protect polar bears and the world we and they inhabit. On screens and magazine covers as well as in advertisements, they are often sad and alone. Humans rarely appear with them, even though out of sight they have negatively impacted polar bears' lives. They are no longer as emotionally complex as many of the examples that appeared before them in stories of dangerous bears, children's literature, and video games. No longer emotionally labile, there polar bears have lost their majesty and their power to threaten. If the long history of how white, mostly male North Americans understand famous bears tracks a shift from human domination to positive cross-species engagement, here they are not dangerous to us but we are to them. Perhaps the legend Boas conveyed, about the loving and reciprocal relationship between a human mother and a polar bear cub, can also serve as the basis for a more modern lesson about our obligation to protect earth and its inhabitants, including very real polar bears, albeit ones more frequently viewed in representations in modern media unknown to Boas. In the early twenty-first century, without elevating any particular one to symbolic fame, the deployment of real and representational polar bears underscores their power as lovable but endangered celebrities.

Yet powerful forces are arrayed against any hopeful prospect that the deployment of the iconography of threatened polar bears aspires to bring about. On Baffin Island and elsewhere, the threats faced by polar bears and the future of the earth they represent are many. Among them are hunting, poaching, toxic wastes, tourism, and extraction of natural resources, including oil and precious metals. Pictures of threatened polar bears connect us with the histories of conservation and the environment. They remind us of the ways capitalism and culture threaten real bears with extinction and more generally predict a bleak future for humanity in the Anthropocene. Juxtaposed against such a possible and dire prospect is playfully hopeful evidence of the representational relationships between bears and humans in the early twenty-first century available in so many forms, including children's literature, collegiate mascots, and nature films. Our future, and theirs, hangs in the balance.

Acknowledgments

Bears here, there, and everywhere, to be sure. And sometimes also here, there, and everywhere were so many human animals who helped in so many ways.

First were those who read what I wrote and helped me clarify and improve what I was saying. Among those who read specific chapters were Peter Alagona, Elizabeth Hanson, Lucas Hilderbrand, Helen L. Horowitz, Sarah Horowitz, Allison Isenberg, Herb Lewis, Julia Mickenberg, Char Miller, Abby Minor, Christen Mucher, Susan Nance, Kim Probolus, Beth Prosnitz, Robert Righter, Carol Rigolot, Nigel Rothfels, Stacey Schmeidel, David Seitz, Carl Smith, Jane Smith, Judy Smith, and Sherry Smith. In addition, and beyond what anyone can possibility expect, Gary S. Cross, Janet M. Davis, and Lynn Dumenil responded to early versions of the entire manuscript with immensely useful suggestions. Though in the end he did not represent me, Peter Bernstein played many roles with this project as he deployed his ample skills as an editor and literary agent.

The Scholars Seminar at the Huntington Library in San Marino, California, has long played a life-sustaining role for me as a citizen and scholar. I am grateful to Sandy Brooke Gordon and Anne Blecksmith for the roles they play at the Huntington, including helping arrange meetings of the seminar. In March 2024 more than three dozen of the seminar's members responded usefully and positively when I gave a talk on America's celebrity bears. So many of its members play such varied roles in my life, but I want to name some of them for the importance of their friendships that have so enriched my life—Hal Baron, Dena Goodman, David Gordon, Kathy Kobayashi, Carol Rigolot, a pack of Smiths (Carl, Jane, Pat, and Sherry), Sharon Strom, and of course the love of my life, Helen L. Horowitz.

Many people in addition to those already mentioned—friends I have known for eons or more recently found ones, as well as knowledgeable scholars—urged me on with evocations of obscure or well-known bears and references to scholarly sources and cheered me on with curiosity and hoorays. Among them are Bob Abzug, Arthur Barsky, Brigitte Buettner, Jon Coleman, Fred Crews, Kathy Dalton, Florrie Darwin, Micaela de Leonardo, John Demos, Susan Faludi, Cori Field, Dan Flores, Michael Gorra, Tina L. Hanlon, Vange Heiliger, Daniel Immerwhar, Nick Jans, Howard Landau, Tom Laqueur, Trent MacNamara, Pam Mendelsohn, Brett Mizelle, Monroe Price, Andy Robichaud, Tony Rotundo, Marni Sandweiss, Stacey Schmeidel, Amanda Seligman, Lewis Siegelbaum, Mark Simpson-Voss, Ted Stebbins, Marianna Szczygielska, Donna Varga, Kari Weil, Richard White, Steve Whitfield, Shari Wilcox, Les Wright, and members of the Children's Literature group on Facebook. As she has done before, Suzie Tibor helped me secure images and copyright for many of the illustrations that enhance the book's appeal.

There is no way this book would have been possible without the work of librarians and the collections they curate. At Smith College, the Resource Sharing Librarian Andy Kretschmar located otherwise difficult-to-access sources. Absolutely essential to my work are the librarians and collections of the Harvard College Library; the Pasadena, California, Public Library; and the Cambridge, Massachusetts, Public Library, which included books from the regional Minuteman Library Network.

The road from preliminary ideas to early chapters, to proposal, and then to publication was long and bumpy—due in part, I assume, to upheavals in the world of publishing and the difficulty many editors had in placing my work in familiar and reassuring categories. After all, there seems to be a robust market for books about animals in the wild but not about many fictional ones. In some cases, editors, backed up by skeptical readings, rejected what I offered or wanted a very different book. Two editors—David Congdon at University Press of Kansas and Linda Henry Kalof at Michigan State University Press—supported by positive and helpful readings, provided a way forward that I very much regretted not being able to take. Eventually my bears came out of hibernation and found a home at Duke University Press. I am grateful to the senior executive editor Ken Wissoker, who early on believed in the importance of what I was doing and then at various points provided guidance and encouragement. Assistant editor Ryan Kendall at Duke University Press deployed her extraordinary skill, understanding, and insights as she helped me transform a manuscript into a book. In addition to reader reports from other presses that were to varying degrees useful, Ken and Ryan secured and interpreted two terrific readings. The anonymous one from a scholar known as Reader #1 was transformatively critical and helpful. Among those who turned the manuscript into a book are copy editor Barbie Halaby and project editor Lisa Lawley.

Notes

PREFACE. POLAR BEARS, FRANZ BOAS, AND ME

1. I am hardly the only person who because of COVID-19 was drawn to bears, as Moses, "Bears Are Having a Moment," reveals. Throughout the book, I offer only a sampling of the rich writing that has informed what I have written.

2. For commercially oriented discussions of these fetishes, see "Zuni Fetish Meanings," *Pueblo Direct*, accessed November 5, 2024, https://www.pueblodirect.com/pages/zuni-fetish-meanings; and "Zuni Fetish Animal Meanings," *Sunshine Studios*, accessed November 5, 2024, https://sunshinestudio.com/pages/zuni-fetishes-animal-meanings.

3. For an assessment of the impact of the trade in Inuit art on this community, see Porter, "Drawn from Poverty."

4. For a celebration of the role of beloved stuffed animals in the lives of adults, see Genecov, "Letter of Recommendation."

5. King, *Gods of the Upper Air*, 29.

6. Boas, *Central Eskimo*, 510, 639. On the relationships between polar bears and the Inuit, see Brunner, *Bears*, 161–69. To learn more about the species, see Fee, *Polar Bear*.

7. "Best of the Western Arctic: Canada and Greenland," *Adventure Life*, accessed November 5, 2024, https://www.adventure-life.com/arctic/cruises/13543/best-of-the-western-arctic-canada-and-greenland#overview.

8. "Why Baffin Island Is Polar Bear Central," Arctic Kingdom, July 15, 2021, https://resources.arctickingdom.com/why-baffin-island-is-polar-bear-central/.

9. Derocher, *Polar Bears*, 1 and 5.

10. McCarthy, "Hank the Tank."

1. Among the books that explore the world of bears generally are Brunner, *Bears*; Bieder, *Bear*; Pastoureau, *Bear*; Grimm, *Bear and Human*; Storl, *Bear*; and Dickie, *8 Bears*.

2. Throughout this book, I contrast humans and animals rather than using the terms common in the field of animal studies—human/nonhuman; for a probing discussion of what is involved in such choices, see Fudge, *Animal*, 158–76. Unfortunately, there are not sufficient studies of what audiences—those who read children's books, watch television and films, go to zoos and theme parks—take away from their engagement with bears. I explore this issue of the relationships between production and consumption of culture in Horowitz, *Consuming Pleasures*.

3. "Lots of Roosevelt Bears."

4. On a different trajectory, see Ritvo, *Animal Estate*, 2–3; Berger, "Why Look"; Robichaud, *Animal City*, 8; Varga, "Babes." Wasik and Murphy, *Our Kindred Creatures*, offers a narrative on a different topic and one in which bears are minor characters.

5. Alagona, *Accidental Ecosystem*, 80 and 96. For a less optimistic assessment, see Dax, *Grizzly West*. For the study of the impact of popular media representations, see Kellert, "Public Attitudes."

6. Douglas and McDonnell, *Celebrity*, 2 and 53; see also especially 1–64, 88–89, and 259–67. See also Marcus, *Drama*.

7. Among discussions of bears' prominence and resemblance to humans are Shepard and Sanders, *Sacred Paw*, xi and 56; Jans, *Grizzly Maze*, 192 and 204; Shepard, *Others*, 167; Brunner, *Bears*, 1 and 235; and Lepore, "Bear Season."

8. Mooallem, *Wild Ones*, 67.

9. Simpson, *Dominion*, explores the contrasting ways we understand bears. In *Wild New World*, Flores considers the history of bears, grizzlies especially, on 191–96, 306–7, and 364–65. Rothfels, *Elephant Trail*, focuses on the history of another species, suggesting how they can evoke contradictory emotions, in this case as both monstrous and miraculous beings. Flores, *Coyote America*, offers some discussion of popular expressions after 1950 but focuses principally on the writings of scientists, conservationists, and those interested in public policy. For one of many examples of an author capturing a series of opposing responses to animals, see Joy, *Why*.

10. On this point more generally, see Ritvo, "Calling the Wild," 105–6.

11. It turns out that even grizzlies are vegetarians: Garcia, "California's Grizzlies."

12. "Bear Intelligence," *Nature*, June 10, 2008, PBS, https://www.pbs.org/wnet/nature /arctic-bears-bear-intelligence/779/. For discussion of issues involved in understanding the intelligence of animals, see Smith and Mitchell, *Experiencing Animal Minds*. On animals as ethical beings, albeit with only one brief reference to bears, see Crane, *Beastly Morality*. In *Not So Different*, Lents explores similarities between humans and animals on issues such as morality, sex and love, grief, fear, and communication.

13. Brunner, *Bears*, 139; see also 131, 132, and 135. PBS has aired a number of shows that explore the abilities and skills of animals: *The Animal Mind* generally and *Bears* specifically emphasize their curiosity, cunning, adaptability, and ability to learn.

14. Herrero, *Bear Attacks*, 8 and 30. See also Jessica Cockroft, "Bear Attack Statistics," *BearVault*, August 25, 2023, updated November 14, 2024, https://bearvault.com/bear -attack-statistics/.

15. The relevant literature is vast, and in addition to works cited elsewhere among the places to begin are Bekoff, *Emotional Lives*; Tawada, *Memoirs*; Singer, *Animal Liberations*; Desmond, *Displaying Death*; Kalof, *Looking at Animals*; Nance, *Historical Animal*; Haraway, *Haraway Reader*; Wolfe, *Animal Rites*; Wolfe, *Posthumanism*; Anderson, *Creatures of Empire*; Daston and Mitman, *Thinking*; and Parkinson, *Animals*. Gruen, *Critical Terms*, provides a useful introduction to key terms in the field. Godfrey-Smith, "Visible and Invisible," focuses on some recent findings. For a discussion of current works in the field of animal welfare, see Sanneh, "Beastly Matters." Among the historians who have followed the call to understand the relationships between human and nonhuman animals in more reciprocal ways are Flores, *Wild New World*; Fudge, *Quick Cattle*; Ritvo, *Noble Cows*; and Anderson, *Creatures of Empire*. Frans de Waal has long been among the most important scholars whose work has focused on the emotional and cognitive capacities of nonhuman animals: *Mama's Last Hug* and *Are We Smart Enough*. Rose, *In the Hearts*, traces this history up to the end of the twentieth century.

16. Demuth, "Labors of Love," 272–73nn3–4, points to many of the most recent studies in animal studies, and her *Floating Coast* reveals what it means to recast the history of the relationships between humans and animals within an environmental framework shaped by competition between capitalism and communism. Weil, *Thinking Animals*, provides a probing discussion of key issues confronting anyone interested in taking seriously what it means to think and write about the relationships between human and nonhuman animals. Davis, *Gospel of Kindness*, explores the relationships between concern for the welfare of humans and that of animals. Nance, *Entertaining Elephants*, provides an exemplary approach of how to combine the scientific and the cultural.

17. Reader #1, Duke University Press. For better or worse, I finished my research before I began to use ChatGPT. However, in March 2025 it answered my inquiry "Why are American bears celebrities?" with this:

> American bears often become celebrities because of their larger-than-life presence in popular culture, as well as real-world stories that capture the public's imagination. Here are a few reasons why they achieve celebrity status:
>
> 1. Social Media Attention: Bears, particularly ones in specific locations like national parks or wildlife reserves, can become internet sensations. For example, famous bears like "Yogi Bear" or real-life bears like the "Yellowstone Grizzly" get attention through viral social media posts, creating a kind of celebrity status. People enjoy watching bears in their natural habitats, and sometimes they become known for their quirky behaviors or interactions with humans.
> 2. Cultural Iconography: Bears have a prominent place in American folklore, mythology, and entertainment. Characters like Yogi Bear, Winnie the Pooh, and Smokey the Bear have been part of American childhoods for decades. They are often depicted as friendly, funny, or heroic, and they represent strength, independence, and resilience.
> 3. Wildlife Conservation Campaigns: Bears, especially endangered species like the polar bear or the grizzly bear, often become symbols for environmental and conservation efforts. These bears sometimes gain celebrity status as part of campaigns

to raise awareness about habitat destruction, climate change, and wildlife preservation.

4. Real-Life Famous Bears: Some individual bears have become famous due to unique, captivating, or tragic events in their lives. For example, the bear known as "Jellystone" in the Smoky Mountains became famous for showing up at tourist attractions, while other bears may become famous for surviving in the wild or for notable rescues.

5. Bear in Entertainment: Beyond TV and films, bears are featured prominently in various forms of media, and some even act as mascots. This often helps keep them in the public eye and elevate their status.

So, whether through fiction, real-life stories, or as part of conservation efforts, American bears have an undeniable celebrity quality. ChatGPT, accessed March 17, 2024, https://chatgpt.com/c/67388279-48e0-8005-b903-4515cb2d07e9.

18. Among the places to engage issues of anthropomorphism are King, *How Animals Grieve*; and Taylor, *Beasts of Burden*.

19. On the issue of actual versus represented bears, see Boggs, *Animalia Americana*; Sherry Simpson, "The Metaphorical Bear," by University of Alaska Southeast, May 5, 2010, YouTube, https://www.youtube.com/watch?v=68A-UkLKsJA; Pearson and Weismantel, "Does 'The Animal' Exist?," 17; Chen, *Animacies*; Woods, *Herds Shot*.

20. The literature on conservation and environmentalism is extensive, but good starting points include Jacoby, *Crimes Against Nature*; Demuth, *Floating Coast*; and Heise, *Imagining Extinction*.

21. To help avoid essentializing Indigenous peoples and Euro-Americans, albeit focusing on different places and times, see Cooley, *Perfection*; and Kreiner, *Legion of Pigs*. Other than the contribution of Sven Haakanson Jr. discussed in the chapter on gay bears, I have not been able to locate ample discussions of bears by Native American scholars. So I have had to rely on scholarship by others, which is often both useful and influenced by the counterculture and/or spiritualism.

1. FOLKLORIC BEARS AND ACTUAL ONES: SACRED AND PROFANE FROM THE BIBLE TO CONTEMPORARY CELEBRITIES

1. Bieder, *Bear*, 48–101, provides a survey of bears in legends, one that crosses time and cultures. Also offering wide-ranging information on how different times and cultures perceived bears is Brunner, *Bear*, 1–7, 19–35, 77–89, 103–15, and 211–19. Cold Warriors were among those who embraced the view of the Russian bear as dangerous and uncontrollable.

2. Here I am relying on "What Animal Is Mentioned Most Often in the Bible?," Bible Answer, December 21, 2017, https://thebibleanswer.org/animal-mentioned-most-often-bible/.

3. "Ursa Major," Chandra X-Ray Observatory, accessed November 5, 2024, https://chandra.harvard.edu/photo/constellations/ursamajor.html.

4. Shepard and Sanders, *Sacred Paw*, xi.

5. Rockwell, *Giving Voice*, 161. There are many guides to sources on how Native Americans understood bears, but among them are Shepard and Sanders, *Sacred Paw*;

Storl, *Bear*; and Rockwell, *Giving Voice*. For specific legends, see "Native American Bear Mythology," Native Languages of the Americas, accessed November 5, 2024, http://www.native-languages.org/legends-bear.htm, a website that provides links to stories.

6. "Two Travelers and a Bear," Aesop for Children, accessed November 5, 2024, http://read.gov/aesop/124.html.

7. The version of the specific story on which I rely appears in Dasent, *Popular Tales*, 409–11.

8. Tatar, *Off with Their Heads!*, and Warner, *Once Upon a Time*, are among the best places to begin to understand how to interpret fairy tales. There is a Freudian feast about fairy tales, most notably in Bettelheim, *Uses of Enchantment*, subject inevitably to critiques, among the most important of which is Dundes, "Bettelheim's Uses."

9. The version I am using appears in *Grimm's Fairy Tales*, translated by Edwardes and Taylor.

10. Brunner, *Bears*, 212–13, points in the right direction but may overstate the case when he writes that "this remarkable denouement represents a revolution in our view of bears: not only does it seem to evoke the ancient cultural bond between our species, but it also foreshadows and accompanies the profound shift in how bears would be perceived in the decades to come. . . . It is tempting to read the story as symbolizing a longing to reinstitute a deeper connection between humans and bears."

11. Kipling, "The White Man's Burden," *New York Sun*, February 1, 1899, https://www.kiplingsociety.co.uk/poem/poems_burden.htm.

12. There is an extensive literature on Kipling as an imperialist; see, as an example, Varley, "Imperialism."

13. Kipling, *Jungle Book*, 53–54. Nath, "'Abandon,'" places the focus on Mowgli in racial and colonial contexts.

14. Waterman, "Perceptions of Race," 3.

15. Waterman, "Perceptions," explores the differences more generally. See also Thompson, "Return of the Empire."

16. Metcalf, "'It's a Jungle Book,'" 87 and 89.

17. "The Jungle Book" in *Disney Classics*, 168–71.

18. *Walt Disney's The Jungle Book*, 39 and 42.

19. Waterman, "Perceptions of Race," 3–5.

20. Bernstein, *Racial Innocence*, 133.

21. I count approximately 12 out of the 185 contained in Chase, *Complete Tales*.

22. Harris, *Uncle Remus*. This also appears in Chase, *Complete Tales*.

23. Chase, *Complete Tales*, 185–88.

24. Joel Chandler Harris, "Why Brother Bear Has No Tail," July 25, 2008, https://freelistens.blogspot.com/2008/07/why-brother-bear-has-no-tail-by-joel.html explores the meanings of the second story.

25. Barnes, "Bayou Overhaul." For a discussion of Disney's version and the controversies surrounding it, see Gates and Tatar, *African American Folktales*, 177–97.

26. For information on Harris and the controversial aspects of his work, see Bickley, *Joel Chandler Harris*.

27. Maria Tatar and Henry Louis Gates Jr. quoted in Robert Siegel, "'Annotated African American Folktales' Reclaims Stories Passed Down from Slavery," *All Things Considered*, November 10, 2017, https://www.npr.org/2017/11/10/563110377/annotated-african-american-folktales-reclaims-stories-passed-down-from-slavery.

28. Gates and Tatar, *African American Folktales*, 179.

29. Julius Lester edited five books retelling Uncle Remus stories: *Tales of Uncle Remus*, *More Tales of Uncle Remus*, *Further Tales of Uncle Remus*, *Last Tales of Uncle Remus*, and *Complete Tales*, which brings together the material in the four previous books. Many of the other stories about bears in Lester's books that do not appear in Chase, *Complete Tales*, confirm my judgment of how bears are outsmarted: for example, "Brer Rabbit Tricks Brer Bear," in Lester, *Tales*, 71–74; or "Brer Bear Gets Tricked by Brer Frog," in Lester, *Further Tales*, 16–19. Several essays by Donna Varga chart key relationships between childhood, animals (including teddy bears), and racism: "Innocence Versus Savagery"; "Babes"; "Gifting the Bear"; and, with Rhoda Zuk, "Golliwogs." Among the many books that explore race in stories about animals is Boggs, *Animalia Americana*.

30. Lester, *Tales*, xiii–xxi.

31. Lester, *More Tales*, viii. See also Lester, *Last Tales*, ix–xv.

32. There may well be more than five, but given variations in the titles it is hard to determine. I also discovered one in Lester's books that appears elsewhere as a story about Brer Bear but not in the book Chase edited: "Brer Rabbit and the Rope Pulling Contest," in Lester, Further Tales of Uncle Remus, Western Libraries, accessed November 16, 2024, https:// onesearch.library.wwu.edu/discovery/fulldisplay?docid=alma9912215773000I451&context =L&vid=01ALLIANCE_WWU:WWU&lang=en&search_scope=DN_and _CI&adaptor=Local%20Search%20Engine&tab=Summit_Plus_Articles&query =creator,exact,Dial%20Books.&facet=creator,exact,Dial%20Books.&offset=0.

33. "The End of Brer Bear," in Lester, *Tales*, 74–75; and "The End of Mr. Bear," in Chase, *Complete Tales*, 84–88.

34. "Brother Bear and the Honey Orchard," in Chase, *Complete Tales*, 451–57; and "Brer Rabbit, Brer Bear, and the Honey Orchard," in Lester, *More Tales*, 50.

35. "Why Brer Bear Has No Tail," in Lester, *Tales*, 100–1.

36. "List of Fictional Bears," *Wikipedia*, accessed November 6, 2024, https://en .wikipedia.org/wiki/List_of_fictional_bears. Throughout the book I have relied on Wikipedia, which is especially useful in offering capacious lists not available elsewhere.

37. Marcus and Zilberdik, "Hamas Teaches Kids."

38. "Oski," The Centennial of the University of California, 1868–1968, Online Archive of California, accessed November 6, 2024, https://oac.cdlib.org/view?docId =hb4v19n9zb&chunk.id=div00238&brand=oac4&doc.view=entire_text; more generally useful is Chris Drew, "42 US Colleges with Bear Mascots," HelpfulProfessor.com, November 21, 2022, https://helpfulprofessor.com/colleges-with-bear-mascots/. For a history of the species, see Storer and Tevis, *California Grizzly*. From 1915 on, Touchdown Bear was the mascot of Cornell University, a series of live ones replaced in the 1970s by a student dressed in a bear costume.

39. "Oski," American Football Database, accessed November 6, 2024, https:// americanfootballdatabase.fandom.com/wiki/Oski.

40. Kell, "Birthday Bear."

41. Jue, "Retro Joe."

42. Jue, "Retro Joe"; this history relies on "UCLA Traditions," UCLA Alumni Association, accessed November 6, 2024, https://alumni.ucla.edu/uclas-story/ucla-history -traditions/.

43. "The Bruin Statue Is Installed, 'Mighty Bruins' Debuts," UCLA 100, accessed November 6, 2024, https://100.ucla.edu/timeline/the-bruin-statue-is-installed.

44. Among the sources on Pooky are "Pooky," Garfield Wiki, accessed November 6, 2024, https://garfield.fandom.com/wiki/Pooky.

45. Davis, *Garfield Complete Works*, 100.

46. The GoComics Team, "Garfield and Pooky Are Friendship Goals, as Is Shown in These Comics," GoComics, May 14, 2024, https://www.gocomics.com/comics/lists /1720956/garfield-comics-teddy-bear-pooky.

47. For a complete listing, see "Garfield," Wikipedia, accessed November 6, 2024, https://en.wikipedia.org/wiki/Garfield.

48. "The Bear Essentials: Top 10 Best Video Game Bears of All Time!," Blockfort, accessed November 6, 2024, https://www.blockfort.com/character-lists/bears/.

49. Madeline Halpert, "Grazer Is Third Female Winner of Fat Bear Week," BBC, October 11, 2023, https://www.bbc.com/news/world-us-canada-67079906.

50. Among the many sources that focus on celebrity bears are Curwood, *Grizzly King*; Seton-Thompson, *Biography*; Stark, *Chasing the Ghost Bear*, which includes a few pages (52–58) on how bears are here, there, and everywhere; and Stonorov, *Watch the Bear*. Bruin, a tame bear who lived in upstate New York in the 1920s, not only tells his own story in Gietz, *Sam Patch*, but also garners attention from a historian in Johnson, *Sam Patch*. Flores, *American Serengeti*, 106, explores how beginning in the early twentieth century writers, in an effort to counter Darwinian notions, emphasized "animal individuality, cooperation, intelligence and reasoning" and narrated tales about grizzlies "telling their stories from the point of view of the animals."

51. Hansen, "Bear Proof." I am grateful to Sherry Smith for alerting me to this story.

52. Thomas D. Mangelsen, *399: Portrait of a Legend*, Mangelsen: Images of Nature Gallery, accessed November 11, 2024, https://www.mangelsen.com/limited-edition -collection/399-portrait-of-a-legend-3332.html.

53. On October 22, 2024, a car hit and killed 399. Thomas D. Mangelsen, "Grizzly 399 (1996–2024)," Mangelsen: Images of Nature Gallery, accessed November 11, 2024, https://www.mangelsen.com/grizzly; Wilkinson, "Famous."

54. Wilkinson, "Famous."

55. Mangelsen, "Grizzly 399."

56. Tatar, *Off with Their Heads*, explores the roles of such stories in the socialization of children.

2. THE STORIES OF HUGH GLASS: THE CASE OF A DISAPPEARING AND REAPPEARING DANGEROUS BEAR

1. Faulkner, "Bear," 193, 241, and 247.

2. Ricciuti, *Backyard*, 185, 231, and 236.

3. Melissa Alonso, Leslie Perrot, and Alaa Elassar, "A Woman Was Found Dead After an Apparent Bear Attack in Colorado," CNN.com, May 2021, https://www.cnn.com /2021/05/01/us/woman-dead-bear-attack-colorado.html.

4. Quammen, *Monster*, 306. The literature on grizzlies is enormous, and among the good places to begin is McCracken, *Beast*.

5. Neihardt, "Song," 127–254.

6. Manfred, *Lord Grizzly*; for important discussions of the text, see Austin, "Legend"; and Myers, *Saga*.

7. What I cover hardly includes the scores if not hundreds of versions of the story of Hugh Glass. I decided to focus on those based on my own judgment and that of Jon T. Coleman.

8. Robert Righter to author, October 26, 2022; Lewis and Clark, *Journals*, 104.

9. Hall, "Letters." Hall wrote the story down after hearing it from someone who in turn had listened to Glass tell the tale at Fort Atkinson. Without analyzing its changing meaning, Edgeley Todd tracks versions of the story from 1825 to 1955: Todd, "James Hall." For a thoughtful consideration of how the story of Hugh Glass morphed, including with *The Revenant*, see Schullery, *Bear Doesn't Know*, 108–20. The website hughglass.org by Museum of the Mountain Man (accessed November 11, 2024) provides much useful information, including a map covering the story's location. The site's "Sources" page (http://hughglass.org/sources/) provides information on and links to versions between 1827 and the publication of Neihardt's version.

10. In very different geographical contexts, Cooley, *Perfection*, underscores the importance of seeing Indigenous groups in differentiated terms.

11. Punke, *Revenant*, 253–54.

12. Coleman, *Here Lies*, 11.

13. "Richard Harris."

14. Manfred, *Lord Grizzly*, 73.

15. On the 1971 date, see Dunaway, *Seeing Green*.

16. Iñárritu, *Revenant*.

17. Punke, *Revenant*, 23.

18. Herrero, *Bear Attacks*.

19. Leonardo DiCaprio and Alejandro J. Iñárritu, quoted in Kroft Talks About Movies, "The Revenant: Secret of Shooting the Bear Scene," YouTube, accessed November 11, 2024, https://www.youtube.com/watch?v=Y-xYlhKpTus. I have slightly modified Iñárritu's phrasing in order to conform to standard English usage.

20. Coleman, *Here Lies*, 159.

21. Coleman, *Here Lies*, x, 11, 15, and 16.

22. For another book that focuses not on how bad a bear attack is but on what humans do to each other after, see Martin, *In the Eye*.

23. This is the central theme of Coleman, *Vicious*.

3. OUT OF HIBERNATION AND INTO CHILDREN'S LITERATURE

1. There is abundant scholarship on bears in children's literature, some of it specifically on bears and some of it useful as background. Among the most suggestive secondary sources are articles by Varga: "Winnie"; "Innocence Versus Savagery"; "Babes": "Teddy's Bear"; and, with Zuk, "Golliwogs." Among the important books are Key, *Century*;

Nodelman, *Hidden Adult*; Nodelman, *Words About Pictures*; Rose, *Peter Pan*; Bader, *American Picturebooks*; Grenby and Immel, *Cambridge Companion*; Melson, *Why*.

2. Lists: Tom, "Ten of the Best Bears in Children's Literature," Nosy Crow, July 26, 2013, https://nosycrow.com/blog/ten-of-the-best-bears-in-children-s-literature/; "Top 10 Bears Books," Bookroo, accessed November 11, 2024, https://bookroo.com/explore /books/topics/bears; "Bear Books for Kids," Growing Book by Book, November 30, 2020, https://growingbookbybook.com/bear-books-for-kids/; historically—"Famous Bears in Literature," The History Press, October 12, 2016, https://www.thehistorypress .co.uk/articles/famous-bears-in-literature. In "'Three Bears,'" Elms discusses the story's origins as well as how scholars have interpreted it. Storl, *Bear*, 257–73, offers an "Encyclo-pedia of Famous Bears," most but not all of which I have discussed here and elsewhere.

3. Anna, "Robert Southey, The Story of the Three Bears, the Original Goldilocks Story," *Words Lost and Regained*, December 9, 2010, http://aversimasini.blogspot.com/2010/12 /robert-southey-story-of-three-bears.html. Opie and Opie, *Classic Fairy Tales*, 199–205, carefully traces the origins and development of the story. For an even more up-to-date telling, see Myrna, "The Three Bears Before Goldilocks: The History of a Fairy Tale," Toronto Public Library, January 25, 2021, https://torontopubliclibrary.typepad.com/arts_ culture/2021/01/the-three-bears-before-goldilocks-the-history-of-a-fairy-tale.html.

4. Tatar, *Off with Their Heads*, xxvii, points out how often in stories for children women appear problematically.

5. Aylesworth, *Goldilocks*, n.p. Marshall, *Goldilocks*, offers a briefer and some-what similar version. In Belle and Caruso-Scott, *Goldilocks*, a book designed for very young children, Goldilocks departs on friendly terms. For versions that adhere closely to the standard story (often relying on Lang, *Green Fairy Book*) but differ mainly in the nature of their illustrations, see Spirin, *Goldilocks*; Eisen, *Goldilocks*; Brett, *Goldilocks*.

6. In finding out about multiple versions, I am relying on Deanna Jump, "Teaching with Versions of Goldilocks and the Three Bears Story," Mrs. Jump's Class, accessed November 12, 2024, https://deannajump.com/versions-of-goldilocks-and-the-three -bears/; Anna Geiger, "Versions of Goldilocks and the Three Bears," The Measured Mom, accessed November 12, 2024, https://www.themeasuredmom.com/versions-of -goldilocks/; and Stephanie, "Favorite Versions of Goldilocks and the Three Bears," Because My Mother Read, April 26, 2018, http://becausemymotherread.com/2018/04 /26/favorite-versions-of-goldilocks-and-the-three-bears/.

7. Willems, *Three Dinosaurs*, n.p.

8. Rosales, *Leola*, [i]. *Goldilocks and the Three Bears: Recitos de Oro y Los Tres Osos* (1976) focuses on bilingualism but not on promoting a Latino perspective of the story.

9. Rosales, *Leola*, 7, 8, 12, 16, 18, 32, 35, and 37.

10. Motion Pictures, "Terrytoons Paul Terry 1939 The Three Bears," YouTube, Janu-ary 4, 2020, https://www.youtube.com/watch?v=mAAWfslDp8w.

11. Jon short (shorty), "Fractured Fairy Tale Goldilocks," YouTube, April 18, 2011, https://www.youtube.com/watch?v=69CXU_KOah4.

12. For a list, see "Goldilocks and the Three Bears," Muppet Wiki, accessed Novem-ber 12, 2024, https://muppet.fandom.com/wiki/Goldilocks_and_the_Three_Bears.

13. "Goldilocks," Muppet Wiki, accessed November 12, 2024, https://muppet.fandom.com/wiki/Goldilocks.

14. TheOriginalTellyMonster, "Sesame Street—Kermit Attempts to Direct 'Goldilocks and the Three Bears,'" YouTube, March 8, 2021, https://www.youtube.com/watch?v=MT3Ww1B1sSE.

15. Milne, *Winnie-the-Pooh*, vii–viii.

16. Milne, *Winnie-the-Pooh*, 122, 240, 147, and 155–56.

17. manlikeisaac, "If Winnie the Pooh Was Black," YouTube, July 7, 2021, https://www.youtube.com/watch?v=dlhoiMG3doo.

18. Stanger, "Feminist Lens," 35 and 48. For children's books on the relationships between Indigenous peoples and bears, see the Birchbark House series by Louise Erdrich, as well as Jose Angutinngurniq, "The Giant Bear: An Inuit Folktale," American Indians in Children's Literature, January 15, 2014, https://americanindiansinchildrensliterature.blogspot.com/2014/01/the-giant-bear-inuit-folktale-by-jose.html.

19. Hoff later published a sequel, *The Te of Piglet*.

20. Crews, *Pooh Perplex*; Crews, *Postmodern Pooh*.

21. Harvey C. Window, "Paradoxical Persona: The Hierarchy of Heroism in *Winnie-the-Pooh*," in Crews, *Pooh Perplex*, 11.

22. Simon Lacerous, "Another Book to Cross Off Your List," in Crews, *Pooh Perplex*, 100; "Note to the 2003 Edition" of *Pooh Perplex*, x, revealed the true identity of Lacerous and Masterson.

23. Lacerous, "Another Book," 106.

24. Felicia Marronnez, "Why? Wherefore? Inasmuch as Which?," in Crews, *Postmodern Pooh*, 3, 6, 9, and 12.

25. See the perceptive review that covers both books: Review of *Postmodern Pooh*, *Publisher's Weekly*, October 2001, www.publishersweekly.com/978-0-86547-626-4.

26. Hoff, *Tao*, xii, 12, 18, 50, 147, and 153.

27. Pauli, "Paddington."

28. Bond, *Bear Called Paddington*, 54.

29. Pauli, "Paddington."

30. Michael Bond, quoted in Reuben, "Paddington Bear"; a somewhat different version on which I have drawn can be found at James Hitchings-Hales, "Paddington Bear Is a Perfect Model for How to Treat Refugees," Global Citizen, June 29, 2017, https://www.globalcitizen.org/en/content/paddington-bear-refugee-michael-bond-migrant/.

31. Roland Miller, "London Will Not Have Forgotten How to Treat a Stranger," accessed November 12, 2024, https://slideplayer.com/slide/13262092/.

32. Smith, "Paddington Bear," 27 and 28. For a positive assessment of *A Bear Called Paddington*, see Smith, "Case Study." On how Paddington stories have figured in campaigns for social justice, see Seitz, "'Migration'"; and Seitz, "'You're Stuffed.'" Hunt and Sands, "View," discuss the role of imperialism in British children's literature.

33. Grayson, "How to Read," 390–91. See also Leslie, "Please."

34. In 1965, soon after the Berenstain books first appeared, Walt Morey introduced Gentle Ben in a children's book of the same name, the title suggesting the nature of a bear who became a boy's friend. And then television and film versions of Gentle Ben began to appear.

35. For some information on the Berenstains and their cultural productions, I am relying on their official site—The Berenstain Bears, https://www.berenstainbears.com/—and on Loviglio, "50 Years Along."

36. Berenstain and Berenstain, *Sunny Dirt Road*, 130.

37. Berenstain and Berenstain, *Sunny Dirt Road*, 149; and Geisel quoted at 157–58.

38. Berenstain and Berenstain, *Sunny Dirt Road*, 158.

39. Geisel, quoted in Mehren, "Bear Facts." For a full rendition of the return to bears, see Berenstain and Berenstain, *Sunny Dirt Road*, 161–62.

40. Mehren, "Bear Facts."

41. Berenstain and Berenstain, *Big Honey Hunt*, 7 and 60.

42. Berenstain and Berenstain, *Sunny Dirt Road*, 167 and 176.

43. Berenstain and Berenstain, *Sunny Dirt Road*, 178.

44. Weeks, "Bear Essentials"; Olney, "Bearly There"; Farhi and Kehayias, "New Children's Books."

45. Mehren, "Bear Facts."

46. Weeks, "Bear Essentials."

47. Weeks, "Bear Essentials."

48. Austerlitz, "Salvation."

49. Krauthammer, "Drown." Bettelheim, *Uses of Enchantment*, 215–24, focused on the story of Goldilocks and the Three Bears.

50. Austerlitz, "Salvation."

51. Rebecca Onion, "How the Berenstain Bears Thanksgiving Book Became the Bane of My Existence," Slate.com, November 24, 2021, https://slate.com/human-interest/2021/11/berenstain-bears-thanksgiving-blessings-conservative.html.

52. For one of many lists, see "Top 10 Bears Books," Bookroo, accessed November 11, 2024, https://bookroo.com/explore/books/topics/bears.

53. One example is Bergen and Nguyen, *Polar Bears' Home*.

54. Of course, Amazon lists of bestsellers are moving targets. See, for instance, https://www.amazon.com/gp/bestsellers/books/2792, accessed October 31, 2024. One encounters a very different world with a search for "young adult bear books," accessed November 15, 2024, https://www.amazon.com/s?k=Young+adult+bear+books&crid=PKBTN8VJRZ55&sprefix=young+adult+bear+books%2Caps%2C138&ref=nb_sb_noss.

55. "I Love You to the Moon and Back," Amazon.com, book listing, accessed November 12, 2024, https://www.amazon.com/I-Love-You-Moon-Back/dp/1589255518.

56. "God Gave Us You," Amazon.com, book listing, accessed November 12, 2024, https://www.amazon.com/God-Gave-You-Lisa-Bergren/dp/0307729915.

57. I echo Christopher Lasch's 1977 book, *Haven in a Heartless World: The Family Besieged*.

58. Krauthammer, "Drown."

59. Austerlitz, "Salvation."

60. This list of alternatives comes from "Top 10 Animals from Children's Books," Imagine Forest, October 2, 2015, https://www.imagineforest.com/blog/top-10-animals-from-childrens-books/.

1. The last five terms appear in Adams, *Hair-Breadth Escapes*, 1.

2. Mizelle, "Man Quite as Much," explores the multiple cultural contexts for understanding Adams and more generally interactions between humans and nonhuman animals. On the connection between his early industrial work in Massachusetts and his later training of bears, and more generally on his management of labor and his entrepreneurial ambitions, see Coleman, "Shoemaker's Circus."

3. "John Adams," *Evening Bulletin*, January 18, 1858.

4. For a description of one attack, see Hittell, *Adventures*, 313–14.

5. Hittell, *Adventures*, 69 and 115.

6. Douglas and McDonnell, *Celebrity*, 72 and 74.

7. Dillon, *Legend*, 198 and 212. On Hittell see Righter, "Theodore Henry Hittell."

8. Hittell, *Adventures*, 12–13.

9. Hittell, *Adventures*, 43–44; for one racially infused statement, see 224. For a history of Native peoples in California in the middle of the nineteenth century, see Madley, *American Genocide*.

10. Hittell, *Adventures*, 17–18 and 25.

11. Hittell, *Adventures*, 66–67 and 71–72.

12. Hittell, *Adventures*, 34, 37, and 66–72; quotes at 68–69. For discussion of his violent taming of the male grizzly General Jackson, see Hittell, *Adventures*, 70–71.

13. Hittel, *Adventures*, 87, 188, 225, 292, and 299.

14. Hittell, *Adventures*, 19 and 58.

15. For some of the remarkably few references to money, see Hittell, *Adventures*, 288, 293–94, 297, and 305.

16. Hittell, *Adventures*, 166, 183, 185, 197, and 224.

17. Hittell, *Adventures*, 373 and 377.

18. Hittell, *Adventures*, 377–78.

19. Adams, *Hair-Breadth Escapes*.

20. See, for example, Adams, *Hair-Breadth Escapes*, 15–18.

21. George Bruns and Thomas W. Blackburn, "The Ballad of Davy Crockett" (theme song for the 1954–1955 ABC television serial *Davy Crockett*, performed by its star, Fess Parker).

22. Adams, *Hair-Breadth Escapes*, 2, 20, and 51.

23. Adams, *Hair-Breadth Escapes*, 1, 3, and 4.

24. Adams, *Hair-Breadth Escapes*, 4, 5, 10, 13, 33, and 37. I cannot identify a South American place named Golina.

25. Without elaboration, Mizelle, "Man Quite as Much," 41, refers to these.

26. Dillon, *Legend*, 10, 14, and 38.

27. Dillon, *Legend*, 151, 200, and 203.

28. Dillon, *Legend*, 26, 128, and 150.

29. Dillon, *Legend*, 206–7, 208, and 222.

30. McClung, *True Adventures*, viii, 27, 35, and 60.

31. McClung, *True Adventures*, 44.

32. McClung, *True Adventures*, 169–70.

33. Phineas Taylor Barnum, *Struggles and Triumphs or, Forty-years Recollections of P. T. Barnum* (1865), quoted in Mizelle, "Man Quite as Much," 40.

34. *Harper's Weekly*, November 10, 1860, quoted in Mizelle, "Man Quite as Much," 41.

35. *New York Weekly*, February 18, 1861, quoted in McClung, *True Adventures*, 177–78.

36. The film is available here: Wm. Thomas Sherman, "Life and Times of Grizzly Adams (1974)—Dan Haggerty, Don Shanks," YouTube, April 25, 2020, https://www .youtube.com/watch?v=1Y-8IOo8BUI. The film relied on Charles Sellier Jr.'s 1972 novel *The Life and Times of Grizzly Adams*. Grizzly Adams makes appearances in several additional films, though not ones that either gave him a major role or gained much traction: among them are *The Life and Times of Judge Roy Bean* (1972), *The Legend of Grizzly Adams* (1990), *Grizzly Adams and the Legend of Dark Mountain* (1999), and *P. T. Barnum* (1999). In addition, Haggerty starred in an updated version of the story of Adams in *Grizzly Mountain* (1997) and *Escape to Grizzly Mountain* (2000). Building on the film's success, between February 1977 and December 1978, NBC aired thirty-seven episodes of *The Life and Times of Grizzly Adams*. Starring Haggerty, the series was even more loosely based on the life of Adams.

37. Mizelle, "Man Quite as Much," 30 and 43.

5. CAPTIVE BEARS AND THEIR CAPTORS AS WORKERS

1. Franz Boas, letter to Roy Chapman Andrews, November 19, 1937, quoted in Rader and Cain, "From Natural History," 155–56.

2. Poliquin, *Breathless Zoo*, which opens with a discussion of polar bears on display, explores how stuffed animals evoke feelings of wonder, beauty, spectacle, order, narrative, allegory, and remembrance.

3. Rader and Cain, *Life on Display*, 268 and 241–42. This discussion draws on their magisterial *Life on Display*, as well as on Rader and Cain, "From Natural History." On how some museums offer an inaccurate vision of bear families, see Asma, *Stuffed Animals*, 224 and 225.

4. Blond, "Imagining the Future," 105. See also Desmond, *Staging Tourism*.

5. "PEM Shows a Changing Planet Through the Eyes of Two Artists," Peabody Essex Museum, February 16, 2022, https://www.pem.org/press-news/pem-shows-a-changing -planet-through-the-eyes-of-two-artists.

6. "The Bulls and Bears in the Market," Google Arts & Culture, accessed November 12, 2024, https://artsandculture.google.com/asset/the-bulls-and-bears-in-the-market -william-holbrook-beard/yAEW2N1zkOAoqA?hl=en.

7. Zoos also exhibited people as captive animals. The most famous case is that of Ota Benga, an African man enslaved by Africans, purchased by an American explorer, and in 1906 displayed in the Bronx Zoo in a cage in the Monkey House along with an orangutan. For the full story, see Newkirk, *Spectacle*.

8. Well before the recent boom in zoo history, Helen L. Horowitz published two essays that foretold much of what was to come: "National Zoological Park" and "Animal and Man." Early in the twenty-first century several important books appeared on the history

of zoos. I have relied most heavily on Rothfels, *Savages and Beasts*; Rothfels, *Representing Animals*, 199–223; and Hanson, *Animal Attractions*. More focused chronologically but especially important on the issue of race is Uddin, *Zoo Renewal*. In *Elephant Trails*, Rothfels explores change and persistence in the understanding of another animal that lived in the wild and in zoos. For an exploration of what zoos mean to people, see Mullan and Marvin, *Zoo Culture*. Berger, "Why Look," is a provocative and influential essay relevant to the experiences at zoos. The most recent contribution to the history of American zoos is Vandersommers, *Entangled Encounters*.

9. Rothfels, *Savages and Beasts*, 42, 163, and 199.

10. For a probing discussion of the park understood within a range of appropriate comparative sites, see Kidd, "Animal Kingdom."

11. Malamud, *Reading Zoos*, 103. For several years, there was a Berenstain Bear section at the Dorney Park and Wildwater Kingdom in Allentown, Pennsylvania, and at the Edaville Family Theme Park in Carver, Massachusetts: TTTTgunner, "Anyone Remember the BerenSTAIN Amusement Park in Dorney Park in PA?," Reddit, accessed November 12, 2024, https://www.reddit.com/r/MandelaEffect/comments/p75xou/anyone _remember_the_berenstain_amusement_park_in/ and "Theme Park Open Featuring Berenstain Bears," Boston Central, 2017, https://www.bostoncentral.com/events/special /p51227.php.

12. Rothfels, *Savages and Beasts*, 197.

13. "About the Walt Disney Company," The Walt Disney Company, accessed November 12, 2024, http://disney.go.com/disneyhand/environmentality/environment/index.html.

14. Rothfels, *Savages and Beasts*, 143–88, discusses how Hagenbeck's enterprises, including the zoo, represented a range of approaches—a paradise and an ark among them—but was fundamentally a business enterprise.

15. This discussion of immersion draws on Rothfels, *Savages and Beasts*, 200–202.

16. For critiques of the turn to conservation and more generally of zoos, see Adams, "Post-Meateating," 55, and Marris, *Wild Souls*, 87–108. DeMello, *Animals and Society*, 107–12, summarizes research on the limits to the effectiveness of these efforts. Hanson, *Animal Attractions*, 162–86, charts the challenges zoos faced beginning in the 1950s. Donahue and Trump, *Politics of Zoos*, offers a political and legal history of fights between the American Association of Zoological Parks and Aquariums and animal welfare advocacy groups. Rothfels, *Elephant Trails*, 122, presents a nuanced assessment of the controversies about zoos. Two award-winning documentaries, *Blackfish* (2013) and *The Conservation Game* (2021), intensified awareness of the conditions animals face in commercialized captivity.

17. Malamud, *Reading Zoos*, 1–2 and 225–26. For a more general analysis, see Malamud, *Introduction to Animals*.

18. Kathryn Sussman, "Humane Wildlife and Nature Alternatives to Zoos," Zoo Check, accessed November 12, 2024, https://www.zoocheck.com/humane-wildlife-and -nature-alternatives-to-zoos/.

19. For a summary of the debate, see Robin McKie, "Is It Time to Shut Down the Zoos?," *The Guardian*, February 2, 2020, https://www.theguardian.com/world/2020 /feb/02/zoos-time-shut-down-conservation-education-wild-animals. On recent legal efforts to change the relationships between zoos and nonhuman animals, see Wright, "Elephant."

20. On bearbaiting and bear pits, see Rothfels, *Savages and Beasts*, 22–24; Rothfels, "Caged Birds Sing," 98–100; Hanson, *Animal Attractions*, 145; Varga, "Babes," 194. Kalof, *Looking at Animals*, discusses bearbaiting and, more generally, animals representationally and in captivity, particularly for the modern period. Kalof, *Looking at Animals*, 89–91 and 137–64.

21. "Exhibits: Big Bears," Bronx Zoo, accessed November 12, 2024, https://bronxzoo .com/things-to-do/exhibits/big-bears.

22. Davis, "Circus Americanized," 44.

23. Davis, *Circus Age*, remains the place to begin to understand the American circus. Among other useful works are Albrecht, *New American Circus*; Nance, *Entertaining Elephants*; Standiford, *Battle*; Simon, *Greatest Shows*. Also of note is the 2018 PBS series *The Circus: American Experience*.

24. Kate Gibson, "Ringling Brothers Circus to Relaunch—Without Animal Acts," CBS News, May 18, 2022, https://www.cbsnews.com/news/ringling-brothers-greatest -show-on-earth-animal-acts-elephants-disney-on-ice/.

25. Nance, *Entertaining Elephants*, 229.

26. Nance, *Entertaining Elephants*, 226. The *Time* article was Corliss, "That Old Feeling."

27. Simon, *Greatest Shows*, 251.

28. Soloski, "Big Apple Circus."

29. Abrams, "New-Look Circus."

30. On the rise of alternative, animal-free circuses, see also Albrecht, *New American Circus*; Simon, *Greatest Shows*, 249–70; and Hammarstrom, *Fall*.

31. See Nance, *Animal Modernity*.

32. Unfootnoted source, quoted in Simon, *Greatest Shows*, 153.

33. On performing bears, including in bear pits and circuses, see Brunner, *Bears*, 183–209; Bieder, *Bear*, 104–5 and 107–9; Fee, *Polar Bear*, 102–36; Adler and Burnham, *Pallenberg Wonder Bears*.

34. Davis, *Circus Age*, 149.

35. Davis, *Circus Age*, 148–63; see also Nance, *Entertaining Elephants*, 5–6.

36. "Bongo the Wonder Bear," Minka's Bear Passion, January 16, 2020, https://www .mibepa.info/bongo-the-wonder-bear/.

37. Amanda, "6 Heartbreaking Reasons Why Bears Shouldn't Be in Circuses or Travel-ing Shows," peta2, March 10, 2023, https://www.peta2.com/news/bears-in-circuses/.

38. Szablowski, *Dancing Bears*, xiv–xvi. Since there are no more dancing bears to res-cue, Dancing Bears Park has been renamed Bear Sanctuary.

39. Grier, *Pets in America*, does not focus on bears but is nonetheless a useful introduc-tion to the more general phenomenon. DeMello, *Animals and Society*, 146–66, provides a useful introduction to how to think about pets.

40. Berenstain and Berenstain, *Trouble with Pets*, a very short book for very young children, is unpaginated.

41. Serpell, "People in Disguise," 132.

42. Samuels, *Molly and Me*, ii–iii, 2, and 4–5.

43. Samuels, *Molly and Me*, 115.

44. Samuels, *Molly and Me*, 132, 134, and 135.

45. For a different story of the commercialization of a pet bear, see "Beast Buddies: I Live with Two Grizzly Bears," posted May 2, 2019, by Beastly, YouTube, 6:01, https://www.youtube.com/watch?v=PJXOkal6roA.

46. ducadelaide, "Brutus, the Pet Grizzly Bear," YouTube, November 10, 2010, https://www.youtube.com/watch?v=CVMBdi4dgME.

47. Real Wild, "This Man Has the World's Only Pet Polar Bear," YouTube, March 8, 2021, https://www.youtube.com/shorts/JR_Llq8aTvg?app=desktop, https://www.buzznicked.com/polar-bear/.

48. The Oregonian, "Nora the Polar Bear Cub Growing Up," YouTube, September 17, 2017, https://www.youtube.com/watch?v=LIHwqDMgbhw.

49. Crystal Long, "Pet Bears Exist, but We're Curious How Possible It Really Is," Wide Open Pets, December 20, 2020, https://www.wideopenpets.com/bears-as-pets/.

50. There is an 1872 photo by him titled *Falls on Yosemite—Great Grizzly Bear Feet*, but I do not see a bear in the picture and assume the reference has to do with the title of a site rather than the presence of an animal.

51. Chris, *Watching Wildlife*, 1–28. Among other books on wildlife films are Bousé, *Wildlife Films*; Mitman, *Reel Nature*; Burt, *Animals in Film*; Wilson, *Culture of Nature*; and Ingram, *Green Screen*, especially 113–18.

52. There are at least two earlier examples—the 1931 animated short *The Clown* and the cartoon *Crazy Horse* in 1940. The discussion that follows covers some but hardly all of the relevant films; also grist for this mill is the 2022 television series *The Bear*, at this writing in its third season on Hulu.

53. Chris, *Watching Wildlife*, 28.

54. Mitman, *Reel Nature*, 110.

55. I chose this film because of its prominence and early date; there is, however, a plethora of Disney bears, both in cartoons and on documentaries. To view the film, see *Bear Country*, directed by James Algar (Los Angeles: Walt Disney Productions, 1952), Internet Archive, May 18, 2017, https://archive.org/details/bearcountry_201705. For a review by a professional mammologist, who acknowledged how the film was staged but nonetheless found it scientifically convincing, see Harold E. Anthony, quoted in Review of *Bear Country*.

56. Chris, *Watching Wildlife*, 36.

57. On how Disney's *True-Life Adventures* promoted typically reassuring 1950s values, including an emphasis on the family, see Palmer, *Shooting*, 36–37; Chris, *Watching Wildlife*, ix and 28; and Mitman, *Reel Nature*, 111.

58. *Bear Country* (dir. Algar), https://archive.org/details/bearcountry_201705.

59. Mitman, *Reel Nature*, 131.

60. Mutual of Omaha commercial, quoted in Palmer, *Shooting*, 40. For discussions of Perkins's career and the surrounding cultural contexts, see Mitman, *Reel Nature*, 132–56; Palmer, *Shooting*, 48–61; and Chris, *Watching Wildlife*, 61–66, 75–76, 107–11, and 114–15.

61. Mutual of Omaha commercial, quoted in Chris, *Watching Wildlife*, 59.

62. Quoted in Mitman, *Reel Nature*, 153.

63. I date this show, which does not appear on easily available lists, to the mid-1960s because Fowler left the show in 1968; a difficult-to-see copyright date seems to be 1963. For the two episodes under consideration here, see *Wild Kingdom*, season 5, episode 6,

"Bears of the High Country," directed by Don Meier, aired January 22, 1967, Mutual of Omaha's Wild Kingdom, accessed November 12, 2024, https://www.mutualofomaha.com/wild-kingdom/classic-episodes/bears-of-the-high-country, and *Wild Kingdom*, season 8, episode 8, "To Rope a Grizzly," directed by Don Meier, aired February 14, 1971, Mutual of Omaha's Wild Kingdom, accessed November 12, 2024, https://www.mutualofomaha.com/wild-kingdom/classic-episodes/to-rope-a-grizzly. Other bear shows featuring Perkins are "Sleeping Bears of Kawishiwi" (1981) and, depending on the dating of his retirement in 1985, "Plight of the Beggar Bears" (1985) and "Polar Bears of the Pack Ice" (1985).

64. On how common drug-and-tag nature films were in the 1970s, see Wilson, *Culture of Nature*, 146.

65. Rosenberg, "New Breed." 41.

66. On National Geographic and Stouffer, see Palmer, *Shooting*, 47–50 and 119–23. Also of note but not under consideration here is the National Geographic Society's *The Grizzlies* of 1987. For another popular film that resembles Stouffer's in many ways, see Jeff Watson's 2016 six-episode series on Animal Planet, *Project Grizzly*, the story of an animal trainer who has raised two grizzlies since they were six weeks old and later struggles with whether to release them into the wild.

67. The film is available on Roku and Tubi.

68. The chapter "Wildlife, Remade for TV" in Chris, *Watching Wildlife*, 78–121, is especially helpful in exploring the situation that began in the last half of the twentieth century, generally and concerning the National Geographic empire.

69. Bousé, *Wildlife Films*, 114–15, discusses the early translation of Curwood's work into film. Also of note, but not discussed here, are films by and about Doug Peacock, including *Peacock's War* (1988), *Grizzly Country* (2019), and *The Beast of Our Time: Grizzly Bears and Climate Change* (2021).

70. Chris, *Watching Wildlife*, 82, underscores how unlikely paternal protection was as well as how this film followed themes found elsewhere.

71. Bousé, review of *The Bear*, 33, which more fully explores how significantly *The Bear* follows genre conventions.

72. For PETA's critique of Working Wildlife for failure to meet reasonable standards of animal care, see "Steve Martin's Working Wildlife: Factsheet," People for the Ethical Treatment of Animals, accessed November 12, 2024, https://www.peta.org/wp-content/uploads/2021/06/SteveMartinWorkingWildlifeFactsheet_2010-06-23.pdf.

73. Among other films that feature bears are *The Edge* (1997), the story of a Kodiak that attacks three men in Alaska, devouring one of them; *Ted* (2012), which features a computer-animated Ted (a.k.a. Teddy Bear), who first appears as the comforting stuffed animal of the film's main character and then comes to life during his adulthood in ways that cause multiple twists and turns in the plot.

74. On the contexts of the Nature programs, see Chris, *Watching Wildlife*, 70–71 and 76–78.

75. *Nature*, season 38, episode 8, "Bears," aired November 20, 2019, PBS, https://www.pbs.org/wnet/nature/bears-preview-7zweov/20402/.

76. Kermode, "*Cocaine Bear* Review." For another film about a violent bear, see David Mamet's *The Edge* (1997).

77. Kermode, "*Cocaine Bear* Review."

78. Chris, *Watching Wildlife*, xi.

79. Rothfels, "Introduction," x.

80. On this issue with *The Bear*, see Berryman, "Why the Worry." For a suggestive critique of the genre in general, see Malamud, "Animals on Film."

81. On these issues see Bousé, "Are Wildlife Films," 116–40; Bousé, *Wildlife Films*, 9–36 and 84–126; Chris, *Watching Wildlife*, 104–8; and Mitman, *Reel Nature*, 110–32. On the avoidance or clouding of political and economic issues, see Wilson, *Culture of Nature*, 142–43.

82. Simpson, *Dominion*, 269; she was relying on Shepard, *Others*, 6.

83. Stouffer, *Wild America*, 134 and 152.

84. Stouffer, *Wild America*, 151 and 160; Geer died shortly before airing and ABC apparently insisted that Henry Fonda serve as narrator (163), though it is possible that Geer remained narrator and Fonda served as host; see *The Man Who Loved Bears*, directed by Marty Stouffer (1979; Marty Stouffer Productions), IMDb, https://www.imdb.com/title/tt1421388/.

85. Stouffer, *Wild America*, 164.

86. McPhee and Carrier, "Wild Photos."

87. Mitman, *Reel Nature*, 203.

88. Associated Press, "Wildlife Photographer Accused of Staging Scenes," *Time*, February 10, 1996, https://www.nwitimes.com/uncategorized/wildlife-photographer-accused-of-staging-scenes/article_1fdf5ab7-a4d4-5160-b56c-bd480d967625.html.

89. Smithsonian's National Zoo (@smithsonianzoo), "#PandaStory," Smithsonian's National Zoo and Conservation Biology Institute, April 19, 2015, https://www.nationalzoo.si.edu/animals/pandastory, accessed October 31, 2024; Nick Schiraldi, "No Panda Party Is Complete Without a Cake," Smithsonian's National Zoo and Conservation Biology Institute, April 26, 2022, https://nationalzoo.si.edu/animals/news/no-panda-party-complete-without-cake.

90. "Giant Panda Cam (Coming Soon)," Smithsonian's National Zoo and Conservation Biology Institute, accessed November 13, 2024, https://nationalzoo.si.edu/webcams/panda-cam.

91. "Disney panda," Google, accessed November 13, 2024, https://www.google.com/search?gs_ssp=eJzj4tVP1zcozMkxNsowqzI1YPTiSckszkutVChIzEtJBAB9WQkA&q=disney+panda&rlz=1C1VDKB_enUS953US953&oq=disney+panda&aqs=chrome.1.0i355i512j46i512j0i512l2j46i512j0i512l5.8559j1j4&sourceid=chrome&ie=UTF-8.

92. Belen Edwards, "'Turning Red's Portrayal of Periods Is a Turning Point for Coming-of-Age Movies," *Mashable*, March 31, 2022, https://mashable.com/article/turning-red-sex-education-coming-of-age-stories.

93. Dino Hazell, "The Panda Party Is Back On as Giant Pandas Will Return to Washington's National Zoo by Year's End," Associated Press News, May 29, 2024, https://apnews.com/article/giant-pandas-washington-zoo-china-764f8016d98c01ab579bdbb6dcc3dd6b#.

94. Kleinfield, "Farewell."

95. Friend, "It's a Jungle," 44; Zuckerman, "Gus."

96. Beard and Boswell, *What's Worrying Gus?*, 2, 6, 16, 24, 69, and 70.

97. DeMello, *Animals and Society*, 338–41, provides a more general discussion of animals on the internet.

98. Instagram, accessed November 13, 2024, https://www.instagram.com/explore /search/keyword/?q=animal%20bears&hl=en; Instagram, accessed November 13, 2024, https://www.instagram.com/explore/search/keyword/?q=bears&hl=en; Adam Schefter, Adam Schefter Podcast, X, accessed November 13, 2024, https://twitter.com/search?q =bears&src=typeahead_click.

99. "Bears sites," YouTube, accessed November 13, 2024, https://www.youtube.com /results?search_query=bears+sites.

100. College Humor, "Cartoon Bears Are Still Bears," Facebook, April 7, 2020, https://www.facebook.com/watch/?ref=search&v=627326087999108&external_log_id =044f6ab5-b06a-4562-a818-ec765cebbc23&q=bears%20videos.

101. Tumin, "Humble Origins."

102. "Brown Bears: Naknek River," explore, accessed October 8, 2022, https://explore .org/livecams/brown-bears/brown-bear-salmon-cam-brooks-falls.

103. Owens, "Internet Loves Otis."

104. Real Wild, "Orphaned Bear Cubs Saved After Man Becomes Surrogate Mother," Facebook, May 16, 2023, https://www.facebook.com/realwild/videos/orphaned-bear -cubs-saved-after-man-becomes-surrogate-mother/185655544379577/.

105. "The Bear Essentials," Blockfort, accessed November 13, 2024, https://www .blockfort.com/character-lists/bears/.

106. Hanson, *Animal Attractions*, 34. Throughout her book, Hanson skillfully explores how art, tourism, and national parks provided interchangeable depictions of animals.

107. On the purchasing of the bears of Grizzly Adams, see Rothfels, *Savages and Beasts*, 48.

6. TEDDY BEAR: ANOTHER ONE QUICKLY DISAPPEARS AND FREQUENTLY REAPPEARS

1. White, *Establishment*, 83. For an insightful discussion of how Roosevelt, concerned that critics saw him as weak and effeminate, emphasized manliness, racism, and civiliza- tion, see Bederman, *Manliness*, 170–215.

2. McCullough, *Mornings*, 344–46; Roosevelt quoted on 345 and McCullough on 346. For another history of the expedition, see Ambrose and Brinkley, "Centennial."

3. Quoted in Varga, "Teddy's Bear," 100.

4. "One Bear Bagged." Buchanan, *Holt Collier*, tells the story of Collier's life and focuses on the legendary hunt (153–83).

5. "Bruin Was in Luck."

6. "Bears in Combine."

7. "Bears Left Behind."

8. "Return of President."

9. In the introduction to Roosevelt, *American Bears*, Paul Schullery gets it right when he remarks that the reference was to the color line and the line between "good sports-

manship and bad" (10). For stories of TR's eagerness to kill bears, see Roosevelt, *Outdoor Pastimes*, especially "A Colorado Bear Hunt," 68–99.

10. Varga, "Gifting the Bear," 76.

11. Varga, "Teddy's Bear," 104. Contextualizing the 1902 story, Mooallem, *Wild Ones*, 61–72, sees the incident as a turning point when Americans shifted their views of bears from monstrous to cuddly because they were no longer a threat where most Americans lived. Mullins, *Teddy Bear Men*, painstakingly explores Berryman's hundreds if not thousands of depictions of Teddy and other bears.

12. "A Happy Day in Bearville, Mississippi," Theodore Roosevelt Center, accessed November 13, 2024, https://www.theodorerooseveltcenter.org/Research/Digital-Library /Record?libID=0274699; untitled illustration by Clifford Berryman, appeared in *Washington Post*, November 9, 1904, NARA and DVIDS Public Domain Archive, accessed November 13, 2024, https://nara.getarchive.net/media/untitled-1335ff.

13. Varga, "Teddy's Bear," 100. On the Boone and Crockett Club, see Horowitz, "Animal and Man."

14. Theodore Roosevelt to Philip Bathell Stewart, in Morison, *Letters*, 378–79.

15. Varga, "Teddy's Bear," 103.

16. "Can the Teddy Bear Speak?" explores the cultural applications of this animal, along with Varga's "Teddy's Bear."

17. Murphy, *Legend*, unpaginated.

18. In "Teddy Bears," Valtonen explores what makes teddy bears so comforting. Among the sources about bears growing in Brooklyn and Germany is Mullins, *Past & Present*, 10–13 and 127. Teddy bears were among the first examples of mass-merchandised toys that had begun to appear in the 1890s, initially, Gary S. Cross shows, representing "a brilliant merging of the fierce and frightening with the cute and the cuddly": *Kids' Stuff*, 94. In Cross, *Cute*, 121–47, he explores how teddy bears in the first decade of the new century represented the shift from frightening to cool and cute and later on explores a rebellion against cuteness.

19. Valtonen, "Teddy Bears," 259.

20. The story of the emergence and spread of teddy bears draws on Charles Moose, "Beginnings"; and Varga, "Gifting the Bear." See also "Sue," "Who Really Created the Teddy (Roosevelt) Bear?," New-York Historical Society Museum & Library (blog), July 25, 2012, https://blog.nyhistory.org/who-really-created-the-teddy-roosevelt-bear/. Varga has cast serious doubt on the story of how the Michtoms commercialized teddy bears, especially how early they had done so. However, many authors have accepted the narrative: See, as an example, Bieder, *Bear*, 126. Waring, *Praise*; and Crisp, *Advertising Art*, offer wonderful illustrations. Günther Pfeiffer has written several books on Steiff teddy bears, including *100 Years of Steiff Teddy Bears*, in which he presents contradictory stories about the Steiff bears lost at sea (22 and 24). Pfeiffer, *Story*, 64–78, relies on research conducted at the Theodore Roosevelt Association and the Steiff company to undermine the widely accepted legend of Steiff's innovation and instead suggests that Berryman's cartoons and Seymour Eaton's poems had a key role. He notes that not until 1908 in company records and 1913 in its catalog did Steiff use the term *teddy bear*.

21. Schullery, Introduction, 11. Fred Patten, "Retrospective: Seymour Eaton's 'The Roosevelt Bears,'" Flayrah, September 30, 2012, https://www.flayrah.com/4178/retrospective

-seymour-eatons-roosevelt-bears, confirms this judgment and offers useful information on Eaton's books, including a bibliography and discussion when the linkage occurred.

22. Eaton, *Roosevelt Bears*, 10.

23. Eaton, *Roosevelt Bears*, 113–14.

24. Eaton, *Roosevelt Bears*, [3] and 113.

25. Moose, "Beginnings," 52.

26. "Lots of Roosevelt Bears."

27. Naughton, "His Christmas."

28. Bieder, *Bear*, 131. It is possible that in the late nineteenth century, P. T. Barnum paraphernalia also proliferated; for a glimpse, see the collections in the Barnum Museum, https://barnum-museum.org/.

29. Retrotor, "Henry Hall & His Orchestra—The Teddy Bear's Picnic (1932)," You-Tube, August 29, 2007, https://www.youtube.com/watch?v=dZANKFxrcKU.

30. On folklore versions of teddy, especially among adults, see Till, "Teddy Bears."

31. "National Teddy Bear Day—September 9," National Day Calendar, accessed November 13, 2024, https://nationaldaycalendar.com/national-teddy-bear-day-september-9/.

32. On how and why this happened, see Varga, "Gifting the Bear."

33. Varga, "Gifting the Bear," 79.

34. Varga, "Gifting the Bear," 80–81.

35. "The Keeper," New Museum, accessed November 13, 2024, https://www .newmuseum.org/exhibitions/view/the-keeper.

36. "Ydessa Hendeles: Partners (The Teddy Bear Project)," Ydessa Hendeles Art Foundation, accessed November 13, 2024, http://yhaf.org/partners/the-teddy-bear-project.html.

37. "The Keeper," New Museum, accessed November 27, 2024, https://www .newmuseum.org/exhibitions/view/the-keeper.

38. Morris, Reddy, and Buntin, "Survival."

39. Beyers, Phipps, and Vorster, "Teddy Bear Therapy," 317 and 325.

40. Bloch and Toker, "Doctor."

41. "Teddy Bear Clinic," UMass Memorial Health, accessed November 13, 2024, https://www.ummhealth.org/umass-memorial-medical-center/patients-visitors/patient -resources/classes-events-screenings/teddy-bear-clinic.

42. Lee, quoted in Friedman, "Alpert Medical Students," 60–61.

43. Salinas, quoted in "Use of Teddy Bear Nebulizers."

44. "The Vermont Teddy Bear Lifetime Guarantee," Vermont Teddy Bear, accessed November 13, 2024, https://www.vermontteddybear.com/lifetime-guarantee.html.

45. Haraway, "Teddy Bear Patriarchy," 21, 45, and 57. The wildly popular movies *Ted* (2012) and *Ted 2* (2015) offer a zany and raunchy take on a teddy bear's role in people's romantic lives.

46. Futter and DeBlasio quoted in Pogrebin, "Roosevelt Statue."

47. "Teddy Bears Raise Awareness for Black Lives Matter Movement in Downtown Los Angeles," ABC7, June 28, 2020, https://abc7.com/bear-the-truth-organization-city -hall-racism-protest/6279134/.

48. The following draws on Varga, "Gifting the Bear"; Varga, "Teddy's Bear"; Varga, "Babes in the Woods"; Varga and Zuk, "Golliwogs and Teddy Bears." For a critique of

Varga's approach, see the Daniel Thomas Cook, in "Response" to her "Gifting the Bear," 89–91.

49. Varga, "Gifting the Bear," 80.

50. Berger, *Objects of Affection*, suggests how teddy bears represent comfort and innocence.

51. Ngai, *Our Aesthetic Categories*, explores the contradictions of cuteness. Among other works that examine these tensions are Parreñas, *Decolonizing Extinction*; and Ticktin, *Casualties of Care*.

7. OFF THE POSTER AND OUT OF THE ZOO: SMOKEY BEAR GOES EVERYWHERE

1. In writing on Smokey Bear, I am relying on Lawter, *Smokey Bear 20252*; Morrison, *Guardian*; "80 Years of Smokey Bear," Smokey Bear Wildfire Prevention, accessed November 13, 2024, https://www.smokeybear.com/en; "History of Smokey Bear," South Dakota Department of Agriculture & Natural Resources, Resource Conservation & Forestry, accessed November 13, 2024, https://danr.sd.gov/Conservation/docs/Education/history-of-smokeybear.pdf; and Bourgon, "Brief History." Kosek, "White Racist Pig," offers an exceptionally insightful analysis.

2. Smith, "Story," 184. For a summary history of the public relations campaign, see Melillo, *How McGruff*, 29–48.

3. United States Forest Service, "Our Carelessness, Their Secret Weapon: Prevent Forest Fires," 1943, University of North Texas Libraries, UNT Digital Library, accessed November 13, 2024, https://digital.library.unt.edu/ark:/67531/metadc494/.

4. Quoted in Haverkampf and Schamel, "Fire Prevention Posters," 165.

5. "Fire Prevention Posters: The Story of Smokey Bear," Original Sources, accessed November 14, 2024, https://www.originalsources.com/Document.aspx?DocID=3YLTK88L8GUWGXN.

6. Jim Richardson memo, September 5, 1944, in Lawter, *Smokey Bear 20252*, 42.

7. Richard Hammatt, August 9, 1944, quoted in Lawter, *Smokey Bear 20252*, 39–40; and Haverkampf and Schamel, "Fire Prevention Posters," 165.

8. "About the Campaign," Smokey Bear Wildfire Prevention, accessed November 14, 2024, https://www.smokeybear.com/en/smokeys-history/about-the-campaign.

9. Coen, *Fu-go*.

10. William Mendenhall, quoted in Kosek, "White Racist Pig," 192.

11. The figure comes from Smith, "Story," 185.

12. On the appearance of the first stuffed animal, see Wilson, *America's Public Lands*, 122.

13. Smith, "Story," 185 and 187.

14. Barker, *Great Wilderness*, 37.

15. Biel, *Do (Not) Feed*, 71.

16. Charlton, "Smokey Bear Dies."

17. Colen, "Fire Fighter."

18. The figure comes from Barker, *Great Wilderness*, 40.

19. Kosek, "White Racist Pig," 211.

20. "Smokey Bear," National Agricultural Library, accessed November 14, 2024, https://www.nal.usda.gov/exhibits/speccoll/exhibits/show/smokey-bear.

21. Sean Munger, "Only You: The Somewhat Depressing History of Smokey the Bear." SeanMunger.com (blog), August 27, 2020, https://seanmunger.com/blog/c/blog/b/only-you-the-somewhat-depressing-history-of-smokey-the-bear. Although not referencing teddy or Smokey, Dunaway, *Seeing Green*, offers a critical assessment of how popular images simultaneously lend support to environmentalism and obfuscate underlying structural issues and the road to enduring solutions.

22. This and other images appear in a *Life Magazine* online slide show titled "The Real Smokey Bear," its date uncertain: https://web.archive.org/web/20100815191406/http://www.life.com/image/first/in-gallery/46761/the-real-smokey-bear. For additional surveys of images and their histories, see also National Archives and Records Administration, "History of Smokey Bear," 2006, https://archive.org/details/gov.nwcg.nfes.2882.3. From 1944 to 1973, the Forest Service employed Rudy Wendelin as Smokey's full-time artist.

23. "Story of Smokey," Smokey Bear Wildfire Prevention, accessed November 14, 2024, https://smokeybear.com/en/smokeys-history?decade=1940. This site also provides links to posters and radio and television shows and even some ephemera.

24. "Smokey Bear Collectibles," Collectors Weekly, accessed November 14, 2024, https://www.collectorsweekly.com/animals/smokey-bear.

25. "History of Smokey Bear," South Dakota Department of Agriculture & Natural Resource, accessed November 27, 2024, https://danr.sd.gov/Conservation/docs/Education/history-of-smokeybear.pdf.

26. Wendelin, quoted in Lawter, *Smokey Bear 20252*, 254–55.

27. Smokey Bear, "Smokey the Bear Song—Eddy Arnold (1952)," YouTube, July 15, 2010, https://www.youtube.com/watch?v=Myz93sXW66Y.

28. Abraham Cartoon, "The Ballad of Smokey the Bear (1966) Rankin_Bass (Animation_Family) (SD)," Dailymotion, https://www.dailymotion.com/video/x8mzz01.

29. "The Smokey Bear Show (1969)," Behind the Voice Actors, accessed November 14, 2024, https://www.behindthevoiceactors.com/tv-shows/The-Smokey-Bear-Show/. Less fully connected to Smokey Bear is the *Smokey and the Bandit* franchise launched in 1977.

30. Gary Snyder, "Smokey the Bear Sutra," *Earth Dharma* 22, no. 1 (2005), https://www.inquiringmind.com/article/2201_27_snyder_smokey-bear-sutra/.

31. Waugh, "'Only You.'"

32. Nichols, *Milagro Beanfield War*, 193. A film version appeared in 1988, directed by Robert Redford.

33. Nichols, *Milagro Beanfield War*, 193 and 195. Jacoby, *Crimes Against Nature*, tells the larger story in which the conflicts between Indigenous peoples and settler colonialists over fire management are important. Demuth, *Floating Coast*, discusses such tensions in another geographical context.

34. Kosek, "White Racist Pig," 184.

35. Don Belding, quoted in Kosek, "White Racist Pig," 203.

36. Kosek, "White Racist Pig," 189 and 225.

37. On these controversies, see Lewis, "Smokey Bear in Vietnam," 602; Lawter, *Smokey Bear 20252*, 315–18 and 325; Abbey, *Monkey Wrench Gang*, 226–27; Lewis and Miller, "Vast, Incredible Damage"; and Miller, "Boiling Point."

38. Donovan and Brown, "Be Careful," 79. For how the Forest Service defended its approach, including its reliance on Smokey Bear, see Melillo, *How McGruff*, 20.

39. Pyne, quoted in Bourgon, "Brief History."

40. Minnich, quoted in Swenson, "Wrong?"

41. Munger, "Only You."

42. Though my interests are somewhat different from hers, in this final discussion, I am relying on Helmers, "Hybridity."

43. Shepard, *Others*, 169–71.

44. Buchanan, *Holt Collier*, vi.

8. OUT OF THE CLOSET: BEARS IN THE GAY WORLD

1. In researching and writing on this topic, I am indebted to the work of Les Wright. Throughout I have relied on two books he edited and contributed to: Wright, *Bear Book*; and Wright, *Bear Book II*. His website, leskwright.com, includes material on his Bear History Project; and he has developed the most important source of archival material: Les K. Wright Papers and Bear History Project Files, Division of Rare and Manuscript Collections, Cornell University Library, collection number 7656, https://rmc.library.cornell.edu/EAD/htmldocs/RMM07656.html. I am grateful to Les Wright for providing information to me during a June 14, 2022, phone conversation. In addition, a good source for leads to this subculture is author Jack Fritscher's website: https://jackfritscher.com/. For a brief discussion of this subculture as an American phenomenon, see Suresha, "You Can Lead," 296–97. Among the scholarly articles on gay bears, which focus mainly on health issues, is Gough and Flanders, "Celebrating 'Obese' Bodies." Among the exceptions to the little written on gay bears outside that community are what Varga says in "Gifting the Bear" and a brief mention in Kipnis, *Bound and Gagged*, 114. See also the X postings of Gabriel Rosenberg, a historian at Duke: bearistotle (@gnrosenberg); and his podcasts at bearistotle.substack.com; as well as his recent publications identified at https://scholars.duke.edu/person/gabriel.rosenberg/publications. In "Furry Fandom," Dunn explores a subculture of people dressing up as animals. Contrast this with what Shepard and Sanders write about in *Sacred Paw*.

2. To a lesser extent than is true with gay bears, sports teams that use bears as mascots project ursine powers onto their athletes. Among the works that provide important contextualization of gay history is D'Emilio, "Capitalism."

3. In *Bear*, Bieder notes that "one of the most universal tales—versions are found from North America to Siberia—is the legend of the woman who marries a bear" (56).

4. Wright, "Concise History," 21. Among other discussions of this history are Suresha, "Bear Roots"; and Fritscher, "Foreword." On the larger context, see Whitesel, *Fat Gay Men*. For products that connect bears and gay culture, see "Gay pride teddy bear," Etsy, accessed November 14, 2024, https://www.etsy.com/market/gay_pride_teddy_bear.

5. Policarpio, "*BEAR* Magazine."

6. Wright, "Introduction," *Bear Book*, 15.

7. For the early statistics, see "A Timeline of HIV and AIDS," HIV.gov, accessed November 14, 2024, https://www.hiv.gov/hiv-basics/overview/history/hiv-and-aids-time-

line. An early identification of gay bears appeared in a July 1979 article in *The Advocate*: Mazzei, "Who's Who." See "#TBT: When *The Advocate* Invented Bears," *The Advocate*, April 17, 2014, https://www.advocate.com/comedy/2014/04/17/tbt-when-advocate -invented-bears. Varga, "Gifting the Bear," notes that "homosexuality, unacknowledged in mainstream bear culture, made" the teddy bear "an artifact of the gay community" in the 1980s, when "giving teddy bears to AIDS sufferers was a means for extending contact in an indirect way to the forbidden bodies of the ill and the dying" (79).

8. Wright, "Introduction," *Bear Book*, 15–16; see also Suresha, "Bear Roots," 48–49.

9. This discussion relies on Wright, "Concise History," 21–39. In the early twenty-first century, in addition to twenty-seven bear clubs elsewhere, there were in excess of sixty in the United States: Hennen, *Faeries*, 97. For another example of gay bears appearing in new media, see this poem: Arnold Zwicky, "Waltzing with Bears," Arnold Zwicky's Blog, May 25, 2010, https://arnoldzwicky.org/2010/05/25/waltzing-with-bears/.

10. Martin, "Foreword," xix–xx. Wright, "Introduction," *Bear Book*, 1–17; and Wright, "Concise History," 21–39, provide a discussion of these debates over definitions. How many gay bears there are in the United States varies over time and depends on parameters used. My guess is that for the United States in the 2020s, we are talking of numbers some- where between 100,000 and 500,000; see also Suresha, *Bears on Bears*, xvii–xviii.

11. See, for example, Ridinger, "Paws," 163–67.

12. Wright, "Introduction," *Bear Book*, 2.

13. Wright, "Concise History," 21–22. On the issue of body image, see Locke, "Male Images."

14. Hill, "Aroused," 65.

15. Wright, *Bear Book II*, contains many contributions that explore multiple aspects of diversity among bears. On the roles race and ethnicity play, see Wright, "Introduction," *Bear Book II*, 4–5; Lopez, "Puerto Rican"; Clark, "One Black Bear"; and Gan, "Asian Bear."

16. Suresha, "Bear Roots," 45. For general discussions of social class in this subculture, see Wright, "Introduction," *Bear Book*, 11–14; Wright, "Introduction," *Bear Book II*, 4–5 and 9; and Rofes, "Academics as Bears."

17. Wright, "Introduction," *Bear Book*, 10.

18. For a probing discussion of the roles gender, class, race, and commercialism play in these communities, see Hennen, *Faeries*. Although it contains no discussion of gay bears, Chasin, *Selling Out*, offers a critical assessment of commercialism's impact on gay culture.

19. The essays in Wright, *Bear Book II*, 287–350, provide a useful entry point to the roles of media in gay bear culture.

20. See the images at Rand's website, https://johnrand.com/portraits/; Nelson, *Bear Cult*.

21. "gay bears," The Movie Database, accessed November 15, 2024, https://www .themoviedb.org/keyword/208135-gay-bears/movie.

22. The film, once hosted at https://www.themoviedb.org/movie/840707-i-f-ck-d -p-dd-ngton-b-r, is inexplicably no longer available on the web. In the 1970s the film director Barry Leith produced a sex tape featuring Paddington, which is also no longer available: Andrew Clark, "Paddington Bear in Sex Tape Scandal," *Press and Journal*, No- vember 30, 2014, https://www.pressandjournal.co.uk/fp/news/uk/416887/paddington -bear-sex-tape-scandal/.

23. bwm Staff, "Are You Ready for Spooky Bear in Provincetown," *Bear World Magazine*, August 30, 2022, https://bearworldmag.com/are-you-ready-for-spooky-bear-in -provincetown-this-october/.

24. "Bear Week," Provincetown Office of Tourism, accessed November 15, 2024, https://ptowntourism.com/events/bear-week/; see also "bearmania Provincetown," Facebook, accessed November 15, 2024, https://www.facebook.com/bearmaniaptown/.

25. Brunner, *Bears*, 171.

26. Mazzei, "Who's Who."

27. Megan Gannon, "Brown Bears Caught Performing Oral Sex," *Live Science*, June 17, 2014, https://www.livescience.com/46364-brown-bears-caught-performing-oral-sex.html.

28. Cohen, *Bear Like Me*, 131.

29. Jaffe, "Licking Voblya," 89; and Suresha, "Acknowledgments," 233. If Henry, *Tales from the Bear Cult*, is typical of collections of short stories of gay male bear porn, then all one would find in terms of references to bears would be a few scattered references to hibernation, Bruins, and grizzlies. From what I can tell, the fact that sex sells and commerce rules fundamentally shapes what is available in bear fiction. See, for example, Suresha, *Biggest Lover*.

30. Hennen, *Faeries*, 95.

31. Hennen, *Faeries*, 98, 109, 110, 112, 115, and 118; Wright, quoted in Hennen, *Faeries*, 109.

32. Hennen, *Faeries*, 118, 130, and 132–33.

33. Kampf, *Bear Handbook*, 120.

34. Ridinger, "Bearaphernalia," 85–86.

35. Fritscher, "Foreword," xxxvii. This discussion relies on material in Wright, *Bear Book* and *Bear Book II*.

36. De Mey, "French Bear," 267.

37. Hill, "Aroused," 65.

38. Suresha, "You Can Lead," 297.

39. Kelly and Kane, "In Goldilocks's Footsteps," 327.

40. https://www.themoviedb.org/movie/840707-i-f-ck-d-p-dd-ngton-b-r; no longer available.

41. Ramsey, "Bear Clan."

42. Ramsey, "Bear Clan," 51–55, 63–64.

43. Wilkinson, "Point of View," 106–7. In *Spaces Between Us*, Morgensen, though he does not reference gay bears, casts a skeptical eye on how some gay people appropriate elements of Indigenous cultures to bolster their claims of legitimacy in contemporary America.

44. Jack Fritscher, quoted in Suresha, *Bears on Bears*, 78.

45. Fritscher, quoted in Suresha, *Bears on Bears*, 94; Suresha, *Bears on Bears*, 93–94; Chris Wittke, quoted in Suresha, *Bears on Bears*, 22, 29.

46. Among relevant explorations of the relationships between sex, love, and violence are Dean et al., "Conversation"; and Bersani, *Rectum*.

47. In an email from June 7, 2022, Les Wright assured me that I would be unlikely to find more relevant material in his extensive collection at Cornell. Only a full exploration of materials will reveal whether there were, in fact, so few visual images of nonhuman bears, an investigation that would include, among other sources, Nelson, *Bear Cult*; and Mazzei, "Who's Who."

1. Coleman, *Here Lies*, 214.
2. Phillips quoted in Lapinski, *Death*, 17.
3. Jans, *Grizzly Maze*, 195.
4. Treadwell and Palovak, *Among Grizzlies*, 1–2.
5. Treadwell and Palovak, *Among Grizzlies*, 2–3.
6. The information on a failed television career and prescribed drugs, as well as other events, comes from Werner Herzog's 2005 documentary film, *Grizzly Man*.
7. Treadwell and Palovak, *Among Grizzlies*, 6–7.
8. Peacock, *Grizzly Years*, 61.
9. Treadwell, "Some Bet."
10. Treadwell and Palovak, *Among Grizzlies*, 10.
11. Treadwell and Palovak, *Among Grizzlies*, 20 and 52. Since the 1980s ecotourism has been an increasingly prominent factor in making it possible for people to encounter animals, including bears, in their natural habitats. Despite its appeal to those committed to environmentalism, because it relies on air travel and often benefits corporations more than nature, it is hardly as socially responsible as its advocates claim or its participants imagine.
12. Zeman, "Man Who Loved."
13. Treadwell and Palovak, *Among Grizzlies*, 19, 21, 69, and 90.
14. Jans, *Grizzly Maze*, 52.
15. Treadwell and Palovak, *Among Grizzlies*, 138.
16. Lapinski, *Death*, 12.
17. Treadwell and Palovak, *Among Grizzlies*, 21, 25, 138, and 190.
18. Treadwell and Palovak, *Among Grizzlies*, 29 and 33.
19. Jans, *Grizzly Maze*, 31. For an example of how a journalist uncritically captured what Treadwell was doing, see Shapiro, Review.
20. These corrective notes rely on Jans, *Grizzly Maze*; Lapinski, *Death*; and Herzog, *Grizzly Man*.
21. For discussions of evidence that contradicts Treadwell's claims, see Lapinski, *Death*, 25–35; and Jans, *Grizzly Maze*, 33–38.
22. Lapinski, *Death*, 74–75; Jans, *Grizzly Maze*, 40–45 and 66–77.
23. Jans, *Grizzly Maze*, 64–66, charts the growing numbers of ecotourists in the region and Treadwell's increasingly hostile encounters with them. "Bear Viewing," Island Air Service, accessed November 15, 2024, https://www.flyadq.com/air-tours/bear-tours/, offers a sense of a flourishing tourism trade. Nor did Treadwell mention how global warming threatened grizzlies, even though it did not fully enter public consciousness until Al Gore and David Guggenheim's film *An Inconvenient Truth* three years after Treadwell's death.
24. Coleman, *Here Lies*, 214–16.
25. Louisa Willcox, quoted in Medred, "Man, Myth, Martyr."
26. Jans, *Grizzly Maze*, 50. On how Treadwell garnered support, see Lapinski, *Death*, 14–24; and Jans, *Grizzly Maze*, 39–40 and 47–51.
27. For key moments in this story, see Jans, *Grizzly Maze*, 47–50, some of which is difficult to locate online, such as a 1995 film, *Timothy and the Bears* by the French Marathon

film company; a 1995 Audubon/Turner Broadcasting documentary called *In the Land of the Grizzlies*; a 1997 Paramount Television short feature for the Fox *Wild Things* series; a 1998 NBC *Dateline* appearance. Or what Jans, *Grizzly Maze*, 49, calls a "tour de force": a 1999 Discovery Channel special, "The Grizzly Diaries."

28. Stambler, "Bears Fan."

29. Treadwell, quoted in Lapinski, *Death*, 16–17.

30. Twinw, "Grizzly Man on David Letterman," YouTube, May 20, 2007, https://www.youtube.com/watch?v=GCi4QgPoHZE&list=PL7rbQpafoAZuzGHhmYlE4ZGRlZO_vfcTx&index=4.

31. Treadwell, quoted in Lapinski, *Death*, 19. Seeing Treadwell come too close to a bear on Snyder's show, the park's superintendent, Deb Liggett, unsuccessfully tried to convince officials at regional headquarters to cite him: Lapinski, *Death*, 72.

32. For a thorough discussion of the risks that bears pose to humans, see Jans, *Grizzly Maze*, 220–37.

33. Treadwell, quoted in Jans, *Grizzly Maze*, 81.

34. Treadwell, quoted in Medred, "Man, Myth, Martyr."

35. Fulton, quoted in Herzog, *Grizzly Man*.

36. Lapinski, *Death*, 103–15; and Jans, *Grizzly Maze*, 76–138, chronicle these final days.

37. Jans, *Grizzly Maze*, 39–45, 148–74, and 212–17, offers a thorough evaluation.

38. Porter, quoted in Jans, *Grizzly Maze*, 215.

39. Bane, letter, quoted in Lapinski, *Death*, 156.

40. Bennett, quoted in Jans, *Grizzly Maze*, 166, 171, and 173. For his comparison of the renderings of the stories of Timothy Treadwell by Herzog in *Grizzly Man* and the more sympathetic treatment of Chris McCandless by Jon Krakauer in *Into the Wild* (1996) and the 2007 film of the same name, see Jans, "Re-Examining."

41. Willcox, quoted in Lapinski, *Death*, 159.

42. Among the scholarly treatments of Herzog's film, several stand out, including Sellbach, "Traumatic Efforts"; Hediger, "Grizzly Love"; and Lulka, "Consuming." The eight episodes of Animal Planet's *Grizzly Man Diaries*, launched in late August 2008, are a sequel to *Grizzly Man* that relied on a decade's worth of Treadwell material. For a critique of this miniseries as compared with the Herzog film, see Genzlinger, "Observer."

43. Bradshaw, "*Grizzly Man* Review." In what follows I am drawing on Herzog's award-winning film; to access it, see *Grizzly Man*, directed by Werner Herzog (2005; Santa Monica, CA: Lionsgate), Tubi, https://tubitv.com/movies/393462/grizzly-man, https://www.youtube.com/watch?v=VBGFONxNpVQ. For a transcript, see "Grizzly Man Script—Dialogue," Drew's Script-O-Rama, accessed November 27, 2024, http://www.script-o-rama.com/movie_scripts/g/grizzly-man-script-transcript-herzog.html.

44. Carman, "Grizzly Love," applies queer, ecological, and postmodernist theories to Treadwell's life and Herzog's film.

45. Ebert, "Grizzly Story."

46. Haakanson, quoted in Herzog, *Grizzly Man*.

47. Fulton, quoted in Herzog, *Grizzly Man*.

48. Engel, *Bear*, 2. Lockwood, "Pull Off My Head," places the novel in the context of Engel's career and laments the "superficiality" of the book's "mass dissemination." Among

the many other stories of interspecies love are Zabor, *Bear Comes Home*; and Straley, *Woman Who Married a Bear*. Among critical assessment of such relationships are Singer, "'Heavy Petting'"; Bakke, "Predicament"; and Elkin, "Making of Ashenden." See also Bieder, *Bear*, 56–60 and 120.

49. Engel, *Bear*, 9.

50. Quoted in Hair, "Engel's 'Bear.'"

51. Hair, "Engel's 'Bear.'" For places to track commentaries on Engel's work, see Fee, "Articulating"; and Gault, "Marian Engel's *Bear*."

52. Engel, *Bear*, 34, 73, and 96.

53. Engel, *Bear*, 93, 99, and 112.

54. Engel, *Bear*, 120, 122, 131, and 132.

55. Engel, *Bear*, 9, 133–34, 136, and 141.

CODA. PRECARITY AND POLAR BEARS

1. Born, "Bearing Witness?," 649, 654, 655, and 659; she was relying on, among other sources, Archibald, "Fierce to Adorable." See also her *Polar Bears*. Mooallem, *Wild Ones*, 11–101, charts Americans' fascination with bears, culminating with the author going to Churchill, Manitoba, as a place to contemplate how climate change threatens polar bears. On grounds that are both ideological and strategic, critics have assailed the campaigns that deploy polar bears as symbols of the dangers of climate change: see Fee, *Polar Bear*, 165–82; and more recently Frankie Adkins, "Why Polar Bears Are No Longer the Poster Image of Climate Change," BBC, November 13, 2023, https://www.bbc.com/future/article/20231113-climate-change-why-photos-of-polar-bears-dont-work.

2. Heise, *Imagining Extinction*, 241–44.

3. Fountain, "Global Warming"; Erdenesanaa, "Polar Bears Struggling."

4. Frazier, "Sell Coca-Cola."

5. Heise, *Imagining Extinction*, 238–40.

6. Greenpeace UK, "The Making of Aurora, Greenpeace's Giant Polar Bear," YouTube, December 23, 2013, https://www.youtube.com/watch?v=KmqmoqSp-nA.

7. "Adopt a Polar Bear," WWFGifts, accessed November 15, 2024, https://gifts.worldwildlife.org/gift-center/gifts/Species-Adoptions/Polar-Bear.aspx.

8. "Why the Polar Bears?," A Warmer Planet, accessed November 15, 2024, https://awarmerplanet.com/why-the-bears/.

9. On the threats to polar bears and the efforts to protect them, see Brunner, *Bears*, 166–69; Bieder, *Bear*, 98–101, 141–43, and 164–69.

10. This summary draws on Zach Fitzner, "Why Polar Bears Became an Icon of Climate Change," Earth.com, October 8, 2018, https://www.earth.com/news/polar-bears-climate-change-2/.

11. Greenemeier, "U.S. Protects Polar Bears." Inhofe quoted in Greenemeier, "U.S. Protects Polar Bears."

Select Bibliography

Abbey, Edward. *The Monkey Wrench Gang*. Lippincott, 1975.

Abrams, Jonathan. "A New-Look Circus Sends in the Clowns, but Loses the Face Paint." *New York Times*, March 2, 2024.

Adams, Carol L. "Post-Meateating." In *Animal Encounters*, edited by Tom Tyler and Manuela Rossini. Brill, 2009.

Adams, Grizzly. *The Hair-Breadth Escapes and Adventures of "Grizzly Adams" in Catching and Conquering the Wild Animals Included in His California Menagerie*. Wynkoop, Hallenbeck and Thomas, 1860.

Adler, Peggy, and Dibrima Jean Burnham. *Pallenberg Wonder Bears—From the Beginning*. BearManor Media, 2022.

Alagona, Peter S. *The Accidental Ecosystem: People and Wildlife in American Cities*. University of California Press, 2022.

Albrecht, Ernest. *The New American Circus*. University Press of Florida, 1995.

Ambrose, Stephen E., and Douglas G. Brinkley. "The Centennial of the Teddy Bear." *Theodore Roosevelt Association Journal* 25 (2003): 17–20.

Anderson, Virginia DeJohn. *Creatures of Empire: How Domestic Animals Transformed Early America*. Oxford University Press, 2004.

Archibald, Kristopher. "From Fierce to Adorable: Representations of Polar Bears in the Popular Imagination." *American Review of Canadian Studies* 45 (2015): 266–82.

Asma, Stephen T. *Stuffed Animals & Pickled Heads: The Culture and Evolution of Natural History Museums*. Oxford University Press, 2001.

Austerlitz, Saul. "How the Berenstain Bears Found Salvation." *New York Times Magazine Section*, October 6, 2016.

Austin, James C. "Legend, Myth, and Symbol in Frederick Manfred's *Lord Grizzly.*" *Critique: Studies in Contemporary Fiction* 6 (1963): 122–30.

Aylesworth, Jim. *Goldilocks and the Three Bears.* Illustrated by Barbara McClintock. Scholastic, 2003.

Bader, Barbara. *American Picturebooks from Noah's Ark to the Beast Within.* Macmillan, 1996.

Bakke, Monica. "The Predicament of Zoopleasures: Human-Nonhuman Libidinal Relations." In *Animal Encounters,* edited by Tom Tyler and Manuela Rossini. Brill, 2009.

Barker, Elliott S. *Smokey Bear and the Great Wilderness.* Sunstone, 1982.

Barnes, Brooks. "Splash Mountain's Bayou Overhaul." *New York Times,* June 14, 2024.

Beard, Henry, and John Boswell. *What's Worrying Gus? The True Story of a Big-City Bear.* Villard, 1995.

"Bears in Combine: Conspiracy to Keep President from Shooting Them." *Washington Post,* November 18, 1902.

"Bears Left Behind." *Washington Post,* November 19, 1902.

Bederman, Gail. *Manliness and Civilization: A Cultural History of Gender and Race in the United States.* University of Chicago Press, 1995.

Bekoff, Marc. *The Emotional Lives of Animals: A Leading Scientist Explores Animal Joy, Sorrow, and Empathy—and Why They Matter.* New World Library, 2007.

Belle, Trixit, and Melissa Caruso-Scott. *Goldilocks and the Three Bears.* Henry Holt, 2014.

Berenstain, Stan, and Jan Berenstain. *The Big Honey Hunt.* Random House, 1962.

Berenstain, Stan, and Jan Berenstain. *Down a Sunny Dirt Road: An Autobiography.* Random House, 2002.

Berenstain, Stan, and Jan Berenstain. *Trouble with Pets.* Random House, 1990.

Bergen, Lara, and Vincent Nguyen. *The Polar Bears' Home: A Story About Global Warming.* Little Simon, 2008.

Berger, Arthur Asa. *The Objects of Affection: Semiotics and Consumer Culture.* Palgrave Macmillan, 2010.

Berger, John. "Why Look at Animals." In John Berger, *About Looking.* Pantheon, 1980.

Bernstein, Robin. *Racial Innocence: Performing American Childhood from Slavery to Civil Rights.* New York University Press, 2011.

Berryman, Annette. "Why the Worry About Anthropomorphism?" *Metro: Media and Education Magazine* 81 (1989): 45–70.

Bersani, Leo. *Is the Rectum a Grave? and Other Essays.* University of Chicago Press, 2010.

Bettelheim, Bruno. *The Uses of Enchantment: The Meaning and Importance of Fairy Tales.* Knopf, 1976.

Beyers, Leandri, Warwick P. Phipps, and Charl Vorster. "An Introduction to Teddy Bear Therapy: A Systems Family Therapy Approach to Child Psychotherapy." *Journal of Family Psychotherapy* 28 (2017): 317–32.

Bickley, Bruce. *Joel Chandler Harris: A Biography and Critical Study.* University of Georgia Press, 1987.

Bieder, Robert E. *Bear.* Reaktion, 2005.

Biel, Alice Wondrak. *Do (Not) Feed the Bears: The Fitful History of Wildlife and Tourists in Yellowstone.* University Press of Kansas, 2006.

Bloch, Yuval H., and Asaf Toker. "Doctor, Is My Teddy Bear Okay? The 'Teddy Bear Hospital' as a Method to Reduce Children's Fear of Hospitalization." *Israel Medical Association Journal* 10 (2010): 597–99.

Blond, Kara. "Imagining the Future of Natural History Exhibitions." In *The Future of Natural History Museums*, edited by Eric Dorfman. Routledge, 2018.

Boas, Franz. *The Central Eskimo: Sixth Annual Report of the Bureau of Ethnology to the Secretary of the Smithsonian Institution, 1884–1885*. Government Printing Office, 1988.

Boggs, Colleen Glenny. *Animalia Americana: Animal Representations and Biopolitical Subjectivity*. Columbia University Press, 2013.

Bond, Michael. *A Bear Called Paddington*. Houghton Mifflin, 1958.

Born, Dorothea. "Bearing Witness? Polar Bears as Icons for Climate Change Communication in *National Geographic*." *Environmental Communication* 13 (2019): 649–63.

Born, Dorothea. *Polar Bears as Cultural Symbols: Threatening Monsters and Threatened Species*. Routledge, 2021.

Bourgon, Lyndsie. "A Brief History of Smokey Bear, the Forest Service's Legendary Mascot." *Smithsonian Magazine*, July 2019. https://www.smithsonianmag.com/history/brief-history-smokey-bear-180972549/.

Bousé, Derek. "Are Wildlife Films Really Nature 'Documentaries'?" *Critical Studies in Mass Communication* 15 (1998): 116–40.

Bousé, Derek. Review of *The Bear*. *Film Quarterly* 43 (1990): 30–34.

Bousé, Derek. *Wildlife Films*. University of Pennsylvania Press, 2000.

Bradshaw, Peter. "*Grizzly Man* Review—Werner Herzog Traces Timothy Treadwell's Steps." *The Guardian*, February 2, 2006.

Brett, Jan. *Goldilocks and the Three Bears*. Putnam and Grosset, 1987.

"Bruin Was in Luck." *Washington Post*, November 16, 1902.

Brunner, Bernd. *Bears: A Brief History*. Translated by Lori Lantz. Yale University Press, 2007.

Buchanan, Minor Ferris. *Holt Collier: His Life, His Roosevelt Hunts, and the Origin of the Teddy Bear*. Centennial, 2002.

Burt, Jonathan. *Animals in Film*. Reaktion, 2002.

BWM Staff. "Are You Ready for Spooky Bear in Provincetown This October?" *Bear World Magazine*, August 30, 2022.

"Can the Teddy Bear Speak?" *Childhood* 18 (2011): 411–18.

Carman, Colin. "Grizzly Love: The Queer Ecology of Timothy Treadwell." *GLQ: A Journal of Lesbian and Gay Studies* 18 (2012): 507–28.

Charlton, Linda. "Smokey Bear Dies in Retirement." *New York Times*, November 10, 1976.

Chase, Richard, ed. *The Complete Tales of Uncle Remus*. Houghton Mifflin, 1955.

Chasin, Alexandra. *Selling Out: The Gay and Lesbian Movement Goes to Market*. St. Martin's, 2000.

Chen, Mel Y. *Animacies: Biopolitics, Racial Mattering, and Queer Affect*. Duke University Press, 2012.

Chris, Cynthia. *Watching Wildlife*. University of Minnesota Press, 2006.

Clark, Jason R. "One Black Bear Speaks Out." In Wright, *Bear Book II*.

Coen, Ross. *Fu-go: The Curious History of Japan's Balloon Bomb Attack on America*. University of Nebraska Press, 2014.

Cohen, Jonathan. *Bear Like Me*. Haworth, 2003.

Coleman, Jon T. *Here Lies Hugh Glass: A Mountain Man, a Bear, and the Rise of the American Nation*. Farrar, Straus and Giroux, 2012.

Coleman, Jon T. "The Shoemaker's Circus: Grizzly Adams and Nineteenth-Century Animal Entertainment." *Environmental History* 20 (2015): 593–618.

Coleman, Jon T. *Vicious: Wolves and Men in America*. Yale University Press, 2004.

Colen, B. D. "S. Bear, Fire Fighter." *Washington Post*, November 10, 1976.

Cook, Daniel Thomas. "Gifting the Bear and a Nostalgic Desire for Childhood Innocence" (Response to Donna Varga). *Cultural Analysis* 8 (2009): 89–96.

Cooley, Mackenzie. *Perfection of Nature: Animals, Breeding, and Race in the Renaissance*. University of Chicago Press, 2022.

Corliss, Richard. "That Old Feeling IV, A Tale of Two Circuses." *Time Magazine*, April 20, 2001.

Crane, Jonathan K., ed. *Beastly Morality: Animals as Ethical Animals*. Columbia University Press, 2016.

Crews, Frederick. *The Pooh Perplex: A Freshman Casebook*. E. P. Dutton, 1963.

Crews, Frederick. *Postmodern Pooh*. Farrar, Straus and Giroux, 2001.

Crisp, Marty. *Teddy Bears in Advertising Art*. Hobby House, 1991.

Cross, Gary S. *The Cute and the Cool: Wondrous Innocence and Modern American Children's Culture*. Oxford University Press, 2004.

Cross, Gary S. *Kids' Stuff: Toys and the Changing World of American Childhood*. Harvard University Press, 1997.

Curwood, James Oliver. *The Grizzly King: A Romance of the Wild*. Grosset & Dunlap, 1918.

Dasent, George Webbe. *Popular Tales from the Norse*. G. P. Putnam's Sons, 1912.

Daston, Lorraine, and Gregg Mitman, eds. *Thinking with Animals: New Perspectives on Anthropomorphism*. Columbia University Press, 2005.

Davis, Janet M. *The Circus Age: Culture and Society Under the American Big Top*. University of North Carolina Press, 2002.

Davis, Janet M. "The Circus Americanized." In *The American Circus*, edited by Susan Weber, Kenneth L. Ames, and Matthew Wittmann. Yale University Press, 2012.

Davis, Janet M. *The Gospel of Kindness: Animal Welfare and the Making of Modern America*. Oxford University Press, 2016.

Davis, Jim. *Garfield: Complete Works*. Vol. 1: 1978–1979. Ballantine, 2018.

Dax, Michael J. *Grizzly West: A Failed Attempt to Reintroduce Grizzly Bears in the Mountain West*. University of Nebraska Press, 2015.

Dean, Tim, Hal Foster, Kaja Silverman, and Leo Bersani. "A Conversation with Leo Bersani." *October* (1997): 3–16.

DeMello, Margo. *Animals and Society: An Introduction to Human-Animal Studies*. Columbia University Press, 2012.

De Mey, Pierre. "A French Bear Asks: Are Bears an American Thing." In Wright, *Bear Book*.

D'Emilio, John. "Capitalism and Gay Identity." In *The Lesbian and Gay Studies Reader*, edited by Henry Abelove, Michèle Aina Barale, and David M. Halperin. Routledge, 1993.

Demuth, Bathsheba. *Floating Coast: An Environmental History of the Bering Strait*. Norton, 2019.

Demuth, Bathsheba. "Labors of Love: People, Dogs, and Affect in North American Arctic Borderlands, 1700–1900." *Journal of American History* 108 (2021): 270–95.

Derocher, Andrew E. *Polar Bears: A Complete Guide to Their Biology and Behavior*. Johns Hopkins University Press, 2012.

Desmond, Jane C. *Displaying Death and Animating Life: Human-Animal Relationship in Art, Science, and Everyday Life*. University of Chicago Press, 2016.

Desmond, Jane C. *Staging Tourism: Bodies on Display from Waikiki to Sea World*. University of Chicago Press, 1999.

de Waal, Frans. *Are We Smart Enough to Know How Smart Animals Are?* Norton, 2016.

de Waal, Frans. *Mama's Last Hug: Animal Emotions and What They Tell Us About Ourselves*. Norton, 2019.

Dickie, Gloria. *8 Bears: Mythic Past and Imperiled Future*. Norton, 2023.

Dillon, Richard. *The Legend of Grizzly Adams: California's Greatest Mountain Man*. Coward-McCann, 1966.

Disney Classics: Storybook Treasury. Disney Press, 2016.

Donahue, Jesse, and Erik Trump. *The Politics of Zoos: Exotic Animals and Their Protectors*. Northern Illinois University Press, 2006.

Donovan, Geoffrey H., and Thomas C. Brown. "Be Careful What You Wish For: The Legacy of Smokey Bear." *Frontiers in Ecology and the Environment* 5 (2007): 73–79.

Douglas, Susan J., and Andrea McDonnell. *Celebrity: A History of Fame*. New York University Press, 2019.

Dunaway, Finis. *Seeing Green: The Use and Abuse of American Environmental Images*. University of Chicago Press, 2015.

Dundes, Alan. "Bruno Bettelheim's Uses of Enchantment and Abuses of Scholarship." *Journal of American Folklore* 104 (1991): 74–83.

Dunn, Kameron. "Furry Fandom, Aesthetics, and the Potential in New Objects of Fannish Interest." *Transformative Works and Cultures* 37 (2022). https://doi.org/10.3983/twc.2022.2133.

Eaton, Seymour. *The Roosevelt Bears: Their Travels and Adventures*. Edward Stern, 1906.

Ebert, Roger. "The Grizzly Story of a Bear Man." August 11, 2005, https://www.rogerebert.com/reviews/grizzly-man-2005.

Eisen, Armand. *Goldilocks and the Three Bears*. Knopf, 1987.

Elkin, Stanley. "The Making of Ashenden" (1972). In *Stanley Elkin's Greatest Hits*. E. P. Dutton, 1980.

Elms, Alan C. "'The Three Bears': Four Interpretations." *Journal of American Folklore* 90 (1997): 257–72.

Engel, Marian. *Bear: A Novel*. Athenaeum, 1976.

Erdenesanaa, Delger. "Videos Show Polar Bears Struggling Not to Starve." *New York Times*, February 14, 2024.

Farhi, Paul, and Lisa Kehayias. "The New Children's Books Grimmer Than Grimm." *Washington Post*, September 3, 1989.

Faulkner, William. "The Bear." In William Faulkner, *Go Down, Moses*. Random House, 1941; Modern Library, 1955.

Fee, Margery. "Articulating the Female Subject: The Example of Marian Engel's Bear." *Atlantis: Critical Studies in Gender, Culture, and Social Justice* 14 (1988): 20–26.

Fee, Margery. *Polar Bear*. Reaktion, 2019.

Flores, Dan. *American Serengeti: The Last Big Animals of the Great Plains*. University Press of Kansas, 2016.

Flores, Dan. *Coyote America: A Natural and Supernatural History*. Basic Books, 2017.

Flores, Dan. *Wild New World: The Epic Story of Animals and People in America*. Norton, 2022.

Fountain, Henry. "Global Warming Is Driving Polar Bears Toward Extinction, Researchers Say." *New York Times*, July 20, 2020.

Frazier, Mya. "Should the Polar Bear Still Sell Coca-Cola?" *New Yorker*, November 6, 2014.

Friedman, Debbie M. "Alpert Medical Students Dispel Fears at Teddy Bear Clinic." *Rhode Island Medical Journal*, January 2014, 60–61.

Friend, Tad. "It's a Jungle in Here." *New York Magazine*, April 25, 1995.

Fritscher, Jack. "Foreword." In Wright, *Bear Book II*.

Fudge, Erica. *Animal*. Reaktion, 2002.

Fudge, Erica. *Quick Cattle and Dying Wishes: People and Their Animals in Early Modern England*. Cornell University Press, 2018.

Gan, Dave. "Asian Bear in Minnesota." In Wright, *Bear Book II*.

Garcia, Karen. "California's Grizzlies: Gargantuan, Dangerous Meat-Lovers. Totally Wrong, Research Shows." *Los Angeles Times*, January 11, 2011.

Gates, Henry Louis, Jr., and Maria Tatar, eds. *The Annotated African American Folktales*. Norton, 2018.

Gault, Cinda. "Marian Engel's *Bear*: Romance or Realism?" *Canadian Literature* 197 (2008): 29–40.

Genecov, Max. "Letter of Recommendation: Stuffed Animals." *New York Times Magazine*, December 13, 2018.

Genzlinger, Neil. "Observer of Grizzly Bears, Seen in Haunting Hindsight." *New York Times*, August 28, 2008.

Gietz, William. *Sam Patch: Ballad of a Jumping Man*. Watts, 1986.

Godfrey-Smith, Peter. "Visible and Invisible Worlds." *New York Review of Books*, June 6, 2024.

Goldilocks and the Three Bears: Recitos de Oro y Los Tres Osos. Adapted by Maria Mata. Translated by Alis Alejandro. Chronicle, 1988.

Gough, Brendan, and Gareth Flanders. "Celebrating 'Obese' Bodies: Gay 'Bears' Talk About Weight, Body Image and Health." *International Journal of Men's Health* 8 (2009): 235–53.

Grayson, Kyle. "How to Read Paddington Bear: Liberalism and the Foreign Subject in *A Bear Called Paddington*." *British Journal of Politics and International Relations* 15 (2013): 378–93.

Greenemeier, Larry. "U.S. Protects Polar Bears Under Endangered Species Act." *Scientific American*, May 14, 2008.

Grenby, M. O., and Andrea Immel, eds. *The Cambridge Companion to Children's Literature*. Cambridge University Press, 2009.

Grier, Katherine C. *Pets in America: A History*. University of North Carolina Press, 2006.

Grimm, Oliver, ed. *Bear and Human: Facets of a Multi-Layered Relationship from Past to Recent Times, with Emphasis on Northern Europe*. 3 vols. Brepols, 2023.

Grimm's Fairy Tales. Translated by Marian Edwardes and Edward Taylor. Maynard and Merrill, 1905.

Gruen, Lori, ed. *Critical Terms for Animal Studies*. University of Chicago Press, 2018.

Hair, Donald S. "Marian Engel's 'Bear.'" *Canadian Literature* 92 (1982): 34–45.

Hall, James. "Letters from the West: The Missouri Trapper." *The Port Folio* 19 (1825): 214–19. http://hughglass.org/wp-content/uploads/2015/09/1825-Hugh-Glass-article.pdf.

Hammarstrom, David Lewis. *Fall of the Big Top: The Vanishing American Circus*. McFarland, 2008.

Hansen, Paul W. "Bear Proof Jackson Hole Now." *Jackson Hole News and Guide*, December 8, 2021.

Hanson, Elizabeth. *Animal Attractions: Nature on Display in American Zoos*. Princeton University Press, 2002.

Haraway, Donna. *The Haraway Reader*. Routledge, 2004.

Haraway, Donna. "Teddy Bear Patriarchy: Taxidermy in the Garden of Eden, New York City, 1908–1936." *Social Text* 11 (1984–85): 20–64.

Harris, Joel Chandler. *Uncle Remus and Brer Rabbit*. Frederick A. Stokes, 1907.

Haverkampf, Beth, and Wynell B. Schamel. "Fire Prevention Posters: The Story of Smokey Bear." *Social Education* 53 (1994): 165–69.

Hediger, Ryan. "Timothy Treadwell's Grizzly Love as Freak Show: The Uses of Animals, Science, and Film." *ISLE: Interdisciplinary Studies in Literature and Environment* 19 (2012): 82–100.

Heise, Ursula K. *Imagining Extinction: The Cultural Meanings of Endangered Species*. University of Chicago Press, 2016.

Helmers, Marguerite. "Hybridity, Ethos, and Visual Representations of Smokey Bear." *JAC* 31 (2011): 45–69.

Hennen, Peter. *Faeries, Bears, and Leathermen: Men in Community Queering the Masculine*. University of Chicago Press, 2008.

Henry, Mark, ed. *Tales from the Bear Cult: Best Bear Stories from the Best Magazines*. Palm Drive, 2001.

Herrero, Stephen. *Bear Attacks: Their Causes and Avoidance*. Rev. ed. Lyons, 2018.

Herzog, Werner. *Grizzly Man*. Discovery Docs and Lionsgate Entertainment, 2005.

Hill, Scott. "Aroused from Hibernation." In Wright, *Bear Book*.

Hittell, Thomas H. *The Adventures of James Capen Adams, Mountaineer and Grizzly Bear Hunter, of California*. Towne and Bacon, 1860.

Hoff, Benjamin. *The Tao of Pooh*. E. P. Dutton, 1982.

Hoff, Benjamin. *The Te of Piglet*. E. P. Dutton, 1990.

Horowitz, Daniel. *Consuming Pleasures: Intellectuals and Popular Culture in the Postwar World*. University of Pennsylvania Press, 2012.

Horowitz, Helen L. "Animal and Man in the New York Zoological Park." *New York History* 56 (1975): 426–55.

Horowitz, Helen L. "The National Zoological Park: 'City of Refuge' or Zoo." In *Records of the Columbia Historical Society of Washington, D.C. 1973–1974*, edited by Francis Coleman Rosenberger. Columbia Historical Society, 1976.

Hunt, Peter, and Karen Sands. "The View from the Center: British Empire and Post-Empire Children's Literature." In *Voices of the Other: Children's Literature and the Postcolonial Context*, edited by Roderick McGillis. Taylor and Francis, 1999.

Iñárritu, Alejandro G., dir. *The Revenant*. 20th Century Fox Studios, 2015.

Ingram, David. *Green Screen: Environmentalism and Hollywood Cinema*. University of Exeter Press, 2000.

Jacoby, Karl. *Crimes Against Nature: Squatters, Poachers, Thieves, and the Hidden History of American Conservation*. University of California Press, 2011.

Jaffe, Daniel M. "Licking Voblya." In Suresha, *Bear Lust*.

Jans, Nick. *Grizzly Maze: Timothy Treadwell's Fatal Obsession with Alaskan Bears*. Penguin, 2005.

Jans, Nick. "Re-Examining Famous Deaths of Timothy Treadwell and Chris McCandless." *Alaska Magazine*, October 10, 2020.

"John Adams." (San Francisco) *Evening Bulletin*, January 18, 1858.

Johnson, Paul E. *Sam Patch, the Famous Jumper*. Hill and Wang, 2003.

Joy, Melanie. *Why We Love Dogs, Eat Pigs, Wear Cows: An Introduction to Carnism*. Conari, 2009.

Jue, Teresa. "Retro Joe to Modern Bruin." *Daily Bruin*, October 18, 2010.

Kalof, Linda. *Looking at Animals in Human History*. Reaktion, 2007.

Kampf, Ray. *The Bear Handbook: A Comprehensive Guide for Those Who Are Husky, Hairy, and Homosexual and Those Who Love 'Em*. Haworth, 2000.

Kell, Gretchen. "Birthday Bear: Iconic Oski Turns 75." *Berkeley News*, September 26, 2016.

Kellert, Stephen R. "Public Attitudes Toward Bears and Their Conservation." *Bears: Their Biology and Management* 9 (1994): 43–50.

Kelly, Elizabeth A., and Kate Kane. "In Goldilocks's Footsteps: Exploring the Discursive Construction of Gay Masculinity in Bear Magazines." In Wright, *Bear Book II*.

Kermode, Mark. "Cocaine Bear Review—Larky Horror Comedy Is Roaring Good Fun." *The Guardian*, February 26, 2023.

Key, Ellen. *The Century of the Child*. Putnam's, 1912.

Kidd, Kenneth B. "Disney of Orlando's Animal Kingdom." In *Wild Things: Children's Culture and Ecocriticism*, edited by Sidney I. Dobrin and Kenneth B. Kidd. Wayne State University Press, 2004.

King, Barbara. *How Animals Grieve*. University of Chicago Press, 2013.

King, Charles. *Gods of the Upper Air: How a Circle of Renegade Anthropologists Reinvented Race, Sex, and Gender in the Twentieth Century*. Doubleday, 2019.

Kipling, Rudyard. *The Jungle Book*. Macmillan, 1894.

Kipling, Rudyard. *The Second Jungle Book*. Macmillan, 1895.

Kipnis, Laura. *Bound and Gagged: Pornography and the Politics of Fantasy in America*. Duke University Press, 1996.

Kleinfield, N. R. "Farewell to Gus, Whose Issues Made Him a Star." *New York Times*, August 28, 2013.

Kosek, Jake. "'Smokey Bear Is a White Racist Pig.'" In *Understories: The Political Life of Forests in Northern New Mexico*. Duke University Press, 2006.

Krauthammer, Charles. "Drown the Berenstain Bears." *Washington Post*, August 18, 1989.

Kreiner, Jamie. *Legion of Pigs in the Early Medieval West*. Yale University Press, 2020.

Lang, Andrew, ed. *The Green Fairy Book*. Dover, 1965.

Lapinski, Mike. *Death in the Grizzly Maze: The Timothy Treadwell Story*. Falcon, 2005.

Lasch, Christopher. *Haven in a Heartless World: The Family Besieged*. Basic, 1977.

Lawter, William Clifford, Jr. *Smokey Bear 20252: A Biography*. Lindsay Smith, 1994.

Lents, Nathan H. *Not So Different: Finding Human Nature in Animals*. Columbia University Press, 2016.

Lepore, Jill. "Bear Season." *New Yorker*, July 24, 2023.

Leslie, Carolyn. "Please Look After This Bear: The Perils of Seeking a New Home in 'Paddington.'" *Screen Education* 77 (2015): 42–51.

Lester, Julius. *Further Tales of Uncle Remus: The Misadventures of Brer Rabbit, Brer Fox, Brer Wolf, the Doodang, and Other Creatures as Told by Julius Lester*. Dial, 1990.

Lester, Julius. *The Last Tales of Uncle Remus*. Dial, 1994.

Lester, Julius. *More Tales of Uncle Remus: Further Adventures of Brer Rabbit, His Legends, Enemies, and Others as Told by Julius Lester*. Dial, 1988.

Lester, Julius. *The Tales of Uncle Remus: The Adventures of Brer Rabbit as Told by Julius Lester*. Dial, 1987.

Lester, Julius. *Uncle Remus: The Complete Tales*. Dial, 1999.

Lewis, James G. "James G. Lewis on Smokey Bear in Vietnam." *Environmental History* 11 (2006): 598–603.

Lewis, James G., and Char Miller. "Vast, Incredible Damage: Herbicides and the U.S. Forest Service." In *Inevitably Toxic: Historical Perspectives on Contamination, Exposure, and Expertise*, edited by Brinda Sarathy, Vivien Hamilton, and Janet Farrell Brodie. University of Pittsburgh Press, 2018.

Lewis, Meriwether, and William Clark. *The Journals of Lewis and Clark*. 1806. Reprint, Viking, 1989.

Locke, Philip. "Male Images in the Gay Mass Media and Bear-Oriented Magazines: Analysis and Content." In Wright, *Bear Book*.

Lockwood, Patricia. "Pull Off My Head." *London Review of Books*, August 12, 2021.

Lopez, Ali. "A Puerto Rican Bear in the USA." In Wright, *Bear Book II*.

"Lots of Roosevelt Bears." *New York Times*, October 13, 1906.

Loviglio, Joann. "50 Years Along, Berenstain Bears a Family Affair." *Washington Times*, January 30, 2011.

Lulka, David. "Consuming Timothy Treadwell: Redefining Nonhuman Agency in Light of Herzog's *Grizzly Man*." In *Animals and Agency: An Interdisciplinary Exploration*, edited by Sarah E. McFarland and Ryan Hediger. Brill, 2009.

Madley, Benjamin. *An American Genocide: The United States and the California Indian Catastrophe: 1846–1873*. Yale University Press, 2016.

Malamud, Randy. "Animals on Film: The Ethics of the Human Gaze." *Spring* 83 (2010): 1–26.

Malamud, Randy. *An Introduction to Animals and Visual Culture*. St. Martin's, 2012.

Malamud, Randy. *Reading Zoos: Representations of Animals and Captivity*. New York University Press, 1998.

Manfred, Frederick. *Lord Grizzly*. 2nd ed. 1954. Reprint, University of Nebraska Press, 1983.

Mangelsen, Tom. "Grizzly 399 and Cub—An Update from Jackson Hole." *Mountain Journal*, June 17, 2023.

Marcus, Itamar, and Nan Jacques Zilberdik. "Hamas Teaches Kids to Kill Jews." *Palestinian Media Watch*, September 23, 2009.

Marcus, Sharon. *The Drama of Celebrity*. Princeton University Press, 2019.

Marris, Emma. *Wild Souls: Freedom and Flourishing in the Non-Human World*. Bloomsbury, 2021.

Marshall, James. *Goldilocks and the Three Bears*. Dial, 1988.

Martin, Natassha. *In the Eye of the Wild*. Translated by Sophie Lewis. New York Review of Books, 2021.

Martin, Tim. "Foreword." In Wright, *Bear Book*.

Mazzei, George. "Who's Who at the Zoo: A Glossary of Gay Animals." *Advocate*, July 26, 1979.

McCarthy, Lauren. "Hank the Tank, a 400-Pound Bear Behind Lake Tahoe Break-Ins, Is Captured." *New York Times*, August 6, 2023.

McClung, Robert M. *The True Adventures of Grizzly Adams: A Biography by Robert M. McClung*. William Morrow, 1985.

McCracken, Harold. *The Beast That Walks Like Man: The Story of the Grizzly Bear*. Roberts Rinehart, 2003.

McCullough, David. *Mornings on Horseback: The Story of an Extraordinary Family, a Vanished Way of Life, and the Unique Child Who Became Theodore Roosevelt*. Simon and Schuster, 1981.

McPhee, Mike, and Jim Carrier. "Wild Photos Called Staged." *Denver Post*, February 9, 1996.

Medred, Craig. "Man, Myth, Martyr." *Los Angeles Times*, December 14, 2003.

Mehren, Elizabeth. "The Bear Facts: Sure, Dad's a Bit of a Buffoon, and Mom's Rigid and Efficient. But More Than 100 Books Later, The 'Berenstain Bears' Clan Is Still Going Strong—As Are Their Seventysomething Creators." *Los Angeles Times*, February 1, 1995.

Melillo, Wendy. *How McGruff and the Crying Indian Changed America*. Smithsonian, 2013.

Melson, Gail F. *Why the Wild Things Are: Animals in the Lives of Children*. Harvard University Press, 2001.

Metcalf, Greg. "'It's a Jungle Book Out There, Kid!': The Sixties in Walt Disney's *The Jungle Book*." *Studies in Popular Culture* 14 (1991): 85–97.

Miller, Char. "Boiling Point: Save Us Smokey Bear." *Los Angeles Times*, November 30, 2023.

Milne, A. A. *Winnie-the-Pooh*. Illustrated by Ernest H. Shepard. E. P. Dutton, 1926.

Mitman, Gregg. *Reel Nature: America's Romance with Wildlife on Film*. Harvard University Press, 1999.

Mizelle, Brett. "'A Man Quite as Much of a Show as His Beasts': James Capen 'Grizzly' Adams and the Making of Grizzly Bears." *Werkstatt Geschichte* 56 (2010): 29–45.

Mooallem, Jon. *Wild Ones: A Sometimes Dismaying, Weirdly Reassuring Story About Looking at People Looking at Animals in America*. Penguin, 2013.

Moose, Charles. "Beginnings of the Big Bear Boom." *Teddy Bear Review*, October 2002, 48–52.

Morgensen, Scott Lauria. *Spaces Between Us: Queer Settler Colonialism and Indigenous Decolonialization*. University of Minnesota Press, 2011.

Morison, Elting E. *The Letters of Theodore Roosevelt*. Vol. 3. Harvard University Press, 1951.

Morrison, Ellen Earnhardt. *Guardian of the Forest: A History of the Smokey Bear Program*. 2nd ed. Morielle, 1989.

Morris, P. H., V. Reddy, and R. C. Buntin. "The Survival of the Cutest: Who's Responsible for the Evolution of the Teddy Bear?" *Animal Behaviour* 50 (1995): 1697–700.

Moses, Claire. "Bears Are Having a Moment." *New York Times*, October 2, 2023.

Mullan, Bob, and Garry Marvin. *Zoo Culture*. Weidenfeld and Nicolson, 1987.

Mullins, Lina. *The Teddy Bear Men: Theodore Roosevelt & Clifford Berryman*. Hobby House, 1998.

Mullins, Lina. *Teddy Bears Past & Present: A Collector's Identification Guide*. Hobby House, 1986.

Murphy, Frank. *The Legend of the Teddy Bear*. Sleeping Bear, 2000.

Myers, John Myers. *The Saga of Hugh Glass: Pirate, Pawnee, and Mountain Man*. University of Nebraska Press, 1963.

Nance, Susan. *Animal Modernity: Jumbo the Elephant and the Human Dilemma*. Palgrave Macmillan, 2015.

Nance, Susan. *Entertaining Elephants: Animal Agency and the Business of the American Circus*. Johns Hopkins University Press, 2013.

Nance, Susan, ed. *The Historical Animal*. Syracuse University Press, 2015.

Nath, Dipika. "'To Abandon the Colonial Animal': 'Race,' Animals and the Feral Child in Kipling's Mowgli Stories." In *Animals and Agency: An Interdisciplinary Exploration*, edited by Sarah E. McFarland and Ryan Hediger. Brill, 2009.

Naughton, Mary Means. "His Christmas." *New York Times*, December 24, 1906.

Neihardt, John G. "The Song of Hugh Glass." In *The Song of Three Friends & The Song of Hugh Glass*. Macmillan, 1924.

Nelson, Chris. *The Bear Cult: Photographs by Chris Nelson*. Gay Men's Press, 1991.

Newkirk, Pamela. *Spectacle: The Astonishing Life of Ota Benga*. HarperCollins, 2015.

Ngai, Sianne. *Our Aesthetic Categories: Zany, Cute, Interesting*. Harvard University Press, 2015.

Nichols, John. *The Milagro Beanfield War*. Holt, Rinehart and Winston, 1974.

Nodelman, Perry. *The Hidden Adult: Defining Children's Literature*. Johns Hopkins University Press, 2008.

Nodelman, Perry. *Words About Pictures: The Narrative Art of Children's Picture Books*. University of Georgia Press, 1988.

Olney, Kathryn. "Bearly There." *Salon*, February 2, 1999.

"One Bear Bagged." *Washington Post*, November 15, 1902.

Opie, Iona, and Peter Opie. *The Classic Fairy Tales*. Oxford University Press, 1974.

Owens, Angela. "The Internet Loves Otis, a Chunky Bear King." *Wall Street Journal*, October 4, 2022.

Palmer, Chris. *Shooting in the Wild: An Insider's Account of Making Movies in the Animal Kingdom*. Sierra Club, 2010.

Parkinson, Claire. *Animals, Anthropomorphism and Mediated Encounters*. Routledge, 2020.

Parreñas, Juno Salazar. *Decolonizing Extinction: The Work of Care in Orangutan Extinction*. Duke University Press, 2018.

Pastoureau, Michel. *The Bear: History of a Fallen King*. Translated by George Holoch. Harvard University Press, 2011.

Pauli, Michelle. "Paddington Stands Up for Things, He's Not Afraid of Going to the Top and Giving Them a Hard Stare." Interview with Michael Bond. *The Guardian*, November 28, 2014.

Peacock, Doug. *Grizzly Years: In Search of the American Wilderness*. Henry Holt, 1990.

Pearson, Susan J., and Mary Weismantel. "Does 'The Animal' Exist? Toward a Theory of Social Life with Animals." In *Beastly Natures: Animals, Humans, and the Study of History*, edited by Dorothee Brantz. University of Virginia Press, 2010.

Pfeiffer, Günther. *100 Years of Steiff Teddy Bears*. HEEL Verlag GmbH, 2001.

Pfeiffer, Günther. *The Story of the Steiff Teddy Bears*. David & Charles, 2003.

Pogrebin, Robin. "Roosevelt Statue to Be Removed from Museum of Natural History." *New York Times*, June 21, 2020.

Policarpio, Joe. "*BEAR* Magazine: Masculinity, Men's Bodies and the Imagination." Media PUP, 1993.

Poliquin, Rachel. *The Breathless Zoo: Taxidermy and the Cultures of Longing*. Penn State University Press, 2012.

Porter, Catherine. "Drawn from Poverty: Art Was Supposed to Save Canada's Inuit. It Hasn't." *New York Times*, October 19, 2019.

Punke, Michael. *The Revenant: A Novel of Revenge*. Picador, 2002.

Quammen, David. *Monster of the God: The Man-Eating Predator in the Jungles of History and the Mind*. Norton, 2003.

Rader, Karen A., and Victoria E. M. Cain. "From Natural History to Science: Display and the Transformation of American Museums of Science and Nature." *Museum and Society* 6 (2008): 151–71.

Rader, Karen A., and Victoria E. M. Cain. *Life on Display: Revolutionizing U.S. Museums of Science and Natural History in the Twentieth Century*. University of Chicago Press, 2014.

Ramsey, Michael S. "The Bear Clan: North American Totemic Mythology, Belief, and Legend." In Wright, *Bear Book*.

"Return of President." *Washington Post*, November 21, 1902.

Reuben, Susan. "Paddington Bear: His Secret Jewish Heritage." *Jewish Chronicle*, June 29, 2017.

Review of *Bear Country*. *Natural History* 62 (March 1953): 138–39.

Ricciuti, Edward R. *Bears in the Backyard: Big Animals, Sprawling Suburbs and the New Urban Jungle*. Countryman, 2014.

"Richard Harris London's No. 1 Bobby Outfoxer." *Los Angeles Times*, November 28, 1971.

Ridinger, Robert B. Marks. "Bearaphernalia: An Exercise in Social Definition." In Wright, *Bear Book*.

Ridinger, Robert B. Marks. "Paws Between the Worlds." In Wright, *Bear Book II*.

Righter, Robert W. "Theodore Henry Hittell: California Historian." *Southern California Quarterly* 48 (1966): 289–306.

Ritvo, Harriet. *The Animal Estate: The English and Other Creatures in the Victorian Age*. Harvard University Press, 1987.

Ritvo, Harriet. "Calling the Wild." In *Gorgeous Beasts: Animal Bodies in Historical Perspective*, edited by Joan B. Landes, Paula Young Lee, and Paul Youngquis. Penn State University Press, 2012.

Ritvo, Harriet. *Noble Cows and Hybrid Zebras: Essays on Animals and History*. University of Virginia Press, 2010.

Robichaud, Andrew A. *Animal City: The Domestication of America*. Harvard University Press, 2019.

Rockwell, David. *Giving Voice to Bear: North American Indian Rituals, Myths, and Images of the Bear*. Roberts Rinehart, 1991.

Rofes, Eric. "Academics as Bears: Thoughts on Middle-Class Eroticization of Working-men's Bodies." In Wright, *Bear Book*.

Roosevelt, Theodore. *American Bears: Selections from the Writing of Theodore Roosevelt*. Edited by Paul Schullery. Roberts Rinehart, 1997.

Roosevelt, Theodore. *Outdoor Pastimes of an American Hunter*. Charles Scribner's Sons, 1905.

Rosales, Melodye Benson. *Leola and the Honeybears: An African-American Retelling of Goldilocks and the Three Bears*. Scholastic, 1999.

Rose, Anne C. *In the Hearts of the Beasts: How American Behavioral Scientists Rediscovered the Emotions of Animals*. Oxford University Press, 2020.

Rose, Jacqueline. *The Case of Peter Pan: Or the Impossibility of Children's Fiction*. Macmillan, 1984.

Rosenberg, Harold. "A New Breed of Nature Show." *The Animals' Agenda*, September/October 2000, 41.

Rothfels, Nigel. *Elephant Trails: A History of Animals and Cultures*. Johns Hopkins University Press, 2021.

Rothfels, Nigel. "How the Caged Birds Sing: Animals and Entertainment." In *A Cultural History of Animals in the Age of Empire*, edited by Kathleen Kete. Berg, 2007.

Rothfels, Nigel, ed. "Introduction." In *Representing Animals*. Indiana University Press, 2002.

Rothfels, Nigel. *Savages and Beasts: The Birth of the Modern Zoo*. Johns Hopkins University Press, 2002.

Samuels, Daniel. *Molly and Me: The Story of a Bear*. D. Samuels, 1997.

Sanneh, Kelefa. "Beastly Matters." *New Yorker*, May 6, 2024.

Schullery, Paul. *The Bear Doesn't Know: Life and Wonder in Bear Country*. University of Nebraska Press, 2021.

Seitz, David K. "'Migration Is Not a Crime': Migrant Justice and the Creative Uses of Paddington Bear." *Annals of the American Association of Geographers*, October 2021, 1–8.

Seitz, David K. "'You're Stuffed, Bear': Geography's Colonial Legacies in the 'Paddington Empire.'" *Transactions of the British Institute of Geographers*, 2021, 1–14.

Sellbach, Undine. "The Traumatic Efforts to Understand: Werner Herzog's *Grizzly Man*." In *Considering Animals: Contemporary Studies in Human-Animal Relations*, edited by Carol Freeman, Elizabeth Leane, and Yvette Watt. Ashgate, 2011.

Serpell, James A. "People in Disguise: Anthropomorphism and the Human-Pet Relationship." In Daston and Mitman, *Thinking with Animals*.

Seton-Thompson, Ernest. *The Biography of a Grizzly*. Century, 1900.

Shapiro, Harriet. Review of Treadwell and Palovak, *Among Grizzlies*. *People*, August 4, 1997.

Shepard, Paul. *The Others: How Animals Made Us Human*. Island Press, 1996.

Shepard, Paul, and Barry Sanders. *The Sacred Paw: The Bear in Nature, Myth, and Literature*. Viking, 1985.

Simon, Linda. *The Greatest Shows on Earth: A History of the Circus*. Reaktion, 2014.

Simpson, Sherry. *Dominion of Bears: Living with Wildlife in Alaska*. University Press of Kansas, 2013.

Singer, Peter. *Animal Liberations: A New Ethics for Our Treatment of Animals*. New York Review of Books, 1975.

Singer, Peter. "'Heavy Petting' and the Politics of Animal Sexual Assault." *Critical Criminology* 10 (2001): 43–55.

Smith, Angela. "A Case Study of Immigration and Otherness." *Children's Literature in Education* 37 (2006): 35–50.

Smith, J. Morgan. "The Story of Smokey Bear." *Forestry Chronicle*, June 1956, 183–88.

Smith, Julie A., and Robert W. Mitchell, eds. *Experiencing Animal Minds: An Anthology of Animal-Human Encounters*. Columbia University Press, 2012.

Smith, Philip. "Paddington Bear and the Erasure of Difference." *Children's Literature Association Quarterly* 45 (2020): 25–42.

Soloski, Alexis. "Big Apple Circus Review: A Show That Bends Over Backward for You." *New York Times*, November 20, 2023.

Spirin, Gennady. *Goldilocks and the Three Bears*. Marshall Cavendish, 2009.

Stambler, Lyndon. "Bears Fan." *People*, October 3, 1994.

Standiford, Les. *Battle for the Big Top: P. T. Barnum, James Bailey, John Ringling, and the Death-Defying Saga of the American Circus*. Public Affairs, 2021.

Stanger, Carol A. "*Winnie the Pooh* Through a Feminist Lens." *Lion and the Unicorn* 11 (1987): 34–50.

Stark, Mike. *Chasing the Ghost Bear: On the Trail of America's Lost Super Beast*. University of Nebraska Press, 2022.

Stonorov, Derek. *Watch the Bear: A Half Century with the Brown Bears of Alaska*. University of Nebraska Press, 2023.

Storer, Tracy I., and Lloyd B. Tevis. *California Grizzly*. University of California Press, 1955.

Storl, Wolf D. *Bear: Myth, Animal, Icon*. North Atlantic, 2018.

Stouffer, Marty, dir. *The Man Who Loved Bears*. United States, first aired June 1, 1979. Television movie, 60 mins.

Stouffer, Marty. *Marty Stouffer's Wild America*. Times Books, 1988.

Stouffer, Marty, dir. *Wild America*. PBS television series, 12 seasons, 1982–94.

Straley, John. *The Woman Who Married a Bear*. Soho Press, 1992.

Suresha, Ron. "Acknowledgments." In *Bear Lust*.

Suresha, Ron, ed. *Bear Lust: Hot, Hairy, Heavy Fiction*. Alyson, 2004.

Suresha, Ron, ed. *Bears on Bears: Interviews and Discussions*. Alyson, 2002.

Suresha, Ron. "Bear Roots." In Wright, *Bear Book*.

Suresha, Ron, ed. *The Biggest Lover: Big-Boned Men's Erotica for Chubs and Chasers*. Bear Bones, 2015.

Suresha, Ron. "You Can Lead a Bear to Culture, but . . . or Bears in Literature and Culture: A Discussion with David Bergman and Michael Bronski." In Wright, *Bear Book II*.

Swenson, Kyle. "Was Smokey Bear Wrong? How a Beloved Character May Have Helped Fuel Catastrophic Fires." *Washington Post*, August 15, 2018.

Szablowski, Witold. *Dancing Bears: True Stories of People Nostalgic for Life Under Tyranny*. Penguin, 2014.

Tatar, Maria. *Off with Their Heads! Fairy Tales and the Culture of Childhood*. Princeton University Press, 1992.

Tawada, Yoko. *Memoirs of a Polar Bear*. Translated by Susan Bernofsky. New Directions, 2016.

Taylor, Sunaura. *Beasts of Burden: Animal and Disability Liberation*. New Press, 2017.

Thompson, Helen. "The Return of the Empire: Representations of Race, Ethnicity and Culture in Disney's *Tarzan* and *The Jungle Book*, and in the Burroughs and Kipling Pre-Texts." *Explorations into Children's Literature* 11 (2001): 5–14.

Ticktin, Miriam I. *Casualties of Care: Immigration and the Politics of Immigration in France*. University of California Press, 2011.

Till, B. G. "Teddy Bears: An Enduring Folk Tradition." *Pennsylvania Folklore* 34 (1985): 78–81.

Todd, Edgeley W. "James Hall and the Hugh Glass Legend." *American Quarterly* 7 (1955): 362–70.

Treadwell, Timothy. "Some Bet on My Death" (Letter to Roland Dixon, September 14, 2003). *Outside*, January 1, 2004, 19.

Treadwell, Timothy, and Jewel Palovak. *Among Grizzlies: Living with Wild Bears in Alaska*. HarperCollins, 1997.

Tumin, Remy. "The Humble Origins of the Fattest Tournament on Earth." *New York Times*, October 6, 2022.

Uddin, Lisa. *Zoo Renewal: White Flight and the Animal Ghetto*. University of Minnesota Press, 2015.

"Use of Teddy Bear Nebulizers Might Make ED Visits Less Stressful." *Emergency Department Management* 11 (1999): 16–17.

Valtonen, Anu. "Teddy Bears." *Consumption, Markets & Culture* 19 (2016): 259–63.

Vandersommers, Daniel. *Entangled Encounters at the National Zoo: Stories from the Animal Archive*. University Press of Kansas, 2023.

Varga, Donna. "Babes in the Woods: Wilderness Aesthetics in Children's Stories and Toys, 1830–1915." *Society and Animals* 17 (2009): 187–205.

Varga, Donna. "Gifting the Bear and a Nostalgic Desire for Childhood Innocence." *Cultural Analysis* 8 (2009): 71–96.

Varga, Donna. "Innocence Versus Savagery in the Recapitulation Theory of Child Study: Depictions in Picture Books and Other Cultural Materials." *International Research in Children's Literature* 11 (2018): 186–202.

Varga, Donna. "Teddy's Bear and the Sociocultural Transfiguration of Savage Beasts into Innocent Children, 1890–1920." *Journal of American Culture* 32 (2009): 98–113.

Varga, Donna. "Winnie: Troubling the Idealization of the Bear as Childhood Innocent." In *Positioning Pooh: Edward Bear After 100 Years*, edited by Jennifer Harrison. University Press of Mississippi, 2021.

Varga, Donna, and Rhoda Zuk. "Golliwogs and Teddy Bears: Embodied Racism in Children's Popular Culture." *Journal of Popular Culture* 46 (2013): 647–71.

Varley, H. L. "Imperialism and Rudyard Kipling." *Journal of the History of Ideas* 14 (1953): 124–35.

Walt Disney's The Jungle Book. Disney Press, 2007.

Waring, Philippa. *In Praise of Teddy Bears: Collector's Edition*. Souvenir, 1997.

Warner, Marina. *Once Upon a Time: A Short History of Fairy Tale*. Oxford University Press, 2014.

Wasik, Bill, and Monica Murphy. *Our Kindred Creatures: How Americans Came to Feel the Way They Do About Animals*. Knopf, 2024.

Waterman, Anna. "Perceptions of Race in Three Generations of *The Jungle Book*." *Continuum: The Journal of African Diaspora Drama, Theatre and Performance* 1 (2015): 1–9.

Waugh, Charles. "'Only You Can Prevent a Forest': Agent Orange, Ecocide, and Environmental Justice." *Interdisciplinary Studies in Literature and Environment* 17 (2010): 113–32.

Weeks, Linton. "The Bear Essentials." *Washington Post*, May 13, 1996.

Weil, Kari. *Thinking Animals: Why Animal Studies Now?* Columbia University Press, 2012.

White, G. Edward. *The Eastern Establishment and the Western Experience: The West of Frederic Remington, Theodore Roosevelt, and Owen Wister*. Yale University Press, 1968.

Whitesel, Jason. *Fat Gay Men: Girth, Mirth and the Politics of Stigma*. New York University Press, 2014.

Wilkinson, Ned. "A Bear Admirer's (Subjective, Fluffy, and Totally Honest) Point of View." In Wright, *Bear Book II*.

Wilkinson, Todd. "Famous Jackson Hole Grizzly 399 Wows Again, But Now What?" *Mountain Journal*, May 18, 2023.

Willems, Mo. *Goldilocks and the Three Dinosaurs*. HarperCollins, 2012.

Wilson. Alexander. *The Culture of Nature: North American Landscape from Disney to the Exxon Valdez*. Blackwell, 1992.

Wilson, Randall K. *America's Public Lands: From Yellowstone to Smokey Bear and Beyond*. Rowman & Littlefield, 2014.

Wolfe, Cary. *Animal Rites: American Culture, the Discourse of Species, and Posthumanist Theory*. University of Chicago Press, 2003.

Wolfe, Cary. *What Is Posthumanism?* University of Minnesota Press, 2010.

Woods, Rebecca. *The Herds Shot Round the World: Native Breeds and the British Empire*. University of North Carolina Press, 2017.

Wright, Lawrence. "The Elephant in the Courtroom." *New Yorker*, March 7, 2022, 44–57.

Wright, Les, ed. *The Bear Book: Readings in the History and Evolution of a Gay Male Subculture*. Haworth, 1997.

Wright, Les, ed. *The Bear Book II: Further Readings in the History and Evolution of a Gay Male Subculture*. Haworth, 2001.

Wright, Les. "Concise History." In Wright, *Bear Book*.

Wright, Les. "Introduction." In Wright, *Bear Book*.

Wright, Les. "Introduction." In Wright, *Bear Book II*.

Zabor, Rafi. *The Bear Comes Home*. Norton, 1998.

Zeman, Ned. "The Man Who Loved Grizzlies." *Vanity Fair*, May 2004.

Zuckerman, Esther. "Gus, Central Park's Famously Depressive Polar Bear, Has Died." *Atlantic Wire*, August 31, 2013.

Index

Page locators in *italics* refer to figures.

Lady Washington (grizzly bear), 77, 78, 80, 81, 86, 87, 92, 201
Legend of Grizzly Adams, The (Dillon), 86–87
Legend of Mor'du (film), 23
Leola and the Honeybears (Rosales), 51–52, *52*
Lester, Julius, 11, 21–23, 178, 220n29, 220n32
Letterman, David, 188
Lewis, Meriwether, 36
Life and Times of Grizzly Adams, The (film), 8, 89–92, 126, 227n36
Life and Times of Grizzly Adams, The (television show), *89*, 227n36
Long, Crystal, 109–10
Lord Grizzly (Manfred), 35, 39, 40, 41
L'Ours. See Bear, The (*L'Ours*, film)

Malamud, Randy, 99, 100
Mandan, 36, 37, 39, 40
Manfred, Frederick, 35, 39, 40, 41
Mangelsen, Thomas, 30
Man in the Wilderness, The (film), 35, 39–41
Man Who Loved Bears, The (television special), 114–16, 232n84
Marronnez, Felicia, 58–59
Martin, Tim, 169
Marty Stouffer's Wild America (Stouffer), 120
masculinity, 7, 9, 98, 130, 178, 184; in gay culture, 125, 167, 168, 169, 173–74
Mathers, Rachel, 103
Mazzei, George, 171
McClung, Robert M., 87–88
McCullough, David, 130–31
McDonnell, Andrea, 3, 78–79
McPhee, Mike, 121–22
Mehren, Elizabeth, 64
Merediz, Olga, 117
Metcalf, Greg, 18
Michtom, Morris, 135–36, 234n20
Michtom, Rose, 135–36, 234n20
Milagro Beanfield War, The (Nichols), 160–61
Milne, A. A., 56–58, 60, 140, 143
Minnich, Richard, 163
Mitman, Gregg, 110, 111, 122
Mizelle, Brett, 92
Monokuma (Japanese video game character), 29, 32, 125
Mooallem, Jon, 4, 234n11, 243n1
Moore, Thomas, 5

Moose, Charles, 136
Mowgli (character in *The Jungle Book*), 17–18
Munger, Sean, 154, 163
Muppets, The, 23
museums, 96–97, 125, 126, 140, 194; exhibits by Grizzly Adams, 77, 83. *See also* American Museum of Natural History; Arizona-Sonora Desert Museum; *Keeper, The* (New Museum exhibit); National Museum of Natural History
Mutual of Omaha's Wild Kingdom (TV series), 111–13, 230–31n63
Muybridge, Eadweard, 110

Nahl, Charles, 75
Nance, Susan, 103
National Museum of Natural History, 96–97
National Zoological Park (National Zoo), 95, 122, 125, 149, 153–54
Native Americans. *See* anthropomorphism: by Indigenous peoples; Glass, Hugh, story of: depictions of Native Americans in; Indigenous peoples; Inuit; Mandan; Native Americans, and bears; racism: and Indigenous peoples; Zuni
Native Americans, and bears, x, 7, 13, 14, 175–76, 194, 196, 218n21; in *Lord Grizzly*, 40; references to, in gay culture, 175, 176–77. *See also* Inuit
Naughton, Mary Means, 140
Neihardt, John G., 35, 41
New York Zoological Society, 95, 99
Nichols, John, 160–61

Oldenburg, Claes, 97, 126
Onion, Rebecca, 68–69
Oski (UC Berkeley mascot), 24–25, *25*

Paddington Bear (character), 59–63, *61*, 70, 118, 140, 165; references in gay film, 170, 175, 239n22
Palovak, Jewel, 181, 182, 184, 186, 187–88
pandas, 4, 101, 122
Peacock, Doug, 183
People for the Ethical Treatment of Animals (PETA), 103, 105, 135
Perkins, Marlin, 111–14, 116
Pogo (comic strip), 23

medicine, 141, 143–44; use in therapy, 141–43. *See also* anthropomorphism: teddy bears and; Roosevelt, Theodore: creation of teddy bear and; Steiff teddy bears

"Three Bears, The" (Terrytoons cartoon), 52–54, 55

Tibbers (*League of Legends* character), 28–29, 32

Time (magazine), 103, 205

Tomorrow's Pioneers (television series), 23, 24

Tournament of Roses. *See* Rose Bowl parade

Treadwell, Timothy (Timothy William Dexter), 9, 181–82, *192*, 199–20; in Alaska, 183–86; death of, 188–90; early life of, 182–83, 186; film about. *See Grizzly Man* (film); self-promotion of, 186–88

Treasury of Pleasure Books for Young Children, A (Cundall), 71, *72*

True Adventures of Grizzly Adams, The (McClung), 87–88, *88*

Tumin, Remy, 124

Turner, Frederick Jackson, 44

Turning Red (film), 122

Uncle Remus (character), 11, 19–23, 64, 140, 220n29

Uncle Remus Stories (Harris), 19. *See also* Harris, Joel Chandler; Uncle Remus (character)

University of California at Berkeley, 24–25, 71, 161

University of California at Los Angeles, 9, 24–26, 32, 71, 204

Ursa Major, 13

Ursa Minor, 13

US Forest Service, 150–54, 160–63

Valtonen, Anu, 136

Van Daele, Larry, 194

Varga, Donna, 132–33, 135, 136, 141, 146, 147, 220n29, 238–39n7

video games, 8, 28–29, 31–32, 35, 71, 125

Vorster, Charl, 142

Waterman, Anna, 18

Weaver, Jackson, 152, 158

Wendelin, Rudy, 157, 237n22

What's Worrying Gus? (Beard and Boswell), 123–24, *123*

"White Man's Burden, The" (Kipling), 17

"Why Brother Bear Has No Tail" (Harris), 19–20

Wilcoxon, Henry, 40–41

Wild America (television series), *115*, 116, 121–22

wildfires. *See* forest fires

Wildlife Conservation Society. *See* New York Zoological Society

Wilkinson, Ned, 176–77

Wilkinson, Todd, 30

Willcox, Louisa, 190

Willems, Mo, 50–51

Winnie the Pooh (character), 56–59, 61, 70, 143, 165

Winnie-the-Pooh (Milne), 55–57

Wittke, Chris, 177

World War II, 60, 62, 63, 150, 151

World Wildlife Fund, 205, 207

Wright, Les, 168, 169, 171, 173, 175, 237–38n1, 240n47

Yellowstone National Park, 5, 113

Yogi Bear (cartoon character), 3, 28, 31, 63, 64, 165, 176, 217–18n17

zoos, 95, 97–101, 103, 104, 125, 127, 227n7. *See also* Bronx Zoo; National Zoological Park (National Zoo); San Diego Zoo Safari Park

Zuni, x

www.ingramcontent.com/pod-product-compliance
Lightning Source LLC
Jackson TN
JSHW080026120725
87553JS00003B/5